APIL Guide to Evidence

APIL Guide to Evidence

General Editor

Stephen Glynn
9 Gough Square, London

Contributor Authors

Laura Elfield
Christopher Goddard
Philip Jones
Linda Nelson
Jennifer Newcomb
Esther Pounder
Shahram Sharghy
Rajeev Shetty
Christopher Stephenson
all of 9 Gough Square, London

and

Edwina Rawson, Partner
Field Fisher Waterhouse LLP

Maria Panteli, Solicitor
Leigh Day & Co

Christine Tallon, Solicitor
Leigh Day & Co

JORDANS

Published by
Jordan Publishing Limited
21 St Thomas Street
Bristol BS1 6JS

British Library Cataloguing-in-Publication Data

A catalogue record for this book is available from the British Library.

ISBN 978 0 85308 756 4

Typeset by Letterpart Ltd, Reigate, Surrey

Printed in Great Britain by CPI Antony Rowe, Chippenham, Wiltshire

PREFACE

PI and clinical negligence claims come in all shapes and sizes. They cover the gamut of human experience from the minor rear-end shunt on the slip road from Watford junction to the M25 to the decades-ago exposure to asbestos whilst working in docks that have long since been developed into luxury flats to the tragic but all too frequent cerebral palsy claim.

All of these cases depend on showing what happened, who did it and why in sufficient detail to impress a defendant, or more likely its insurer, to pay up or a judge, if it goes that far, to order the defendant and its insurer to do so.

Whilst we all press our claims for the benefit of our injured clients, we are all, every day, in the running (and turning down) of our cases dealing with, or looking for, or assessing evidence. Without knowing what the rules of evidence are and in particular how to use evidence and what the court-imposed limits are in using evidence a claim is likely to founder. No properly advised defendant is going to admit liability or make a decent offer if the evidence is not there or cannot be used.

Although we know that the vast majority of personal injury and clinical negligence cases never see the inside of a court room, the best prepared cases (and therefore the most profitable for the claimant and for his solicitors) are those that are prepared on the basis that the case will end up before a judge. Understanding this then fully means that a practitioner knows early on which cases to run as well as which ones to drop. Whether pursuing a particular line of enquiry is worth the effort or even necessary.

In this book the editorial team, which consists of both barristers and solicitors, hope to provide the practitioner with all the detail necessary to understand the fundamental importance of evidence and how the court will allow the parties to use it, from the initial steps of investigating a case through to the trial itself and the appellate process.

We have tried our best to state the law as we understand it as at February 2011 but any mistakes and errors remain mine as editor. My thanks also to Lycia Parker, who was my pupil at the time of the birth of the book, for all her hard work and help on the text.

I hope you find the text useful.

Stephen Glynn

9 Gough Square
London
EC4A 3DG

sglynn@9goughsquare.co.uk

February 2011

ASSOCIATION OF PERSONAL INJURY LAWYERS (APIL)

APIL is the UK's leading association of claimant personal injury lawyers, dedicated to protecting the rights of injured people.

Formed in 1990, APIL now represents around 5,000 solicitors, barristers, academics and students in the UK, Republic of Ireland and overseas.

APIL's objectives are:

- to promote full and just compensation for all types of personal injury;
- to promote and develop expertise in the practice of personal injury law;
- to promote wider redress for personal injury in the legal system;
- to campaign for improvements in personal injury law;
- to promote safety and alert the public to hazards;
- to provide a communication network for members.

APIL is a growing and influential forum pushing for law reform, and improvements, which will benefit injured people.

APIL has been running CPD training events, accredited by the Solicitors Regulation Authority and Bar Standards Board, for nearly 20 years and has a wealth of experience in developing the most practical up-to-date courses, delivered by eminent leading speakers, either publicly or in-house.

APIL training now runs almost 200 personal injury training events nationally each year, plus up to a further 100 meetings of our regional and special interest groups. Topics cover a wide range of subjects and are geared towards giving personal injury lawyers a thorough grounding in the core areas of personal injury law, whilst keeping lawyers thoroughly up to date in all subjects.

APIL is also an authoritative information source for personal injury lawyers, providing up-to-the-minute PI bulletins, regular newsletters and publications, information databases and online services.

For further information contact:

APIL
3 Alder Court
Rennie Hogg Road
Nottingham
NG2 1RX
DX 716208 Nottingham 42
Tel 0115 9580585
Email mail@apil.org.uk
Website www.apil.org.uk

CONTENTS

TABLE OF CASES

References are to paragraph numbers.

TABLE OF STATUTES

References are to paragraph numbers.

TABLE OF STATUTORY INSTRUMENTS

References are to paragraph numbers.

CHAPTER 1

INTRODUCTION

Stephen Glynn

1.1 THE IMPORTANCE OF EVIDENCE

Evidence forms the very foundation of any legal system and no claim can succeed at trial or before without sufficiently good evidence to support its constituent parts.

Whatever the potential value, there will be little point in pursuing a claim unless the evidence is there to substantiate it. It is a trite but true statement that the court process is often not really about the truth but, rather, it is about the 'proof' or, as we shall see, the existence and quality of the evidence gathered by each side, in particular, by the claimant, in any claim for personal injury.

Judicial decision-making is entirely dependent on there being evidence to support or contradict any assertion made by either side in the litigation. Personal injury litigation is no different. Evidence can take many forms but the most common form is the witness statement, whether this is made by the party in question, a lay witness or by the legal representative made in relation to any interim hearing.

Evidence in its broadest sense includes everything that is used to determine or demonstrate the truth of an assertion. Evidence is the currency by which the burden of proof is fulfilled. Without evidence there can, in effect, be no claim. Without sufficiently probative evidence the claim is likely to fail.

The legal burden of proof in all aspects of a civil claim is on the claimant. Where the defendant alleges contributory negligence or failure to mitigate, the legal burden rests on the defendant to plead and prove these contentions. However once such issues are raised sufficiently in the pleadings, the onus shifts back to the claimant to disprove the allegation. This is sometimes called the evidential as distinct from the legal burden. We shall see later in Chapter 3 how the onus of proof shifts for example where the defendant has been convicted of an offence arising out of the circumstances of the accident.

However, it is important to be aware of where the burden of proof lies in employer's liability claims based on breach of a statutory provision. For example, the statutory provision relied on to found the claim may be defended by establishing that it was not 'reasonably practicable' to comply with the obligation in question. 'Reasonable practicability' is a common phrase found in a number of statutory provisions designed to protect employees at work (the so-called Six Pack[1]). The burden of pleading and proving that compliance with a statutory duty was not reasonably practicable (where the obligation in questions provides such a defence) lies on the defendant.[2] In *King v RCO Support Services*,[3] the Court of Appeal made it clear that if the employer defendant fails to establish that it was reasonably practicable to avoid the need or reduce the risk of injury (the case concerned the duty so to do under reg 4 of the Manual Handling Operations Regulations 1992) the claim succeeds without the court needing to find that it was reasonably practicable to avoid the risk or reduce it.

The well-informed practitioner then should be alive not just to the importance of evidence but also on which party the burden of pleading and proving the relevant allegations lie.

1.2 INTEGRAL TO ALL ASPECTS OF PERSONAL INJURY LITIGATION

Obtaining sufficiently probative evidence to prove all the parts of a claim is integral to a personal injury claim. In such a claim there must be evidence to establish the essential elements in a successful claim on the balance of probabilities:

• the existence of the duties said to be owed by the defendant to the claimant (whether at common law or under statutory provision);

• the breach of duty itself;

• the loss and how this was the result of the breach.

1.3 SCOPE OF THIS GUIDE

This book intends to equip the reader with a comprehensive and detailed understanding of both the substantive and procedural rules of evidence necessary to bring and maintain a successful personal injury, including clinical negligence, claim.

---

[1]   Although the number of statutory instruments regulating health and safety at work now well exceed six.

[2]   *Jenkins v Allied Ironfounders Ltd* [1969] 3 All ER 1609, HL; and *Larner v British Steel plc* [1993] ICR 551, CA.

[3]   [2001] ICR, 608, CA.

1.4 SOURCE MATERIAL

The source material dealing with matters pertaining to the evidence, the form it should take, its admissibility and deployment at trial are to be found as follows:

- Courts and Legal Services Act 1990, s 5

- Civil Evidence Act 1995

- CPR Part 22 – statements of truth

- CPR Part 32 – evidence (witness statements)

- CPR Part 33 – miscellaneous rules about evidence (hearsay and plans and photographs)

- CPR Part 34 – depositions and court attendance by witnesses

- CPR Part 35 – expert evidence.

The provisions of CPR Part 32 are supplemented by a practice direction that details the provisions about the form and content of written evidence in the form of witness statements and exhibits. It also contains provisions about agreed bundles of documents for hearings, and video-conferencing.

A further source material often overlooked by practitioners is contained in the Queen's Bench Guide which supplements the CPR. The part of this guide relevant to this book is contained in para 7.10.4, which we set out here for completeness although reference should be made to Chapter 7 below on witness evidence generally:

'In addition to the information and provisions for making a witness statement mentioned in paragraph 7.10.2, the following matters should be borne in mind:

(1) a witness statement must contain the truth, the whole truth and nothing but the truth on the issues it covers,

(2) those issues should consist only of the issues on which the party serving the witness statement wishes that witness to give evidence in chief and should not include commentary on the trial bundle or other matters which [may arise during the trial or] may have arisen during the proceedings,

(3) a witness statement should be as concise as the circumstances allow, inadmissible or irrelevant material should not be included,

(4) the cost of preparation of an over-elaborate witness statement may not be allowed,

(5) Rule 32.14 states that proceedings for contempt of court may be brought against a person if s/he makes, or causes to be made, a false statement in a document verified by a statement of truth without an honest belief in its truth,

(6) if a party discovers that a witness statement, which they have served, is incorrect they must inform the other parties immediately.'

1.5   PART 32 WRITTEN EVIDENCE

The core rules concerning the nature and use of evidence in a personal injury claim are set out in CPR Part 32 (written evidence) and also in CPR Part 35, which deals with expert evidence.

Part 32.1 is central to this book. It provides as follows:

'32.1 Power of court to control evidence

(1) The court may control the evidence by giving directions as to—
(a)   the issues on which it requires evidence;
(b)   the nature of the evidence which it requires to decide those issues; and
(c)   the way in which the evidence is to be placed before the court.

(2) The court may use its power under this rule to exclude evidence that would otherwise be admissible.

(3) The court may limit cross-examination.'

Under the CPR and related practice directions the court has extensive powers to manage cases and these powers are to be used flexibly. The nature of case management may vary, depending on whether a case is allocated to the fast track or multi-track, and, in the latter event, on whether the case is straightforward or less simple.

The general power to 'control the evidence' is an unfettered discretion, crucial to the effective operation of the CPR and the proper management of cases and must be applied by the court in accordance with the overriding objective.[4] A number of rules in Part 32 are subject to CPR 32.1. If a party wishes to challenge the admissibility of evidence often CPR 32.1 is cited as the source of the court's power so to do, even though the main reason for the alleged exclusion, for example where a document sought to be relied upon by one party said by the other to be privileged, is more properly based in substantive law.[5]

In exercising its powers of case management, the court may make rulings which are complemented by directions under CPR 32.1 such as restricting

---

[4]   *O'Brien v Chief Constable of South Wales* [2005] UKHL 26; [2005] 2 AC 534, HL.
[5]   See *GE Capital Commercial Finance Ltd v Sutton* [2003] EWHC 1648, QB.

a party to his previous schedule or counter-schedule and the evidence in support thereof as a sanction for failing to serve an updated one by a certain time (as occurred in *Walsh v Misseldine*.[6]

Practitioners should always be cognisant of the fact that written evidence, as identified by the CPR, is not restricted to witness statements but include the statements of case, the schedule and counter-schedule as well as any notices of application that are all to be verified by a 'statement of truth'.

As to whether a judge in civil proceedings has much if any discretion other than under its case management powers to exclude relevant and admissible evidence has been questioned by some commentators[7] but clearly the pursuit of the overriding objective means that the courts in personal injury claims regularly exclude evidence that is otherwise relevant and admissible, for example where a court directs that expert evidence be limited to one discipline and be the product of a joint instruction or where it directs that any further witness statement served by the claimant be limited to certain issues but not others.

Older practitioners may recall the limits imposed on the use of hearsay evidence in civil proceedings and until relatively recently there was a degree of parity between civil and criminal proceedings limiting if not entirely excluding the use of hearsay evidence. The position now is that such common law rules as there remain excluding hearsay evidence are almost entirely negated by the Civil Evidence Act 1995, which provides that evidence is not to be excluded in civil proceedings on the ground only that it is hearsay.[8]

The 1995 Act though provides that it is for the court to decide the weight, if any, to be given to hearsay evidence and this requires the court to concentrate its attention on the question of weight in the individual circumstances of the evidence and the case.

Chapter 7 below deals with the factors the court will take account in deciding how much weight should be attached to hearsay evidence but it is probably fair to say that such evidence will rarely be given the same importance as direct oral testimony subject to cross-examination. As a result of this process the hearsay evidence may in fact be given no weight at all, which would essentially equate to the position as if the evidence had never been admitted in the first place.

---

[6]   [2000] CP Rep 74; [2000] CPLR 201.
[7]   *Cross and Tapper on Evidence* (9th edn, 1999), p 195.
[8]   Section 1.

1.6   PART 35 EXPERT EVIDENCE

In almost all personal injury and probably all clinical negligence cases some form of expert evidence will be required. This will predominantly involve medical or clinical experts but other types of expert are often necessary as to liability but also as to quantum, such as an engineer, or accommodation expert.

One of the progenitors of the CPR was the recognition that the use of expert evidence had led to increased expense and delay. Of real concern was the failure by some experts to maintain their independence from the instructing party, and who often became the party's advocate instead.[9] Since the advent of the CPR the court's control over the use of expert evidence is more or less absolute and covers the pre-issue as well as post-issue period. Chapter 6 below deals with expert evidence and the restriction upon its use in detail.

It is the 'Protocol for the Instruction of Experts to give Evidence in Civil Claims', which is annexed to Part 35, that governs the way in which experts are to be used in civil litigation now.[10] The Protocol replaces the earlier Codes of Guidance on Expert Evidence produced by the Expert Witness Institute and the Academy of Experts. The Protocol offers guidance to experts and those who instruct them in compliance with CPR Part 35. It is intended to assist in interpretation, not to replace the rules or any practice direction.

The Protocol does not apply to an expert who advises only before proceedings and whose advice will remain privileged unless this is waived. The Protocol though does apply if the same expert is later relied upon by the same party in the proceedings and this is often forgotten in the context of personal injury claims, and often by defendant practitioners who sometimes wrongly insist on the disclosure of expert reports obtained by the claimant before proceedings begin.

This pre-CPR concern about the proliferation and misuse of expert evidence generated CPR 35.1, which directs that: 'Expert evidence shall be restricted to that which is reasonably required to resolve the proceedings.' The court then will generally attempt always to control expert evidence by directing the issues on which it allows such evidence and the way in which the evidence is to be placed before the court. The rule exhorts the court to restrict the excessive or inappropriate use of expert evidence. Yet it would be wrong to think that the court's discretion to permit the use of expert evidence is to be fettered. Again, the overriding objective must inform the application of CPR 35.1.

---

9   See chapter 13 of the Access to Justice final report.
10   Published by the Civil Justice Council in July 1995.

The wariness of the court in allowing expert evidence has been seen in a number of cases, including *Liddle v Middleton*[11] and *Hawkes v Southwark London Borough Council*.[12] When considering whether to grant permission for a party to use expert evidence the CPR do not provide any further express guidance, but the issue was considered in *Mann v Chetty & Patel*,[13] when the Court of Appeal considered the following factors ought to be borne in mind in considering whether to allow a party to rely upon a particular expert:

- How useful will the expert evidence be to the court in resolving the issues at stake?

- How expensive will it be to use the expert in relation to the type and size of case in question?

- How cogent or probative will the evidence be?

Practitioners should also carefully consider whether the evidence sought to be adduced from an expert is available from another source. This is sometimes the reason why the courts do no permit the evidence of an employment consultant, for example, who often do not make their reports specific enough to a claimant for it to be said that the evidence sought to be relied upon is not otherwise available elsewhere. Often it is said that the statistics upon which employment consultants rely are available publicly. However, while this might strictly be true, clearly a busy practitioner would find it more difficult to access the information and make it readily understandable without the help of an expert. The court needs to be told why permission is sought to be relied upon even if the reason is as described. It may often be cheaper and easier for an expert to do the research and present the evidence.

In summary the conduct of a successful personal injury or clinical negligence claim is dependent on a thorough understanding of what expert evidence is, how it should be used and what the potential court-imposed limitations will be.

1.7 PROTOCOLS

There are three pre-action protocols relevant to this book, which are dealt with in detail in Chapter 3. They are:

- the Pre-action Protocol for Personal Injury Claims;

- the Pre-action Protocol for the Resolution of Clinical Disputes; and

---

[11] [1996] PIQR P36.
[12] (unreported) 20 February 1999.
[13] (unreported) 26 October 2000.

- the Pre-action Protocol for Clinician Negligence Claims.

The protocols are designed to enable parties to a dispute to embark on meaningful negotiations as soon as the possibility of litigation is identified and to ensure that as early as possible they have the relevant information to define their claim and make realistic offers to settle. Lord Woolf said that the protocols:

- are intended to build on and increase the benefits of early but well-informed settlements that genuinely satisfy both parties to the dispute;

- should make litigants focus on the desirability of resolving disputes without litigation;

- should enable them to obtain information they reasonably need in order to enter an appropriate settlement ('cards on the table');

- should encourage litigants to make an appropriate offer (of a kind that can have costs consequences if litigation ensues); and

- should lay the ground for expeditious conduct of proceedings (if they do not settle pre-action.

In this book we will concentrate on the 'cards on the table' approach, emblematic of the protocols. The court now expects litigants to co-operate at an early stage in disclosing their case in outline in letters of claim and response, and by exchanging information, including key documents.

Failure to comply with the spirit of the protocols, including a failure to provide evidence in the form of key information and documents will be the subject of potential judicial criticism and sanction when the issue of costs arises.[14]

Therefore the protocols exhort claimant solicitors to obtain more information from clients on instruction and possibly from key witnesses at an early stage. Defendants have to make enquiries and respond to claims on a similarly prompt basis.

The Personal Injury Protocol is intended to apply mainly to potential fast-track cases with a value of up to £25,000,[15] but the general approach should still be followed in larger claims, except cases of occupational disease and clinical negligence, which have their own protocols. The

---

[14] See CPR 44.1 and 44.3(5)(b) and the Practice Direction to the Pre-Action Protocols generally.

[15] The limit was £15,000 in respect of claims issued before 6 April 2009 after which the limit was increased to £25,000.

defendant is asked to acknowledge the letter of claim within 21 days of receipt and respond in full within three months of the acknowledgment, either admitting or denying liability with reasons.

The protocol specifically requires the parties to co-operate on the selection of an expert, especially the medical expert providing a condition and prognosis report on the accident victim and this aspect of the protocol is dealt with below in Chapter 3 (liability investigations and enquiries) and Chapter 6 (expert evidence).

The personal injury protocol also recommends that the claimant's solicitor should be responsible for arranging access to the claimant's medical records and a specimen letter of instructions to a medical expert is annexed to the protocol. This aspect is dealt with in Chapter 4 (medical records).

The personal injury protocol includes as an annex, specimen non-exhaustive detailed lists of documents that defendants should disclose with any denial of liability in particular types of case, eg highway accidents and employers' liability cases. See Chapter 3 below (liability investigations and enquiries).

What about pre-action admissions made by defendants made in the course of protocol compliant behaviour? Are admissions any more than evidence against the defendant or are they binding? Until April 2007 the personal injury protocol required defendants to undertake to stand by an admission of liability for claims up to £15,000. This was a concession made by the insurers during the drafting stage. Before the CPR the Court of Appeal had indicated that a pre-action admission did not bind a defendant.[16] After the advent of the CPR between 2000 and 2005 the courts considered that pre-issue admissions ought to have a binding nature but that CPR 14.1 gave them the power to order the withdrawal of an admission whether made before or pre-action or during the proceedings, including in multi-track cases, depending on the circumstances.[17]

The Court of Appeal took a markedly different approach in *Sowerby v Charlton*.[18] The claimant suffered serious injuries in falling off steps leading to her flat. She fell into the basement courtyard below. The defendant's insurer admitted liability pre-issue but denied liability in the defence. At first instance and on appeal the relevant parts of the defence were struck out because of the pre-issue admission. The Court of Appeal

---

[16] *Gale v Superdrug Stores plc* [1996] 1 WLR 1089.

[17] *Hackman v Hounslow* [2000] CLY 354; *Flinn v Wills* [2001] CLY 412; *Sollitt v Broady Ltd* [2000] CPLR 259; *Browning v Oates* [2002] CLY 284; *Flaviis v Pauley* (unreported) 29 October 2002 (QB), Nelson J; *Hamilton v Hertfordshire CC* [2003] EWHC 3018, QB; *Barnard v Sappi Europe Ltd* [2005] EWHC 2169, QB.

[18] [2005] EWCA Civ 1610.

concluded that the CPR were concerned with the regulation of cases *after* an action is started and not with pre-issue conduct. They did not think that Part 14 was meant to cover anything other than post-issue admissions by when the claimant's case was fully formed and the subject of formal pleadings in comparison with the situation before the issue and service of proceedings. The Court of Appeal noted also that in multi-track claims the presumption against resiling from pre-action admissions of liability in the protocol was not repeated. Smith LJ, who gave the lead judgment, considered that *Gale v Superdrug*[19] should now be approached with caution as it was concerned with the pre-CPR rules.[20]

Since *Sowerby* CPR Part 14 has subsequently been amended in relation to pre-action admissions made after 6 April 2007 in personal injury, clinical negligence and disease and illness claims (Part 14A). The admission must be made after a letter of claim has been received, or states expressly that Part 14 applies. CPR 14.1A(3) provides that a pre-action admission may be withdrawn either (a) at any time by consent, or (b) when proceedings have been commenced, only with the court's permission.

New guidance is given in para 7 of the Practice Direction to Part 14 as follows:

> '7.1 An admission made under Part 14 may be withdrawn with the court's permission.
>
> 7.2 In deciding whether to give permission for an admission to be withdrawn, the court will have regard to all the circumstances of the case, including—
> (a)   the grounds upon which the applicant seeks to withdraw the admission including whether or not new evidence has come to light which was not available at the time the admission was made;
> (b)   the conduct of the parties, including any conduct which led the party making the admission to do so;
> (c)   the prejudice[21] that may be caused to any person if the admission is withdrawn;
> (d)   the prejudice that may be caused to any person if the application is refused;
> (e)   the stage in the proceedings at which the application to withdraw is made, in particular in relation to the date or period fixed for trial;
> (f)   the prospects of success (if the admission is withdrawn) of the claim or part of the claim in relation to which the offer was made; and
> (g)   the interests of the administration of justice.'

---

[19]   [1996] 1 WLR 1089.

[20]   In *Sowerby*, although the defendant was not prevented from applying to resile from its earlier admission the Court of Appeal nevertheless, pursuant to CPR Parts 23 and 3, declined to set aside judgment on the basis that the defendant did not in fact have a realistic prospect of success in any event. See also *Stoke on Trent City Council v Walley* [2006] EWCA Civ 1137.

[21]   As to what constitutes prejudice see *Ashraf v Devon CC* (unreported) 30 August 2007.

CHAPTER 2

INITIAL STEPS

Christine Tallon

2.1 INTRODUCTION

For many injured claimants the first appointment with you may be the first time that they have had contact with a solicitor. The process of coming to terms with an accident which may have caused them permanent physical and/or psychological symptoms, and of seeking compensation for those injuries, will be daunting for them.

The claimant may, in the case of serious injury in particular, feel uncertain about the future and uneasy in the presence of a solicitor. It will be important to build up a relationship of trust with the client at an early stage. The first appointment with the client will be vital both in terms of gaining the client's trust and in managing the client's expectations.

Empathy in relation to the claimant's symptoms, both physical and emotional, will greatly assist in gaining the claimant's trust, which should, in turn, lead him or her to talk more openly to you, making it easier to obtain the information required to formulate the claim and assess prospects of success fully. It is important to remember that the litigation process will be a stressful experience in itself.

This chapter will cover the principal initial steps that a practitioner needs to go through when preparing a personal injury case. Whilst the specifics of what is required in each case will vary depending on the facts, this chapter should serve as a useful initial guide.

2.2 WITNESS EVIDENCE

The Civil Procedure Rules ('CPR') Part 32 provides as follows:

CPR 32.2:

(1) The general rule is that any fact which needs to be proved by the evidence of witnesses is to be proved:

    (a) at trial, by their oral evidence given in public; and
    (b) at any other hearing, by their evidence in writing.

CPR 32.4:

(1) A witness statement is a written statement signed by a person that contains the evidence that that person would be allowed to give orally.

(2) The court will order a party to serve on the other parties any witness statement of the oral evidence that the party serving the statement intends to rely on in relation to any issues of fact to be decided at the trial

CPR 32.5:

(1) If:

  (a) a party has served a witness statement; and
  (b) he wishes to rely at trial on the evidence of the witness who made the statement,

  he must call the witness to give oral evidence unless the court orders otherwise or he puts the statement in as hearsay evidence.

(2) Where a witness is called to give oral evidence under para (1), his witness evidence shall stand as his evidence in chief unless the court orders otherwise.

(3) A witness giving oral evidence at trial may with the permission of the court:

  (a) amplify his witness statement; and
  (b) give evidence in relation to new matters that have arisen since the witness statement was served on the other parties.

(4) The court will give permission under para (3) only if it considers that there is good reason not to confine the evidence of the witness to the contents of his witness statement.

Importantly, CPR 32.10 provides that:

> 'If a witness statement or witness summary for use at trial is not served in respect of an intended witness within the time specified by the court then the witness may not be called to give oral evidence unless the court gives permission.'

2.3 THE CLAIMANT'S FIRST STATEMENT

When drafting any statement it is essential to think about who will be reading it, namely the defendant, the experts and the judge. It is important for the statement to give a clear picture of how the accident occurred, how it has affected the claimant and for the statement to support all the losses claimed. The statement effectively needs to tell a story.

The following is a list of some of the questions to be asked when taking instructions for the statement:

- If liability is in dispute or contributory negligence has been or may be raised, the statement should set out the accident circumstances. What happened? Where did it happen? How did it happen?

- The events immediately post-accident (assuming your client remained conscious) – were they taken to hospital by ambulance? What happened at hospital? What were the injuries sustained? What tests were undertaken (if the claimant is aware)? What were they told? How long was your client in hospital?

- When was your client discharged? Was this to his home or elsewhere eg a rehabilitation unit, care home etc?

- What difficulties did the client experience following his return home as a result of his injuries? Provide a property description. Did adaptations need to be made to the home, even if only temporary (eg moving a bed downstairs, using a commode)?

- Were there any personality changes (eg increased irritability, frustration, anger) and/or any effects on relationships with others?

- Is there any relevant past medical history?

- What was the claimant's pre-accident employment? What did he earn? What qualifications and experience does the claimant have? Have they returned to work? If not, what is the position regarding a return in the future? Should the claimant's CV be exhibited to the statement?

- What care did your client receive (consider care both whilst in hospital and following his return home)? Was any gratuitous care given by a friend or family member (bear in mind that gratuitous care includes emotional support, which may be particularly important during the period in hospital)? Was care paid for? If so, who funded that care? Did the carer give up work or take time off work? If so did the carer lose earnings? If so, how much?

- What out-of-pocket expenses were incurred? Examples might include costs relating to a damaged vehicle or damaged or destroyed clothes, travel to and/or from a hospital, GP or other treatment providers, treatment itself, medication, travel to work as a result of the accident (eg loss of use of a bicycle or car or additional expenses incurred as a result of travel anxiety) and increased costs incurred at home (eg higher heating bills as a result of the claimant having to stay at home, payments to others to undertake domestic activities such as DIY, decorating, window cleaning).

- Have any hobbies been affected? How?

- Were any planned holidays affected? Was the client able to obtain a refund?

- What are the claimant's future plans and hopes? Have they had to change as a result of the accident? How have they changed?

When drafting the statement consider also the likely weak points in the case and try to address them eg pre accident medical history, previous depression, previous accidents as these will almost inevitably be referred to in the medical records and will be raised by the defendant.

Bear in mind also that the statement needs to be in the claimant's own words and whilst it is likely that you will be drafting the statement for your client, avoid using words or phrases which it is clear would not be used by your client as this will become obvious if the matter proceeds to a trial and your client has to give evidence.

In fatal accident cases, witness statements are usually taken from a dependant or dependants. It is important to set out clearly the nature of the relationship between the dependant(s) and the deceased, the nature and extent of the dependency, which apart from financial dependence may also involve a loss of care claim, as well as the general claims for loss of household services or loss of a spouse or mother's care and affection. The statement should include details of:

- the deceased's job, earnings details including any overtime, bonuses and benefits or, if self-employed, the business and profits;

- the deceased's future career plans eg promotion, future changes in career due to retraining, further education and qualifications, etc;

- the deceased's state of health generally (this will need to be verified by the medical records);

- the dependant's own employment and earnings;

- any pension schemes of which the deceased and the dependant(s) were members;

- any children: Whose are they? Were they dependant on the deceased? Their ages; any childcare arrangements pre- and post-accident and any assistance provided to grandchildren (eg babysitting etc);

- the dependant(s) and, where the deceased was a spouse, the plans for the future, retirement etc;

- where future loss of household services is to be claimed, the tasks that the deceased would do around the home (eg DIY, gardening, cooking, cleaning etc);

- where the deceased was a parent, their involvement with the children (eg doing homework or providing financial support whilst at university).

2.4   EXHIBITING DOCUMENTS

Consider whether exhibits to the statement would assist. There will of course be documents which will be disclosed in any event, but it may greatly assist in bringing home some key points if certain documents are exhibited to the statement. By way of example, photographs showing the claimant immediately following the accident will give an indication of the likely level of pain and suffering, and photographs of residual scarring will assist in quantifying the claim. Similarly, exhibiting photographs and/or a plan of the locus of the accident is often very helpful. However, be careful not to exhibit more documentation than is necessary to prove the claim, as it is important that the statement and its exhibits are concise and other key documents will have been included in the disclosure list in any event. A detailed statement will help focus the mind of the claimant, give both solicitors and barristers the best information with which to assess prospects of success and assist medical experts as, particularly in catastrophic injury cases, there will be insufficient time during a medical assessment to discuss the many different ways in which the accident may have affected the claimant.

2.5   CPR REQUIREMENTS FOR A WITNESS STATEMENT

It should be remembered that a witness statement must comply with the requirements set out in CPR Practice Direction 32 – that is to say that the statement should:

- be produced on A4 paper with a 3.5cm margin;

- be fully legible and should normally be typed on one side of the paper only;

- in the top right-hand corner of the first page there should clearly be written:

  (1) the party on whose behalf it is made,
  (2) the initials and surname of the witness,
  (3) the number of the statement in relation to that witness,
  (4) the identifying initials and number of each exhibit referred to, and
  (5) the date that the statement was made;

- bear the initials of the witness on each page;

- be divided into numbered paragraphs and page numbered;

- be headed with the title of the proceedings;

- be expressed in the first person and in the witness's own words (see *Alex Lawrie Factors v Morgan*[1]) and should also state:

  (1) the full name of the witness,
  (2) his place of residence or, if he is making the statement in his professional, business or other occupational capacity, the address at which he works, the position he holds and the name of his firm or employer,
  (3) his occupation or, if he has none, his description,
  (4) the fact that he is a party to the proceedings or his relationship to a party in the proceedings.

Any exhibits should be separate from the statement and clearly marked as such, eg 'this is the exhibit referred to as "XYZ1" in the witness statement of XYZ'. Where a witness makes more than one witness statement to which there are exhibits in the same proceedings, the numbering of the exhibits should run consecutively throughout and not start again with each witness statement.

Further, CPR Part 22 requires a witness statement to be verified by a statement of truth.

CPR 22.2 provides as follows:

(1) If a party fails to verify his statement of case by a statement of truth:

  (a) the statement of case shall remain effective unless struck out; but
  (b) the party may not rely on the statement of case as evidence of any of the matters set out in it.

---

[1] (1999) *The Times*, 18 August.

(2) The court may strike out a statement of case that is not verified by a statement of truth.

CPR 22.3:

> 'If the maker of a witness statement fails to verify the witness statement by a statement of truth the court may direct that it shall not be admissible as evidence.'

Those giving witness statements should be reminded that proceedings for contempt of court may be brought against a person if he makes, or causes to be made, a false statement in a document verified by a statement of truth without an honest belief in its truth.

2.6 OBTAINING THE POLICE ACCIDENT REPORT

Where a road traffic accident has resulted in police attendance or where an accident has subsequently been reported to the police, there will generally be a police accident report ('PAR') relating to the collision. Such reports may include interviews with the parties to the collision (possibly under caution), statements from independent witnesses to the incident, comments from the officers that attended the scene about what they found, sketch diagrams of the scene post-collision and information about the speed limit for the road, traffic conditions at the time and weather conditions at the time.

It is always a good idea to make contact with the police as soon as possible, if only to put them on notice of your involvement on behalf of the claimant. They will hopefully then notify you when their investigations have been completed or when a decision has been reached regarding any prosecution. If they do not contact you, this should be followed up. If there is a prosecution arising from the investigation, you will have an opportunity to attend the prosecution trial in the event that liability is unclear or an allegation of contributory negligence is likely to be or has already been raised by the defendant.

In a case concerning a summary offence (in other words where the offence is only triable by the magistrates' court), for example an offence of driving without due and attention, the Crown Prosecution Service have a period of six months from the date of the accident within which to investigate and to decide whether there is to be a prosecution and to lay an information against the proposed defendant. In respect of offences that are triable by either the magistrates' court or the Crown Court (usually at the defendant's instance) or solely by the Crown Court by reason of the seriousness of the offence, such as death by dangerous driving, the CPS are not so limited. In any case it will not usually be possible to obtain a copy of the PAR until such time as the investigation and prosecution has been concluded. It can often take several weeks or months to obtain a copy of the report.

In the meantime, however, the police should confirm third party details and the registration numbers of the vehicles involved, which will enable a basic search to be undertaken at www.askmid.com to check that the vehicle(s) was/were insured and with whom. This website provides access to the Motor Insurance Database ('MID'). This is a database that was set up by the Motor Insurers' Bureau and is an up-to-date central record of all insured vehicles in the United Kingdom. Information can be obtained from this website on a one-off basis at the cost of £3.75 (at the time of writing) or an annual subscription can be purchased.

The lack of a copy of the PAR does not prevent a letter of claim being sent, though it may be that the defendant will attempt to avoid making a decision on liability pending the outcome of a prosecution, notwithstanding the requirements of the Personal Injury Pre-Action Protocol ('PI Protocol'). A civil claim is of course not dependent upon there being a successful police prosecution, though a conviction will greatly assist in establishing liability and almost inevitably leads to primary liability being admitted. However, this does not prevent an allegation of contributory negligence being successfully made in certain cases.[2]

To obtain a copy of the third party details or PAR, you will need to write to the police. A fee is payable, which varies from force to force. The Metropolitan Police require a form 518, which may be downloaded from their website,[3] to be submitted together with a fee. This will provide you with the basic report, but a further fee is payable should you require the full report.

Where liability is admitted in full, there is generally no need to obtain a copy of the PAR. However it is important to bear in mind that a defendant may later seek to withdraw from an admission or raise contributory negligence, at which point the report may become relevant. PARs are often destroyed after three years and upon receipt of an admission of liability, therefore, you should advise the defendant that in reliance upon that admission, you will not be undertaking any further investigations into liability. In the event that the defendant subsequently seeks to withdraw a full admission you will be able to refer to the unavailability of the PAR and your reliance upon the admissions in maintaining potential prejudice in any court application made by the defendant for permission to withdraw the earlier admission.

Where a copy of the PAR is obtained, check the statement made by your client to the police carefully to make sure that it accords with the

---

[2]   See Chapter 3 and the evidential significance of a conviction.
[3]   www.met.police.uk/index.shtml.

information provided by the client to you. If it does not, find out why not. The PAR will also contain copies of any other witness statements provided and details of any other witnesses including those from whom statements may not have been obtained. Due to the Data Protection Act 1998, the witness statements will have the contact details removed and it will therefore be necessary for a request to be made to the police for contact information to be provided, which will involve the police writing to the witnesses to seek authority to disclose this information, or an application would need to be made to the court under CPR 31.17 for an order for disclosure of witness details (for further information on how to make such an application, see Chapter 9).

2.7   THE RIDDOR REPORT AND ACCIDENT BOOK

The Reporting of Diseases, Injuries and Dangerous Diseases Regulations 1995 ('RIDDOR') place a legal duty on employers, self–employed people and people in control of premises to report all:

- work-related deaths;

- major injuries;

- injuries that last more than three days – that is to say that the injured person is absent from work or unable to perform their normal duties for over three days;

- work-related diseases;

- dangerous occurrences (eg near-miss accidents);

- injuries to members of the public or people not at work where they are taken from the scene of an accident to hospital.

Gas-safe registered fitters must also report dangerous gas fittings they find and gas conveyors/suppliers must report certain flammable gas incidents.

Under reg 7 of RIDDOR there is an obligation to keep a record of any reportable injury, disease or dangerous occurrence. The form in which this record should be kept is not specified and therefore could presumably take the form of an accident book entry, computer record, accident form or other written record.

Employers are required to keep any RIDDOR report (including any accident book entry made under these regulations) for at least three years from the date on which it was made (RIDDOR 1995, reg 7(3)). An injured party or, in the event of an accident involving a child, their parent or legal guardian, is entitled to a copy of the RIDDOR report. In order to obtain the report the injured party, parent or legal guardian, must make a request to the employer and under reg 7(1) of the Safety Representatives and Safety Committees Regulations 1978. The employer is obliged to comply with the request.

2.8   EARNINGS DETAILS

Apart from the claimant's basic wage, it is important not to overlook additional payments the claimant would have received 'but for' the accident, such as overtime payments, bonuses, shift or weekend work allowances and benefits in kind (eg company car, private medical insurance, gym membership, etc). Check whether the client has a second part-time job or whether he does any voluntary work that may pay a stipend. Even in situations in which the claimant is lucky enough to remain in receipt of full pay for a period of time off work following an accident, he may well only be receiving his basic pay. A claimant's contract of employment may provide that in the event that the employee recovers loss of earnings from a third party, the employer would have a right to seek repayment of their outlay. This should be determined by writing to the employer and obtaining a copy of the relevant part of the contract of employment before the witness statement and schedule of loss is finalised.

Earnings details should be obtained for at least three months, or 13 weeks, prior to the accident, but bear in mind that there may be seasonal variations that would necessitate earnings records being obtained for a longer period. Request copy P60s from the claimant or his employer and check when annual salary reviews are scheduled. Where the claimant is self-employed, it will generally be appropriate to consider a three-year history of earnings by reference to tax returns, annual company financial statements and profit and loss accounts. Where a claimant is the sole director/shareholder in a business that has been growing over a number of years and where there may have been a particular reason for a dip in a more recent year, accounts covering a longer period may be useful to show a general trend and support a higher loss claim than three years alone might justify.

An incorporated company cannot claim loss of profits as a result of an employee's absence from work.

2.9   PENSION LOSS

In addition to loss of earnings, the claimant's pension may be affected, particularly where he is unable to return to his former employment or is only able to obtain employment at a lesser salary or part-time or even not at all. Details should be obtained of any pensions to which the claimant contributed prior to the accident, together with details of any employer contributions which would have been made.

The claimant's state pension may also have been affected and a pension forecast should be requested from the Department for Work and Pensions by following the simple instructions supplied on their website.[4]

2.10 SPECIAL DAMAGES

The fundamental principle in UK law is that the injured party should be restored, so far as is possible, to the position he or she would have been in, but for the accident. Clearly where a claimant has sustained permanent injuries, no amount of financial compensation will change that however in practical terms the principle does mean that the claimant will be able to claim for all losses and expenses which have reasonably arisen and/or will reasonably arise in the future as a result of the accident (*Livingstone v Rawyards Coal Co*[5]).

Consider what expenditure or other out-of-pocket losses have been incurred as a result of the accident. The most obvious examples are:

- loss of earnings;

- loss of pension;

- gratuitous and/or paid care;

- travel expenses;

- additional household costs as a result of the claimant being at home, e g heating, electricity;

- medication purchased;

- equipment purchased and adaptations made;

- treatment paid for by the claimant including travelling costs incurred;

- home maintenance e g gardening/DIY;

- loss of holiday;

- future treatment and/or surgery costs;

---

[4]   www.direct.gov.uk/en/Pensionsandretirementplanning/StatePension/
      StatePensionforecast/DG_10014008.
[5]   (1879-80) LR 5 App Cas 25.

- hire/purchase costs of a replacement vehicle.

It is always wise to advise a client to keep a running record of all out-of-pocket expenses incurred, starting from immediately after the accident, together with receipts in support. A table provided to the client for completion as the expenses are incurred is useful, but providing the claimant regularly with a large envelope in which to keep all relevant receipts is usually the most reliable way of ensuring that the claimant retains the necessary evidence. The absence of supporting documentation will not be an absolute bar to recovery however where there is no or insufficient evidence to support a particular head of loss, the claimant runs the risk that the court will award a nominal amount only or in particular where the amount is too speculative, nothing at all.

Think ahead to disclosure – what documents are you going to need to prove the various elements of the claimant's claim? The client should be made aware of the ongoing obligation to disclose any documentation relevant to the case that comes into being throughout the duration of the case – whether or not it is supportive to the claim. For further details about disclosure obligations, see Chapter 9.

Check whether the client has received any payments as a result of the accident or injury. If payments have been made as a result of an insurance policy (for example, critical illness or mortgage protection plans), details will be required. Usually such benefits will not be deductible against any earnings or pension loss claim but they are relevant generally to the claim. Often it will be necessary to explain how the claimant is managing to survive despite the injuries and his inability to work and earn to assuage any concerns that the claimant has found alternative employment and not disclosed this. In addition, it is important to bear in mind that certain benefits that the claimant may have received could be recoverable by the Department for Work and Pensions on the claimant receiving their compensation from the defendant.

2.11   OTHER WITNESSES

You need to consider the elements that will need to be proved in order for the claim to be successful and how statements other than that of the claimant may support certain aspects of the claim. Any such evidence should be obtained as soon as possible, even if only in draft form, as memories will inevitably fade with the passage of time or witnesses will move on and the opportunity to obtain their evidence will be lost. This will also provide you with an early indication of those elements of the claim which can be supported by independent witness evidence and those which cannot or which require further investigation.

Where liability is in issue or contributory negligence raised, statements will be required from witnesses to the accident, though you may need to await the PAR to obtain names and addresses. In addition to statements from witnesses relevant to liability, consideration should be given to how other witnesses might support the quantum part of the case. In particular, where the claimant has received gratuitous care, statements should be obtained from those who provided the care. If a report from a care expert is required, such a statement will greatly assist in its preparation. Such statements should detail what type of care was required and the amount of care provided per day and at what time of day (enhanced rates may apply where night time care is required), whether this included emotional support, over what period the care was provided, how the amount of care provided changed over time and the current continuing care provided, if any. If carers travelled to hospital, the statement should also detail the number of journeys made, expenses incurred in travelling to hospital such as mileage and parking costs and the time taken to travel.

Where the claimant's employment has been affected, whether temporarily or permanently, statements from his employer or former employers should be obtained, and should include the following information:

- details of the nature of the claimant's employment,

- confirmation of earnings including overtime,

- confirmation of the claimant's absence and loss of earnings following the accident,

- whether the claimant has returned to work and, if so, whether this is at pre-accident capacity,

- whether the claimant has needed to be placed on light duties,

- promotion prospects both pre- and post-accident.

The above information should support your loss of earnings claim. Other work colleagues may be useful comparators particularly where they have received promotions, bonuses etc.

Where the claimant is a child, consider obtaining witness statements from the headmaster of his school, or his teacher, detailing the claimant's character, academic achievements, anticipated successes and involvement in extra-curricular activities, both before and after the index accident. Any significant changes should be highlighted.

Particularly in cases in which the claimant has been permanently affected, witness statements that provide a description of the claimant's life and personality pre and post accident are also useful.

Remember that under the CPR, the general rule is that a witness statement will stand as the witness's evidence in chief and it is therefore crucial to ensure that the statements cover all relevant matters that you would wish to bring to the attention of the court. It should not be assumed that a judge at trial will grant permission to ask additional questions of the claimant or a witness, as many will not.

2.12   PHOTOGRAPHS

Where possible, obtain colour photographs of the scene of the accident. This is particularly important in tripping and slipping cases as, once reported to the relevant defendant, the defect is likely to be rectified expeditiously. Proving a case without such evidence can be very difficult indeed.

Photographs of the injuries themselves are also helpful. If possible, obtain photographs showing the claimant's injuries in hospital when they were likely to be at their worst, to give an impression of the likely level of distress. Such detail should assist in maximising a claim for pain suffering and loss of amenity.

In serious injury cases where the claimant's accommodation is unsuitable (eg where the claimant is in rented accommodation that does not have wheelchair access) and alternative accommodation is sought prior to the instruction of an accommodation expert, photographs of the property should be obtained to support the assertion that the accommodation was unsuitable.

2.13   THE REHABILITATION CODE 2007 (ANNEX D OF THE PI PROTOCOL)

The purpose of personal injury claims is to put the injured party, as far as and as quickly as possible, back into the position in which they would have been but for the accident. With this in mind, the Rehabilitation Code was originally launched in 1999 and subsequently revised in 2007. Whilst it is not mandatory for parties to follow the Code, it is widely accepted as good practice and has been appended to the PI Protocol though, interestingly, not to the protocol relating to clinical negligence claims.

The road to recovery may be a long one for the claimant. If steps can be taken as soon as is reasonably practicable to assist the claimant in regaining some form of normality, all parties will benefit.

Under s 4 of the PI Protocol, reiterated in the Rehabilitation Code, 'The claimant or the defendant or both shall consider as early as possible whether the claimant has reasonable needs that could be met by rehabilitation treatment or other measures.' In other words, consideration should be given to whether there is anything that can be done to improve the claimant's present and/or long-term physical and mental wellbeing. Parties should liaise with a view to implementing the Code. The claimant's solicitor should provide notification of the claim and of the requirement for the claimant's rehabilitation needs to be addressed to the defendant as soon as possible following receipt of instructions. An example letter on behalf of the claimant is contained at annex A to the PI Protocol. There is no requirement for the letter of claim to have been sent or for the defendant to have concluded its liability investigations before this letter is sent.

2.14   THE IMMEDIATE NEEDS ASSESSMENT

The parties should attempt to agree the instruction of a suitable person or organisation (generally an occupational therapist, specialist nurse or other person with the appropriate skill to be able to assess the claimant's needs) to carry out immediate assessment of the claimant's needs (referred to as the Immediate Needs Assessment or 'INA') although under the Code, the costs of the assessment will be met by the compensator. Preferably, the assessment should be carried out in person but it may be carried out by telephone. It is not regarded as an expert report and is therefore excluded from the provisions of Parts 3.15–3.21 of the PI Protocol.

The INA should:

- provide a very brief summary of the accident circumstances. This can be limited to just one sentence (eg 'The claimant was travelling as a passenger in a vehicle which collided with a tree'). The report should not attempt to provide a detailed account of the accident circumstances and should not comment on any issues relating to liability;

- summarise the injuries sustained – at this early stage, medical records may not have been obtained, but the person carrying out the INA should at least have access to any discharge summary which the claimant received from hospital, a copy of which will have been provided to the claimant's GP;

- summarise the claimant's current disability/incapacity arising as a result of the injuries sustained;

- describe the claimant's domestic circumstances. This will be particularly important if, for example, the claimant has sustained injuries which makes their current accommodation inaccessible (eg with a wheelchair) or wholly inadequate;

- highlight those injuries that it is considered may be alleviated by early intervention (eg counselling, physiotherapy);

- indicate the likely cost of the recommended treatment and the likely benefit of that treatment.

It is unlikely that the person carrying out the INA will be able to give an indication of the likely number of sessions of treatment required: this will be clarified once the initial assessments have been carried out by the appointed physiotherapist, counsellor etc. Any treatment costs that are authorised by the compensator under the Rehabilitation Code will not be repayable by the claimant in the event that the claim fails, is discontinued or an element of contributory negligence is found.

2.15 APPENDIX: THE 2007 REHABILITATION CODE

Introduction

The aim of this code is to promote the use of rehabilitation and early intervention in the compensation process so that the injured person makes the best and quickest possible medical, social and psychological recovery. This objective applies whatever the severity of the injuries sustained by the claimant. The Code is designed to ensure that the claimant's need for rehabilitation is assessed and addressed as a priority, and that the process of so doing is pursued on a collaborative basis by the claimant's lawyer and the compensator. Therefore, in every case, where rehabilitation is likely to be of benefit, the earliest possible notification to the compensator of the claim and of the need for rehabilitation will be expected.

1. Introduction

1.1 The purpose of the personal injury claims process is to put the individual back into the same position as he or she would have been in, had the accident not occurred, insofar as money can achieve that objective. The purpose of the rehabilitation code is to provide a framework within which the claimant's health, quality of life and ability to work are restored as far as possible before, or simultaneously with, the process of assessing compensation.

1.2 Although the Code is recognised by the Personal Injury Pre-Action Protocol, its provisions are not mandatory. It is recognised that the aims of the Code can be achieved without strict adherence to the terms of the Code, and therefore it is open to the parties to agree an alternative framework to achieve the early rehabilitation of the claimant.

1.3 However, the Code provides a useful framework within which claimant's lawyers and the compensator can work together to ensure that the needs of injured claimants are assessed at an early stage.

1.4 In any case where agreement on liability is not reached it is open to the parties to agree that the Code will in any event operate, and the question of delay pending resolution of liability should be balanced with the interests of the injured party. However, unless so agreed, the Code does not apply in the absence of liability or prior to agreement on liability being reached.

1.5 In this code the expression 'the compensator' shall include any loss adjuster, solicitor or other person acting on behalf of the compensator.

2. The claimant's solicitor

2.1 It should be the duty of every claimant's solicitor to consider, from the earliest practicable stage, and in consultation with the claimant, the claimant's family, and where appropriate the claimant's treating physician(s), whether it is likely or possible that early intervention, rehabilitation or medical treatment would improve their present and/or long term physical and mental well being. This duty is ongoing throughout the life of the case but is of most importance in the early stages.

2.2 The claimant's solicitors will in any event be aware of their responsibilities under section 4 of the Pre-Action Protocol for Personal Injury Claims.

2.3 It shall be the duty of a claimant's solicitor to consider, with the claimant and/or the claimant's family, whether there is an immediate need for aids, adaptations, adjustments to employment to enable the claimant to keep his/her existing job, obtain suitable alternative employment with the same employer or retrain for new employment, or other matters that would seek to alleviate problems caused by disability, and then to communicate with the compensators as soon as practicable about any such rehabilitation needs, with a view to putting this Code into effect.

2.4 It shall not be the responsibility of the solicitor to decide on the need for treatment or rehabilitation or to arrange such matters without appropriate medical or professional advice.

2.5 It is the intention of this Code that the claimant's solicitor will work with the compensator to address these rehabilitation needs and that the assessment and delivery of rehabilitation needs shall be a collaborative process.

2.6 It must be recognised that the compensator will need to receive from the claimants' solicitors sufficient information for the compensator to make a proper decision about the need for intervention, rehabilitation or treatment. To this extent the claimant's solicitor must comply with the requirements of the Pre-Action Protocol to provide the compensator with full and adequate details of the injuries sustained by the claimant, the nature and extent of any or any likely continuing disability and any suggestions that may have already have been made concerning the rehabilitation and/or early intervention.

2.7 There is no requirement under the Pre-Action Protocol, or under this code, for the claimant's solicitor to have obtained a full medical report. It is recognized that many cases will be identified for consideration under this code before medical evidence has actually been commissioned or obtained.

3. The Compensator

3.1 It shall be the duty of the compensator, from the earliest practicable stage in any appropriate case, to consider whether it is likely that the claimant will benefit in the immediate, medium or longer term from further medical treatment, rehabilitation or early intervention. This duty is ongoing throughout the life of the case but is most important in the early stages.

3.2 If the compensator considers that a particular claim might be suitable for intervention, rehabilitation or treatment, the compensator will communicate this to the claimant's solicitor as soon as practicable.

3.3 On receipt of such communication, the claimant's solicitor will immediately discuss these issues with the claimant and/or the claimant's family pursuant to his duty set out above.

3.4 Where a request to consider rehabilitation has been communicated by the claimant's solicitor to the compensator, it will usually be expected that the compensator will respond to such request within 21 days.

3.5 Nothing in this or any other code of practice shall in any way modify the obligations of the compensator under the Protocol to investigate claims rapidly and in any event within 3 months (except where time is extended by the claimant's solicitor) from the date of the formal claim letter. It is recognized that, although the rehabilitation assessment can be done even where liability investigations are outstanding, it is essential that such investigations proceed with the appropriate speed.

4. Assessment

4.1 Unless the need for intervention, rehabilitation or treatment has already been identified by medical reports obtained and disclosed by either side, the need for and extent of such intervention, rehabilitation or treatment will be considered by means of an assessment by an appropriately qualified person.

4.2 An assessment of rehabilitation needs may be carried out by any person or organisation suitably qualified, experienced and skilled to carry out the task. The claimant's solicitor and the compensator should endeavour to agree on the person or organisation to be chosen.

4.3 No solicitor or compensator may insist on the assessment being carried out by a particular person or organisation if [on reasonable grounds] the other party objects, such objection to be raised within 21 days from the date of notification of the suggested assessor.

4.4 The assessment may be carried out by a person or organisation which has a direct business connection with the solicitor or compensator, only if the other party agrees. The solicitor or compensator will be expected to reveal to the other party the existence of and nature of such a business connection.

5. The Assessment Process

5.1 Where possible, the agency to be instructed to provide the assessment should be agreed between the claimant's solicitor and the compensator. The method of providing instructions to that agency will be agreed between the solicitor and the compensator.

5.2 The assessment agency will be asked to carry out the assessment in a way that is appropriate to the needs of the case and, in a simple case, may include, by prior appointment, a telephone interview but in more serious cases will probably involve a face to face discussion with the claimant. The report will normally cover the following headings:-
1. The Injuries sustained by the claimant.
2. The current disability/incapacity arising from those Injuries. Where relevant to the overall picture of the claimant's needs, any other medical conditions notarising from the accident should also be separately annotated.
3. The claimant's domestic circumstances (including mobility accommodation and employment) where relevant.
4. The injuries/disability in respect of which early intervention or early rehabilitation is suggested.
5. The type of intervention or treatment envisaged.
6. The likely cost.
7. The likely outcome of such intervention or treatment.

5.3 The report should not deal with issues relating to legal liability and should therefore not contain a detailed account of the accident circumstances.

5.4 In most cases it will be expected that the assessment will take place within 14 days from the date of the letter of referral to the assessment agency.

5.5 It must be remembered that the compensator will usually only consider such rehabilitation to deal with the effects of the injuries that have been caused in the relevant accident and will normally not be expected to fund treatment for conditions which do not directly relate to the accident unless the effect of such conditions has been exacerbated by the injuries sustained in the accident.

6. The Assessment Report

6.1 The report agency will, on completion of the report, send copies onto both the claimant's solicitor and compensator simultaneously. Both parties will have the right to raise questions on the report, disclosing such correspondence to the other party.

6.2 It is recognised that for this assessment report to be of benefit to the parties, it should be prepared and used wholly outside the litigation process. Neither side can therefore, unless they agree in writing, rely on its contents in any subsequent litigation.

6.3 The report, any correspondence related to it and any notes created by the assessing agency to prepare it, will be covered by legal privilege and will not be disclosed in any legal proceedings unless the parties agree. Any notes or documents created in connection with the assessment process will not be disclosed in any litigation, and any person involved in the preparation of the report or involved in the assessment process, shall not be a compellable witness at Court. This principle is also set out in paragraph 4.4 of the Pre-Action Protocol.

6.4 The provision in paragraph 6.3 above as to treating the report etc as outside the litigation process is limited to the assessment report and any notes relating to it. Any notes and reports created during the subsequent case management process will be covered by the usual principle in relation to disclosure of documents and medical records relating to the claimant.

6.5 The compensator will pay for the report within 28 days of receipt.

6.6 This code intends that the parties will continue to work together to ensure that the rehabilitation which has been recommended proceeds smoothly and that any further rehabilitation needs are also assessed.

7. Recommendations

7.1 When the assessment report is disclosed to the compensator, the compensator will be under a duty to consider the recommendations made and the extent to which funds will be made available to implement all or some of the recommendations. The compensator will not be required to pay for intervention treatment that is unreasonable in nature, content or cost or where adequate and timely provision is otherwise available. The claimant will be under no obligation to undergo intervention, medical or investigation treatment that is unreasonable in all the circumstances of the case.

7.2 The compensator will normally be expected to respond to the claimant's solicitor within 21 days from the date upon which the assessment report is disclosed as to the extent to which the recommendations have been accepted and rehabilitation treatment would be funded and will be expected to justify, within that same timescale, any refusal to meet the cost of recommended rehabilitation.

7.3 If funds are provided by the compensator to the claimant to enable specific intervention, rehabilitation or treatment to occur, the compensator warrants that they will not, in any legal proceedings connected with the claim, dispute the reasonableness of that treatment, nor the agreed costs, provided of course that the claimant has had the recommended treatment. The compensator will not, should the claim fail or be later discontinued, or any element of contributory negligence be assessed or agreed, seek to recover from the claimant any funds that they have made available pursuant to this Code

A copy of the 2007 Rehabilitation Code and of the 'Rehab Lite' version may be downloaded at www.bicma.org.uk/cobp.php.

CHAPTER 3

LIABILITY INVESTIGATIONS/ENQUIRIES

Linda Nelson

3.1   DISCLOSURE & THE PRE-ACTION PROTOCOLS

3.1.1   The pre-action protocols generally

When commencing enquiries into a case, the pre-action protocols ('PAPs') will often be a useful starting point. The first of the PAPs were introduced with the Civil Procedure Rules ('CPR') in 1999 and are intended to enable litigants to obtain information at an early stage; to focus attention on resolving disputes without litigation and to expedite the conduct of proceedings should pre-action settlement not be achieved. The PAPs are a key part of the current 'cards-on-the-table' approach to litigation and require a significantly greater degree of cooperation between the parties than was previously the norm.

The PAPs are codes of best practice rather than rules to be followed slavishly and courts are more interested in compliance with the spirit of a protocol than with its letter.[1] However parties should take care to follow them where possible: when making directions a court will take into account whether a party has complied with the Pre-Action Conduct Practice Direction and any relevant PAP[2] and failure to comply may have costs implications. For example, the Personal Injury Pre-action Protocol ('PI Protocol') specifically provides that once the letter of claim has been sent to the defendant no further investigation on liability should normally be carried out until a response is received from the defendant indicating whether liability is disputed.[3] Use of the word 'normally' is key and means that investigations need not grind to a halt in cases where the defendant does not respond within the prescribed period.

There are currently 11 PAPs in force. They are:

- clinical disputes

- disease and illness

---

[1]   Pre-Action Conduct Practice Direction 4.3(1).
[2]   CPR 3.1(4).
[3]   PI Protocol 2.10.

- personal injury

- construction and engineering

- defamation

- housing disrepair

- judicial review

- pre-action protocol for low value personal injury claims in road traffic accidents

- professional negligence

- possession claims based on mortgage arrears etc

- possession claims based on rent arrears

3.1.2 The Personal Injury Protocol

Each of the PAPs specifies the types of case to which it applies. The PI Protocol for example does not apply to occupational disease claims[4] and is intended to apply to fast-track cases – primarily road traffic, tripping and slipping and accident at work cases.[5] Even in cases where no PAP is applicable, they may still provide a useful template for pre-action enquiries.

Early disclosure at the pre-action stage must not be used as a 'fishing expedition' and requests must therefore be limited to those documents likely to assist in clarifying issues and resolving disputes. Useful lists of documents falling within standard disclosure are annexed to the PI Protocol. These lists are specimen and non-exhaustive.[6] There are individual lists for:

- road traffic accident ('RTA') cases;

- highway tripping claims;

- workplace claims (with specific sub-lists to be used where specific health and safety regulations apply).

These lists are reproduced at appendix 1 to this chapter.

---

[4]   PI Protocol 2.2.
[5]   PI Protocol 2.3.
[6]   Eg PI Protocol 3.11.

The RTA list includes documents identifying damage, MOT and maintenance records if relevant and further documents applicable to cases involving commercial vehicles or allegations of highway design defect. The highway tripping list includes inspection, maintenance, accident and complaints records and minutes of meetings where maintenance or repair policy has been discussed. The workplace list includes accident book entries, accident investigation report, Reporting of Injuries, Diseases and Dangerous Occurrences Regulations 1995 ('RIDDOR') report to the HSE, risk assessments (pre- and post-accident), employee training, information and documents relating to previous accident(s) identified by the claimant (note: *not* documents relating to 'any previous similar accident'), as well as documents relevant to the various health and safety regulations.

3.1.3 Clinical Negligence Protocol

The Pre-Action Protocol for the Resolution of Clinical Disputes ('Clinical Negligence Protocol') provides that requests for copies of clinical records should be made using the Law Society and Department of Health approved standard forms, which are at Annex B of the protocol (and reproduced at appendix 2 to this chapter), adapted as necessary. The purpose of the form is to standardise and streamline the disclosure of medical records and obviate the need for further correspondence and queries. The information to be provided on the form, which can also be used in personal injury cases, includes basic details about the claimant (name, address, date of birth, national insurance number etc); summary of the reason for the request for records (where, when and by whom was the treatment provided), a confirmation that reasonable copying charges will be paid and the solicitor's contact details.

3.1.4 Disease and Illness Pre-Action Protocol and the Mesothelioma Practice Direction

The Disease and Illness Pre-Action Protocol ('Disease and Illness Protocol') applies to all personal injury claims where the injury results not from an accident but takes the form of an illness or disease. 'Disease' means: 'any illness physical or psychological, any disorder, ailment, affliction, complaint, malady or derangement other than a physical or psychological injury solely caused by an accident or other single event'.[7] This PAP therefore applies to asbestos claims for example.

The Royal Courts of Justice in London operates a 'fast-track' process for mesothelioma cases and all asbestos-related claims (asbestosis, lung cancer etc). The process, designed by Senior Master Whitaker, aims to complete claims within four months of service of the claim form (where the victim is still alive) or within six months (in all other claims). The

---

[7]   Disease and Illness Protocol 2.1 and 2.2.

process is contained in CPR Practice Direction 3D and applies only once the claim has been issued. It allows the court to operate a show cause procedure, which applies unless there is good reason for it not to.[8] Where it applies, at the first case management conference ('CMC') the defendant must show cause (by identifying the evidence and legal arguments that give the defendant a real prospect of success on any or all issues of liability[9]) why judgment on liability should not be entered against the defendant.[10] This process may curtail the litigation but initial investigations are still required before the claim can be issued. In order for the court to adopt the show cause procedure the claimant must file and serve a witness statement regarding liability with the claim form (or not less than seven days before the CMC[11]). The statement must identify as far as possible:[12]

- the alleged victim's employment history and history of exposure to asbestos;

- the identity of any employer where exposure to asbestos of the alleged victim is alleged;

- details of any self-employment in which the alleged victim may have been exposed; and

- details of all claims made and payments received under the Pneumoconiosis etc (Workers' Compensation) Act 1979.

The claimant must also attach to the claim form a work history from HM Revenue and Customs where available.[13]

Disease and illness claims often entail additional lines of enquiry: to identify the employment(s) where the disease was contracted; to determine the appropriate limitation date and to establish causation. The Disease and Illness Protocol recognises these factors and therefore differs from the PI Protocol in many respects. Particular features of the Disease and Illness Protocol include:

- 4.1: a claimant may request occupational health records and personnel records before sending a letter of claim (in contrast to the procedure under the PI Protocol, where relevant documents need only be disclosed once the defendant has made its decision on liability). At annexes A and A1 to the Disease and Illness Protocol are a standard letter of request and application for documents,

---

8   Practice Direction 3D para 6.2.
9   Practice Direction 3D para 6.1.
10 Practice Direction 3D para 6.2.
11 Practice Direction 3D para 3.2.
12 Practice Direction 3D para 3.3.
13 Practice Direction 3D para 3.4.

which are very similar to the standard form of request for records annexed to the Clinical Negligence Protocol (see appendix 2 to this chapter).

- 5.1: third party record holders (such as previous employers and GPs) are also expected to cooperate with requests for disclosure. It will be a rare case where a decision on prospects of success can be reached without sight of GP records.

Where a defendant fails to comply with its PAP disclosure obligations a pre-action disclosure application may be made. This topic is addressed in Chapter 9. Further consideration is given elsewhere in this chapter to the investigations applicable particularly to disease claims.

3.2 INVESTIGATIONS IN INDUSTRIAL DISEASE CASES

Disease and illness claims often entail lines of enquiry that are not necessary in basic personal injury claims. Identification of the employment(s) where and when the breach of duty occurred giving rise to the subsequent disease (which may manifest itself many years later) and determination of the appropriate limitation date are two issues regularly encountered.

Identification of the correct defendant is often more complex in disease cases than in other personal injury cases. A claimant will frequently have worked for a number of employers over the course of his working life, any of which is potentially a defendant. Further, an employment history may be obscured by a company's change of name or transfers of employment. The following are good sources of this basic, but often hard-to-ascertain, information and if all else fails an enquiry agent may be necessary:

- A claimant's record of employment can be requested from the Inland Revenue and National Contributions Office (for contact details see www.hmrc.gov.uk). Records are available in respect of all employers who made national insurance contributions on behalf of their employees from 1961 to date. Making such requests is not always straightforward: records may be retained under the name of a parent company or may simply be incomplete or inaccurate.

- In order to determine the correct name of a defendant company, searches can be made on the Companies House website (www.companieshouse.gov.uk). Certain information about limited companies is provided free of charge, such as registered office, date of incorporation, date of last accounts and previous names, all of which may be useful in tracing the evolution of a company. Records are held for 20 years. Any further information may be obtainable on the site for a fee. In cases where a company has been struck off the register the company must be restored to the register before a claim can be brought. This is done by way of an application under sections 1029–1033 Companies Act 2006 to the Companies Court in the Chancery Division.

Where a defendant company has no assets (eg where it has been restored to the register) litigation will be pointless unless the company had insurance, in which case the claimant has a claim to the benefit of the insurance policy under the Third Parties (Rights Against Insurers) Act 1930 and/or Third Parties (Rights Against Insurers) Act 2010.[14] Not all companies will have employer's liability insurance as it has only been compulsory since 1972.[15] The following sources may yield details of any insurer:

- the APIL database of insurers, which can be searched via the members' section of the website (www.apil.com);

- the defendant's insurance broker;

- liquidator's report or list of creditors;

- bank account records (which may show payments to insurers);

- trade unions and/or local solicitors (some of which keep their own database);

- the Association of British Insurers' tracing scheme, which keeps details of dissolved companies. Enquiries are free of charge and are made by completing an online form. See www.abi.org.uk/EL_Code/Employers_Liability_Tracing_Service.aspx.

In a mesothelioma case the insurer at the relevant time may seek to argue that the terms of the insurance policy did not cover the mesothelioma claim in question. In *Durham v BAI (Run Off) (in scheme of arrangement) and other appeals*[16] the question arose whether it was the time of the cause of the mesothelioma (the time of the inhalation of the asbestos dust) or the time of the occurrence of the disease that served to identify a particular policy liability. It was decided that when an insurance policy included the phrase 'sustaining injury' this referred to the time when the injury was first suffered and not to the cause of the injury. The phrase 'disease contracted' was concerned with the causal origins of the disease. This is an issue which practitioners need to be alert to in cases concerning possible multiple defendants when considering which insurers the claim should be brought against.

---

14   The 2010 Act has yet to be given a commencement date at the time of writing.
15   Since the introduction of the Employer's Liability (Compulsory Insurance) Act 1969 on 1 January 1972.
16   [2010] EWCA Civ 1096.

Given the nature of disease claims, limitation is often a significant preliminary issue. By s11 of the Limitation Act 1980 the three-year limitation period runs from either the accrual of the cause of action or the date of knowledge (if later). In asbestos-related cases the date of exposure does not start time running: without damage (symptoms) there is no cause of action and there is typically a delay of 15–40 years between exposure and onset of symptoms. Even once a claimant has developed symptoms (breathlessness, etc) he will not necessarily have the relevant knowledge for time to start running. The date of knowledge is when the claimant knows or ought to have known:[17]

- that the injury in question was significant; and

- that it was attributable in whole or in part to the act or omission that is alleged to constitute negligence, nuisance or breach of duty; and

- the identity of the defendant; and

- if it is alleged that the act or omission was that of a person other than the defendant, the identity of the person and the additional facts supporting the bringing of an action against the defendant.

Detailed consideration of limitation is outside the scope of this chapter but it will be clear from this summary that an investigation into limitation will include consideration of the claimant's medical records and personnel or occupational health file, as well as taking a detailed statement from the claimant.

3.3 PROVING BREACH OF DUTY: CONSIDERATION OF RELEVANT SAFETY STANDARDS

Once a claimant's instructions have been considered and potential breaches of duty identified, further investigation may be required to determine whether there is in fact an arguable case.

There are a number of publications that provide greater insight into and analysis or explanation of the health and safety regulations that may be applicable to a workplace accident. These are considered below.

3.3.1 Health and Safety Executive Guidance

The Health and Safety Executive guidance publications are available from www.hsebooks.com and have been issued in relation to:

- the Manual Handling Operations Regulations 1992;

---

[17] Section 14 Limitation Act 1980.

- the Management of Health and Safety at Work Regulations 1999;

- Personal Protective Equipment at Work Regulations 1992;

- Provision and Use of Work Equipment Regulations 1998; and

- Workplace (Health, Safety and Welfare) Regulations 1992.

The publications contain more than just a simple explanation of the legal framework: they also contain background information and materials that may assist in assessing a claim. For example, the manual handling guidance contains tables of guideline weights that may be lifted by men and women in various circumstances. The guidance is produced to assist employers to comply with their obligations under the regulations and does not of itself impose any further duties. The HSE states within the guidance that:

> 'Following this guidance is not compulsory and you are free to take other action. But if you do follow the guidance you will normally be doing enough to comply with the law. Health and Safety inspectors seek to secure compliance with the law and may refer to this guidance as illustrating good practice.'

3.3.2   Health and Safety Executive approved codes of practice

The Health and Safety Executive ('HSC') publishes approved codes of practice ('ACoPs'). These are available from www.hsebooks.com. ACoPs have been issued in respect of a number of regulations, including:

- the Construction (Design and Management) Regulations 2007;

- the Workplace (Health, Safety and Welfare) Regulations 1992; and

- the Control of Asbestos Regulations 2006.

The HSE has the power to issue or approve an ACoP to provide practical guidance to regulations made under the Health and Safety at Work Act 1974.[18] A failure on the part of any person to observe any provision of an ACoP shall not in itself render him liable to any civil or criminal proceedings.[19] However where in any criminal proceedings a party is alleged to have committed an offence by reason of breach of a regulation in respect of which an ACoP is in effect, any provision of the ACoP relevant to the offence alleged shall be admissible in evidence in the proceedings and, where there is a failure to comply with a relevant part of an ACoP, that breach shall be taken as proved unless the court is satisfied that the relevant duty imposed by the regulation was complied with in

---

[18]   Section 16 Health and Safety at Work Act 1974.
[19]   Section 17(1) Health and Safety at Work Act 1974.

some way other than by observance of the ACoP.[20] In other words, ACoPs have the effect of reversing the burden of proof. There is no parallel provision applicable to civil proceedings but the codes will of course be of assistance to a court when determining whether there has been a breach of a particular regulation. A breach of an ACoP may be referred to in submissions as an aid to construction. It is not essential that the particular breaches of the ACoP relied upon are pleaded or put to the witnesses in evidence.[21] However in *Ellis v Bristol City Council* the court highlighted that it is necessary to treat the guidance with caution as it may be wrong.

- **International Organisation for Standardisation.** The International Organisation for Standardisation ('ISO') has operated since 1947 and aims to facilitate the international coordination and unification of industrial standards. Its catalogue of standards is available to view at www.iso.org/iso/catalogue_ics.htm. An ISO standard is a documented agreement containing technical specifications or other precise criteria to be used consistently as rules, guidelines or definitions of characteristics to ensure that materials, products, processes and services are fit for their purpose. The standards may apply to the safety, reliability and efficiency of machinery and tools, means of transport, toys or medical devices for example. ISO standards are voluntary and ISO has no power to enforce the implementation of the standards it develops. However the standards may be adopted as part of the regulatory framework or referred to in legislation.

- **Royal Society for the Prevention of Accidents.** The Royal Society for the Prevention of Accidents ('ROSPA') provides information and guidance on safety on the road, at work, at home, at leisure and on child safety and provides safety and risk education and inspections.

- **British Standards Institute.** The British Standards Institute ('BSI') was established in 1901 and develops private, national and international standards, certifies products, provides testing and certification of products and services and provides training and information on standards. BSI has 27,000 current standards, from health and safety (including personal protective equipment) to toy manufacture and food and drink. The full catalogue is available to view at http://shop.bsigroup.com.

Failure to comply with a BSI standard is not in itself a breach of duty but when considering allegations of breach of duty courts may take the BSI standards into account along with all the circumstances of the case.

---

[20] Section 17(2) Health and Safety at Work Act 1974.
[21] *Ellis v Bristol City Council* [2007] EWCA Civ 685, per Smith LJ at para 33 of his judgment.

In *Doherty & others v Rugby Joinery (UK) Ltd*[22] the Court of Appeal found the defendant employer to be in breach of duty for failing to respond to information published in 1990 in a book[23] on vibration-induced white finger ('VWF'). The claimants worked for the defendant in its door and window manufacturing factories and suffered VWF as the result of frequent use of hand-held vibratory tools. At first instance the court[24] found that the claimants had contracted VWF in the course of their employment with the defendant and it was agreed between the parties that at no time did the defendant in fact have knowledge that the tools used by the claimants carried a risk of VWF. A finding of breach of duty therefore depended on the defendant's constructive knowledge. The parties further agreed that the defendant's duty of care in such circumstances had best been defined in *Stokes v GKN (Bolts and Nuts) Ltd*:[25]

> 'The overall test is the conduct of the reasonable employer taking positive thoughts for the safety of his workers in the light of what he knew or ought reasonably to have known . . . Where there is developing knowledge, he must keep reasonably abreast of it and not be too slow to apply it.'

The claimants had also alleged a breach of duty for failing to respond to earlier key developments in knowledge, namely a 1975 BSI 'Draft for Development'[26] and a 1987 British Standard Guide.[27] The Court of Appeal upheld a finding that although the defendant should reasonably by 1976–77 and/or 1988–89 have reacted to those publications, no one in the industry had contemplated that they applied to the wood-working industry and they did not therefore trigger a duty on the defendant to monitor and assess for VWF. But for this point of fact, introduced by expert evidence, the failure to respond to the publication of the BSI Draft and Guide would have been the basis for a finding of breach of duty.

The nature of the duty that arises following such publications was described by the Court of Appeal. In the circumstances of this particular case, Wilson J found[28] that had the claimants been warned of the risk of VWF, they would have reported to the defendant the symptoms they were experiencing (instead of saying nothing, as they in fact had done). Once told, the defendant, acting in accordance with the BSI Draft, would have

---

22 [2004] All ER(D) 292 (Feb).
23 Written by Professor Griffin of Southampton University, called: '*Handbook of Human Vibration*'. It made the first reference to wood-sanders (as opposed to metalwork equipment) posing a risk of VWF.
24 HHJ Moore at Sheffield County Court.
25 [1968] 1 WLR 1776 at 1783D, per Swanwick J.
26 Not a standard: it was a provisional document as no definite conclusions could yet be reached on safe vibration levels. It was called 'Guide to the evaluation of exposure of the human hand-arm system to vibration.'
27 BS 6842:1987. Published on 30 October 1987 and entitled 'Measurement and evaluation of human exposure to vibrations transmitted to the hand'. This suggested that a VWF risk arose at substantially lower levels of vibration than the 1975 draft had suggested.
28 Paragraph 41.

removed the claimants from work with vibratory tools. As this was not in fact done, the defendant was in breach of duty. Hale LJ made the further general observation that employers are routinely expected to scan such publications to see whether they contain advice that might affect them and that what steps it is reasonable for an employer to take will depend on all the circumstances of the case.[29] In the course of argument the Court of Appeal were referred to *Armstrong v British Coal Corporation (No 1)*[30] in which it was held:

> 'It is trite law that an employer paying proper attention to the safety of his employees cannot rely on the absence of complaints from them as providing an impenetrable shield against possible liability.'

3.3.3   Highways Maintenance Code of Practice

In Highways Act ('HA') 1980 cases consideration must be given to whether the highway authority is in breach of its s 41 HA 1980 duty and to whether it will be able to rely on the s 58 defence. Assistance may be derived from the Department for Transport publication 'Well-maintained Highways. Code of Practice for Maintenance Management'. The latest edition was published on 6 July 2005 and is designed to help local authorities establish and maintain a road maintenance policy. It contains an introduction to the code, its scope and purpose, an analysis of the legal framework and principles for developing strategy and network hierarchy, inspection standards and monitoring of all service aspects. It is a useful document to compare with a defendant highway authority's own regime and it provides background information to highway inspections (how highways are classified, what should be recorded in an inspection report etc). A copy can be obtained for £53 from The Stationary Office (www.tsoshop.co.uk).

3.4   OBTAINING DOCUMENTS FROM THE HEALTH AND SAFETY EXECUTIVE

If the Health and Safety Executive ('HSE') are considering or are in the process of prosecuting, or have already prosecuted the defendant employer(s) concerned, it can often be useful to obtain the documents which form(ed) part of its investigation. Although the HSE is not party to the proceedings, under CPR 31.17 an application can be made for disclosure against it. The application must be supported by evidence (CPR 31.17(2)). The court can only make an order under this part where the documents are likely to support the case of the applicant or adversely affect the case of one of the other parties to the proceedings (CPR 31.17(3)(a)) and disclosure is necessary in order to dispose fairly of the claim or to save costs (CPR 31.17(3)(b)). In response to this

---

[29]   Paragraphs 47–49.
[30]   28 November 1996, unreported.

application, the HSE can apply, without notice, for an order permitting it to withhold disclosure of a document on the ground that disclosure would damage the public interest (CPR 31.19(1)). Paragraph 31.3.33 of the White Book states that the test is in effect whether withholding the documents is necessary for the proper functioning of the public service. Although public interest immunity cannot be waived, it can 'evaporate' if those involved in the giving and receiving of the information concerned consent to its disclosure. In deciding whether the administration of justice should prevail over public interest immunity, the fact that partial disclosure has already eroded the immunity is a relevant consideration (*Multi Guarantee Co v Cavalier Insurance Co Ltd*[31]). The decision ultimately rests with the judge as to whether there are reasonable grounds for apprehending danger to the public interest. In practice, the HSE will usually not disclose documents relevant to their prosecution until after they have decided not to proceed with their prosecution or until after any prosecution and appeal process has been completed.

3.5 EXPERTS' REPORTS

Instructing an expert is a step often required at the later stages of litigation and Chapter 6 addresses this topic in detail. However in some circumstances instruction of an expert will be required at the stage of initial liability investigations – generally in claims which turn not on points of law but on particular points on which only experts can give an opinion. This is often the case in clinical negligence claims.

The Clinical Negligence Protocol gives guidance regarding expert evidence.[32] It notes that the CPR encourages economy in the use of experts and a less adversarial expert culture but recognises that in clinical negligence disputes the parties will require flexibility in their approach to expert evidence. An expert opinion will generally be needed on breach of duty and causation before the prospects of success can be adequately analysed. Joint instructions are therefore rarely practicable. Whilst the parties are encouraged, as with the other PAPs, to discuss the need for experts and the appropriate instruction, the protocol is not prescriptive as to the form of instruction and the decision ultimately rests with the parties.

Where a report is obtained solely on one party's instruction (rather than a joint instruction) and the identity of the expert has not been revealed, then even if the instruction was agreed upon by the parties in accordance with the PI Protocol (ie the claimant indicated a list of potential experts, the defendant indicated any of those experts to which it objected and the claimant then instructed one of the remaining experts) the report remains

---

[31]   (1986) *The Times*, 24 June.
[32]   At s 4.

privileged and the court cannot order its production.[33] The instruction remains a single instruction by the claimant and although the PI Protocol encourages voluntary disclosure, the court cannot require it.

The instruction of an expert represents a significant financial commitment to a case and recovery of that cost will be of concern to the instructing party. It is worth noting therefore that the court's power to order a party to pay such costs may be limited:

- On the small claims track the court may order a maximum of £200 per expert.[34]

- Where CPR 45 II (fixed recoverable costs) applies, the court may allow a claim for the cost of only a medical report or engineer's report by way of expert evidence.[35] There is no cap on the amount recoverable.

- Where CPR 45 VI (pre-action protocol for low value personal injury claims in road traffic accidents) applies, the court may allow a claim for the cost of only a medical report or engineer's report or report as provided for in the RTA protocol.[36] The RTA protocol defines 'medical expert' as a person who is (a) registered with the General Medical Council; (b) registered with the General Dental Council; or (c) a Psychologist or Physiotherapist registered with the Health Professions Council.[37] It provides that it is expected that most claimants will obtain a medical report from one expert, but that a claimant may also obtain:

    - a report from a second medical expert in a different discipline where it is clear that one expert cannot deal with all elements of the injury;[38]
    - a further initial medical report from a medical expert in a different discipline on the recommendation of each of the two initial experts (ie the claimant may obtain a maximum of one initial medical report from four different disciplines);[39]
    - a subsequent medical report from an initial medical expert if the first medical report recommends that further time is required before a prognosis of the claimant's injuries can be determined, or where the claimant is receiving continuing treatment.[40]

---

[33] *Carlson v Townsend* [2001] 3 All ER 663.
[34] CPR 27.14(2)(f) and CPR Practice Direction 27, para 7.3(2).
[35] CPR 45.8(b) and 45.10(2)(a).
[36] CPR 45.28(b) and 45.30.
[37] CPR 1.1(13).
[38] CPR 7.4.
[39] CPR 7.5.
[40] CPR 7.6.

- On the fast track and multi track the costs will be assessed at the court's discretion, giving consideration to the factors at CPR 44.3.

3.6   EVIDENTIAL STATUS OF PREVIOUS JUDGMENTS

When investigating liability it may transpire that the relevant accident (or other tort or breach of duty) has previously been litigated in the civil courts or resulted in a prosecution in the criminal courts or has been considered at an inquest. It may be that a defendant employer has been convicted of a health and safety offence or a defendant in a road traffic accident has been convicted of a driving offence or successfully sued by another vehicle involved in the accident. Careful consideration must be given to the extent to which the subject matter or finding of those previous proceedings may be relied upon as evidence in the current claim.

3.6.1   General rule

The general rule at common law was laid down in *Hollington v Hewthorn & Co Ltd,*[41] a claim arising from a RTA, where the claimant sought permission to rely on a certificate of the defendant's conviction for driving without due care and attention. The claimant accepted that the certificate could not be conclusive but argued that it would be prima facie evidence of the defendant's negligent driving to which the court should attach such weight as it thought proper. The Court of Appeal upheld the lower court's decision that the certificate was not admissible, holding that the conviction was only proof that another court considered that the defendant was guilty of careless driving. A subsequent court could not know what evidence was before that court, what arguments were addressed or what influenced that court in arriving at its decision and the opinion of that court was therefore irrelevant.[42]

The rule in *Hollington* has not survived without criticism: in *Hunter v Chief Constable of the West Midlands*[43] Lord Diplock noted that *Hollington* 'is generally considered to have been wrongly decided'. However, the rule has been confirmed by the Court of Appeal in a number of cases, most recently in *Secretary of State for Business Enterprise and Regulatory Reform v Aaron,*[44] in which the court had to decide whether a report by the Financial Services Authority was admissible in disqualification proceedings under the Company Directors Disqualification Act 1986. The court held:[45]

> 'Despite criticism of the rule in *Hollington v Hewthorn* (as for example in the opinion of Lord Hoffmann in *Arthur JS Hall v Simons* [2002] 1 AC 615 at

---

[41]   [1943] KB 27; on appeal [1943] KB 587.
[42]   Per Goddard LJ at p 40.
[43]   [1982] AC 529.
[44]   [2008] EWCA Civ 1146.
[45]   Per Thomas LJ at para 20.

page 702D and the observations of Toulson J in *Lincoln National v Sun Life* [2004] EWHC 343 Comm at paragraph 92), the rule remains a clear rule of evidence – see the cases referred to in *Cross & Tapper on Evidence* 11th edition (2007) at page 119'.

3.6.2   Exceptions to the rule in *Hollington* (prior convictions)

There are some exceptions to this rule, the most significant of which is s 11 of the Civil Evidence Act ('CEA') 1968 in which Parliament went some way to reversing the rule in *Hollington*.

By s 11(1) CEA 1968:

> 'In any civil proceedings the fact that a person has been convicted of an offence by or before any court in the United Kingdom or of a service offence anywhere shall (subject to subsection (3) below) be admissible in evidence for the purpose of proving, where to do so is relevant to any issue in those proceedings, that he committed that offence, whether he was so convicted upon a plea of guilty or otherwise and whether or not he is a party to the civil proceedings; but no conviction other than a subsisting one shall be admissible in evidence by virtue of this section.'

Subsection (3) provides that nothing in s 11(1) shall prejudice the operation of s 13 of this Act or any other enactment, whereby a conviction or a finding of fact in any criminal proceedings is for the purposes of any other proceedings made conclusive evidence of any fact. Section 13 ('Conclusiveness of convictions for purposes of defamation actions') provides at sub-s (1) that in an action for libel or slander in which a relevant issue is whether the claimant did or did not commit a criminal offence, proof that the claimant stands convicted of that offence shall be conclusive evidence that he committed that offence and his conviction thereof shall be admissible in evidence accordingly.

The difference between ss 11 and 13 is the conclusiveness of the evidence of the prior conviction. Whereas in proceedings to which s 13 applies the conviction is conclusive, where s 11 applies the conviction is admissible and creates a rebuttable presumption: by s 11(2), where there is evidence of a person's conviction he shall be taken to have committed that offence unless the contrary is proved. The standard of proof is the ordinary burden in a civil action: the balance of probabilities. The defendant does not have to show that the conviction was obtained by fraud or collusion and does not have to adduce fresh evidence that is conclusive of his innocence, but in the face of a conviction after a full hearing, discharging the burden of proof is likely to be an uphill task.[46]

---

[46]   Per Lord Diplock in *Hunter* at p 736.

Documents admissible as evidence of the conviction and to identify the facts on which the conviction was based include the information, complaint, indictment and charge-sheet.[47]

The CEA has no parallel provision making acquittals admissible in evidence. In *Hunter* Lord Diplock observed that this is because the standard of proof in criminal proceedings (beyond all reasonable doubt) is higher than in civil proceedings (balance of probabilities) and a person's acquittal is not therefore inconsistent with a finding against him in civil proceedings.[48]

Section 11 will usually be used by a claimant who wants to rely on a conviction of the defendant, but the section is not expressly confined to prior convictions of defendants in civil proceedings. It is difficult to imagine circumstances in which a claimant could assist his civil action by relying on his own conviction for a criminal offence but a claimant may be tempted to use s 11 to initiate a collateral attack on his own conviction. In *Hunter* Lord Diplock observed that the general rule of public policy applies and the use of civil actions for this purpose would be an abuse of the process of the court,[49] the only exception being where there is fresh evidence that 'entirely changes the aspect of the case'. It should be noted that this test is more rigorous than that applied to applications to admit fresh evidence for the purpose of an appeal (where fresh evidence may be admitted if it would probably have an important influence on the result of the case, although it need not be decisive).

3.6.3   Prior civil judgments

As between the parties to civil proceedings the judgment in those proceedings will of course be conclusive. In this regard, the principles of *res judicata,* issue estoppel and abuse of process operate to prevent decided issues being raised in subsequent proceedings. Detailed analysis of these topics is outside the scope of this chapter, but some points of note are:

*   Even if a decision is based upon a view of the law that is subsequently expressly overruled by a higher court, the judgment itself remains *res judicata* and cannot be set aside.[50]

---

[47]   Section 11(2)(b) CEA 1968.
[48]   At p 734.
[49]   At pp 735 and 736.
[50]   See *Re Waring (decd), Westminster Bank Ltd v Burton-Butler* [1948] 1 All ER 257, [1948] Ch 221, as cited by Lord Hoffmann in *Arthur JS Hall & Co v Simons* [2000] 3 All ER 673 at para 24 of his judgment, at pp 705 and 706.

- An issue estoppel created by earlier litigation is binding, subject to narrow exceptions.[51]

However, non-parties will not be bound by that judgment: the rule in *Hollington* applies in this situation as it would where one party seeks to rely on prior convictions.[52] The reasoning is the same as that applied to convictions, namely the impossibility of determining what weight should be given to the judgment without retrying the former case. Where, for example, there has been a multi-vehicle collision and one claimant has successfully sued a defendant, a second claimant pursuing his own claim cannot rely on that judgment as evidence of the defendant's negligence, or of the facts found in that judgment.

The prohibition of collateral attacks applies to civil judgments as it does to convictions and the court has an inherent power to strike out a claim for abuse of process. Not every case which can be said to be a collateral attack on a previous judgment will be an abuse of process and nor is there a presumption to that effect. The court's power to strike out for abuse of process may be exercised where relitigation of an issue previously decided:

- would be 'manifestly unfair' to a party; or

- would bring the administration of justice into disrepute.[53]

Whether a claim falls into one of those categories is a matter for judicial consideration of the facts of each case.[54] In *Arthur JS Hall v Simons* Lord Hoffmann observed that in civil cases it will seldom be possible to say that an action for negligence against a legal adviser would bring the administration of justice into disrepute.[55] Whether the original decision was right or wrong is usually a matter of concern only to the parties and has no wider implications. The action for negligence may however be manifestly unfair to someone not a party, in which case it could be struck out as an abuse of the process of the court.

A judgment will be conclusive, as against all persons, of the state of things which it actually affects – eg that *A* must pay damages to *B*. It is not evidence of anything more eg that *A* was negligent or that the judgment sum was the true measure of damages.[56]

---

[51]   See *Arnold v National Westminster Bank plc* [1991] 2 AC 93, [1991] 3 All ER 41, as cited by Lord Hoffmann in *Arthur JS Hall & Co v Simons* [2000] 3 All ER 673 at para 24 of his judgment, at pp 705 and 706.

[52]   *Hollington,* per Goddard LJ at p 41.

[53]   *Arthur JS Hall & Co v Simons* [2000] 3 All ER 673, per Lord Hoffmann at p 703.

[54]   Ibid, per Lord Hoffmann at p 705, para 24 of the judgment.

[55]   At p 706.

[56]   *Hollington,* per Goddard LJ at p 41.

A similar but distinct point, considered in the case of *Al-Hawaz v Thomas Cook Group Ltd*[57] (a case referred to by Potter LJ in his judgment in *Secretary of State for Trade and Industry v Bairstow*[58] without specific approval or doubt) is the use of findings in earlier cases being put by way of cross-examination as to credit. In *Hawaz*, although the High Court upheld a ruling that a decision in earlier civil proceedings (that the claimant had forged travellers cheques) was inadmissible in subsequent civil proceedings between him and another person by virtue of the similar fact evidence test, the court had to be careful not to overly constrain an area of enquiry. In the instant case, the financial position of the claimant was relevant to the accusations of fraud and the alleged frauds were relevant as to his credit. The judge should therefore have allowed the defendant some limited cross-examination in respect of those matters:

> '... the principles adumbrated in Hollington v Hewthorn remain applicable in cases where none of the statutory or common law exceptions operate. Those principles prevent the findings made in earlier civil cases from being used subsequently as evidence of the facts found. They do not in themselves operate as a bar to the findings being put by way of cross-examination as to credit, subject to the control of the court, but that is a different topic with which it will be necessary to deal later in this judgment. But in so far as it was sought to adduce the findings of Ferris J in order to establish that the Respondent had committed fraud and forgery ... and had therefore been involved in a fraudulent claim on the travellers cheques in this action the learned judge was correct to rule that those findings were inadmissible in law.'[59]

3.6.4   Inquest

In many personal injury cases a coroner's inquest will be held in relation to the index accident. Coroners' offices are often very reluctant to give interested parties disclosure of the documentation gathered in advance of the inquest, but such documentation can be requested from the coroner's office after the inquest has closed. Attendance at the inquest is usually a good source of information: not only can one ascertain the content of witness statements etc, but it is also a chance to assess the witnesses as they give their evidence. Coroners' findings do not, of course, bind a civil court subsequently considering a particular injury or accident.

---

[57]   [2000] All ER (D) 1568.
[58]   [2003] EWCA Civ 321, at para 23.
[59]   Per Keene J.

3.7 APPENDIX 1: PRE-ACTION PERSONAL INJURY PROTOCOL STANDARD DISCLOSURE LISTS

FAST TRACK DISCLOSURE

RTA CASES

SECTION A

In all cases where liability is at issue –

(i) Documents identifying nature, extent and location of damage to defendant's vehicle where there is any dispute about point of impact.

(ii) MOT certificate where relevant.

(iii) Maintenance records where vehicle defect is alleged or it is alleged by defendant that there was an unforeseen defect which caused or contributed to the accident.

SECTION B

Accident involving commercial vehicle as defendant –

(i) Tachograph charts or entry from individual control book.

(ii) Maintenance and repair records required for operators' licence where vehicle defect is alleged or it is alleged by defendant that there was an unforeseen defect which caused or contributed to the accident.

SECTION C

Cases against local authorities where highway design defect is alleged.

(i) Documents produced to comply with Section 39 of the Road Traffic Act 1988 in respect of the duty designed to promote road safety to include studies into road accidents in the relevant area and documents relating to measures recommended to prevent accidents in the relevant area.

HIGHWAY TRIPPING CLAIMS

Documents from Highway Authority for a period of 12 months prior to the accident –

(i) Records of inspection for the relevant stretch of highway.

(ii) Maintenance records including records of independent contractors working in relevant area.

(iii) Records of the minutes of Highway Authority meetings where maintenance or repair policy has been discussed or decided.

(iv) Records of complaints about the state of highways.

(v) Records of other accidents which have occurred on the relevant stretch of highway.

WORKPLACE CLAIMS

(i) Accident book entry.

(ii) First aider report.

(iii) Surgery record.

(iv) Foreman/supervisor accident report.

(v) Safety representatives accident report.

(vi) RIDDOR (Reporting of Injuries, Diseases and Dangerous Occurrences Regulations) report to HSE.

(vii) Other communications between defendants and HSE.

(viii) Minutes of Health and Safety Committee meeting(s) where accident/matter considered.

(ix) Report to DSS.

(x) Documents listed above relative to any previous accident/matter identified by the claimant and relied upon as proof of negligence.

(xi) Earnings information where defendant is employer.

Documents produced to comply with requirements of the Management of Health and Safety at Work Regulations 1992 –

(i) Pre-accident Risk Assessment required by Regulation 3.

(ii) Post-accident Re-Assessment required by Regulation 3.

(iii) Accident Investigation Report prepared in implementing the requirements of Regulations 4, 6 and 9.

(iv) Health Surveillance Records in appropriate cases required by Regulation 5.

(v) Information provided to employees under Regulation 8.

(vi) Documents relating to the employees health and safety training required by Regulation 11.

WORKPLACE CLAIMS – DISCLOSURE WHERE SPECIFIC REGULATIONS APPLY

SECTION A – Workplace (Health Safety and Welfare) Regulations 1992

(i) Repair and maintenance records required by Regulation 5.

(ii) Housekeeping records to comply with the requirements of Regulation 9.

(iii) Hazard warning signs or notices to comply with Regulation 17 (Traffic Routes).

SECTION B – Provision and Use of Work Equipment Regulations 1998

(i) Manufacturers' specifications and instructions in respect of relevant work equipment establishing its suitability to comply with Regulation 5.

(ii) Maintenance log/maintenance records required to comply with Regulation 6.

(iii) Documents providing information and instructions to employees to comply with Regulation 8.

(iv) Documents provided to the employee in respect of training for use to comply with Regulation 9.

(v) Any notice, sign or document relied upon as a defence to alleged breaches of Regulations 14 to 18 dealing with controls and control systems.

(vi) Instruction/training documents issued to comply with the requirements of regulation 22 insofar as it deals with maintenance operations where the machinery is not shut down.

(vii) Copies of markings required to comply with Regulation 23.

(viii) Copies of warnings required to comply with Regulation 24.

SECTION C – Personal Protective Equipment at Work Regulations 1992

(i) Documents relating to the assessment of the Personal Protective Equipment to comply with Regulation 6.

(ii) Documents relating to the maintenance and replacement of Personal Protective Equipment to comply with Regulation 7.

(iii) Record of maintenance procedures for Personal Protective Equipment to comply with Regulation 7.

(iv) Records of tests and examinations of Personal Protective Equipment to comply with Regulation 7.

(v) Documents providing information, instruction and training in relation to the Personal Protective Equipment to comply with Regulation 9.

(vi) Instructions for use of Personal Protective Equipment to include the manufacturers' instructions to comply with Regulation 10.

SECTION D – Manual Handling Operations Regulations 1992

(i) Manual Handling Risk Assessment carried out to comply with the requirements of Regulation 4(1)(b)(i).

(ii) Re-assessment carried out post-accident to comply with requirements of Regulation 4(1)(b)(i).

(iii) Documents showing the information provided to the employee to give general indications related to the load and precise indications on the weight of the load and the heaviest side of the load if the centre of gravity was not positioned centrally to comply with Regulation 4(1)(b)(iii).

(iv) Documents relating to training in respect of manual handling operations and training records.

SECTION E – Health and Safety (Display Screen Equipment) Regulations 1992

(i) Analysis of work stations to assess and reduce risks carried out to comply with the requirements of Regulation 2.

(ii) Re-assessment of analysis of work stations to assess and reduce risks following development of symptoms by the claimant.

(iii) Documents detailing the provision of training including training records to comply with the requirements of Regulation 6.

(iv) Documents providing information to employees to comply with the requirements of Regulation 7.

SECTION F – Control of Substances Hazardous to Health Regulations 1999

(i) Risk assessment carried out to comply with the requirements of Regulation 6.

(ii) Reviewed risk assessment carried out to comply with the requirements of Regulation 6.

(iii) Copy labels from containers used for storage handling and disposal of carcinogenics to comply with the requirements of Regulation 7(2A)(h).

(iv) Warning signs identifying designation of areas and installations which may be contaminated by carcinogenics to comply with the requirements of Regulation 7(2A)(h).

(v) Documents relating to the assessment of the Personal Protective Equipment to comply with Regulation 7(3A).

(vi) Documents relating to the maintenance and replacement of Personal Protective Equipment to comply with Regulation 7(3A).

(vii) Record of maintenance procedures for Personal Protective Equipment to comply with Regulation 7(3A).

(viii) Records of tests and examinations of Personal Protective Equipment to comply with Regulation 7(3A).

(ix) Documents providing information, instruction and training in relation to the Personal Protective Equipment to comply with Regulation 7(3A).

(x) Instructions for use of Personal Protective Equipment to include the manufacturers' instructions to comply with Regulation 7(3A).

(xi) Air monitoring records for substances assigned a maximum exposure limit or occupational exposure standard to comply with the requirements of Regulation 7.

(xii) Maintenance examination and test of control measures records to comply with Regulation 9.

(xiii) Monitoring records to comply with the requirements of Regulation 10.

(xiv) Health surveillance records to comply with the requirements of Regulation 11.

(xv) Documents detailing information, instruction and training including training records for employees to comply with the requirements of Regulation 12.

(xvi) Labels and Health and Safety data sheets supplied to the employers to comply with the CHIP Regulations.

SECTION G – Construction (Design and Management) (Amendment) Regulations 2000

(i) Notification of a project form (HSE F10) to comply with the requirements of Regulation 7.

(ii) Health and Safety Plan to comply with requirements of Regulation 15.

(iii) Health and Safety file to comply with the requirements of Regulations 12 and 14.

(iv) Information and training records provided to comply with the requirements of Regulation 17.

(v) Records of advice from and views of persons at work to comply with the requirements of Regulation 18.

SECTION H – Pressure Systems and Transportable Gas Containers Regulations 1989

(i) Information and specimen markings provided to comply with the requirements of Regulation 5.

(ii) Written statements specifying the safe operating limits of a system to comply with the requirements of Regulation 7.

(iii) Copy of the written scheme of examination required to comply with the requirements of Regulation 8.

(iv) Examination records required to comply with the requirements of Regulation 9.

(v) Instructions provided for the use of operator to comply with Regulation 11.

(vi) Records kept to comply with the requirements of Regulation 13.

(vii) Records kept to comply with the requirements of Regulation 22.

SECTION I – Lifting Operations and Lifting Equipment Regulations 1998

(i) Record kept to comply with the requirements of Regulation 6.

SECTION J – The Noise at Work Regulations 1989

(i) Any risk assessment records required to comply with the requirements of Regulations 4 and 5.

(ii) Manufacturers' literature in respect of all ear protection made available to claimant to comply with the requirements of Regulation 8.

(iii) All documents provided to the employee for the provision of information to comply with Regulation 11.

SECTION K – Construction (Head Protection) Regulations 1989

(i) Pre-accident assessment of head protection required to comply with Regulation 3(4).

(ii) Post-accident re-assessment required to comply with Regulation 3(5).

SECTION L – The Construction (General Provisions) Regulations 1961

(i) Report prepared following inspections and examinations of excavations etc to comply with the requirements of Regulation 9.

SECTION M – Gas Containers Regulations 1989

(i) Information and specimen markings provided to comply with the requirements of Regulation 5.

(ii) Written statements specifying the safe operating limits of a system to comply with the requirements of Regulation 7.

(iii) Copy of the written scheme of examination required to comply with the requirements of Regulation 8.

(iv) Examination records required to comply with the requirements of Regulation 9.

(v) Instructions provided for the use of operator to comply with Regulation 11.

3.8 APPENDIX 2: MEDICAL NEGLIGENCE AND PERSONAL INJURY CLAIMS, A PROTOCOL FOR OBTAINING HOSPITAL MEDICAL RECORDS

CIVIL LITIGATION COMMITTEE

REVISED EDITION JUNE 1998

APPLICATION ON BEHALF OF A PATIENT FOR HOSPITAL MEDICAL RECORDS FOR USE WHEN COURT PROCEEDINGS ARE CONTEMPLATED

Purpose of the forms

This application form and response forms have been prepared by a working party of the Law Society's Civil Litigation Committee and approved by the Department of Health for use in NHS and Trust hospitals.

The purpose of the forms is to standardise and streamline the disclosure of medical records to a patient's solicitors, who are investigating pursuing a personal injury claim against a third party, or a medical negligence claim against the hospital to which the application is addressed and/or other hospitals or general practitioners.

Use of the forms

Use of the forms is entirely voluntary and does not prejudice any party's right under the Access to Health Records Act 1990, the Data Protection

Act 1984, or ss 33 and 34 of the Senior Court Act 1981. However, it is Department of Health policy that patients be permitted to see what has been written about them, and that healthcare providers should make arrangements to allow patients to see all their records, not only those covered by the Access to Health Records Act 1990. The aim of the forms is to save time and costs for all concerned for the benefit of the patient and the hospital and in the interests of justice. Use of the forms should make it unnecessary in most cases for there to be exchanges of letters or other enquiries. If there is any unusual matter not covered by the form, the patient's solicitor may write a separate letter at the outset.

Charges for records

The Access to Health Records Act 1990 prescribes a maximum fee of £10. Photocopying and postage costs can be charged in addition. No other charges may be made.

The NHS Executive guidance makes it clear to healthcare providers that 'it is a perfectly proper use' of the 1990 Act to request records in that framework for the purpose of potential or actual litigation, whether against a third party or against the hospital or trust.

The 1990 Act does not permit differential rates of charges to be levied if the application is made by the patient, or by a solicitor on his or her behalf, or whether the response to the application is made by the healthcare provider directly (the medical records manager or a claims manager) or by a solicitor.

The NHS Executive guidance recommends that the same practice should be followed with regard to charges when the records are provided under a voluntary agreement as under the 1990 Act, except that in those circumstances the £10 access fee will not be appropriate.

The NHS Executive also advises –
- that the cost of photocopying may include 'the cost of staff time in making copies' and the costs of running the copier (but not costs of locating and sifting records);
- that the common practice of setting a standard rate for an application or charging an administration fee is not acceptable because there will be cases when this fails to comply with the 1990 Act.

Records: what might be included

X-rays and test results form part of the patient's records. Additional charges for copying X-rays are permissible. If there are large numbers of X-rays, the records officer should check with the patient/solicitor before arranging copying.

Reports on an 'adverse incident' and reports on the patient made for risk management and audit purposes may form part of the records and be disclosable: the exception will be any specific record or report made solely or mainly in connection with an actual or potential claim.

Records: quality standards

When copying records healthcare providers should ensure –
1. All documents are legible, and complete, if necessary by photocopying at less than 100% size.
2. Documents larger than A4 in the original, eg ITU charts, should be reproduced in A3, or reduced to A4 where this retains readability.
3. Documents are only copied on one side of paper, unless the original is two sided.
4. Documents should not be unnecessarily shuffled or bound and holes should not be made in the copied papers.

Enquiries/further information

Any enquiries about the forms should be made initially to the solicitors making the request. Comments on the use and content of the forms should be made to the Secretary, Civil Litigation Committee, The Law Society, 113 Chancery Lane, London WC2A 1PL, telephone 0171 320 5739, or to the NHS Management Executive, Quarry House, Quarry Hill, Leeds LS2 7UE.

The Law Society

May 1998

Application on behalf of a patient for hospital medical records for use when court proceedings are contemplated

This should be completed as fully as possible

Insert Hospital Name and Address

To: Medical Records Officer

Hospital

1	(a) Full name of patient (including previous surnames)	
	(b) Address now	
	(c) Address at start of treatment	
	(d) Date of birth (and death, if applicable)	
	(e) Hospital ref. no. if available	
	(f) N.I. number, if available	
2	This application is made because the patient is considering	

	(a) a claim against your hospital as detailed in para 7 overleaf	YES/NO
	(b) pursuing an action against someone else	YES/NO
3	Department(s) where treatment was received	
4	Name(s) of consultants at your hospital in charge of the treatment	
5	Whether treatment at your hospital was private or NHS, wholly or in part	
6	A description of the treatment received, with approximate dates	
7	If the answer to Q2(a) is 'Yes' details of	
	(a) the likely nature of the claim	
	(b) grounds for the claim	
	(c) approximate dates of the events involved	
8	If the answer to Q2(b) is 'Yes' insert	
	(a) the names of the proposed defendants	
	(b) whether legal proceedings yet begun	YES/NO
	(c) if appropriate, details of the claim and action number	
9	We confirm we will pay reasonable copying charges	
10	We request prior details of	
	(a) photocopying and administration charges for medical records	YES/NO
	(b) number of and cost of copying x-ray and scan films	YES/NO

11	Any other relevant information, particular requirements, or any particular documents <u>not</u> required (e g copies of computerized records)	
	Signature of Solicitor	
	Name	
	Address	
	Ref.	
	Telephone Number	
	Fax number	

	Please print name beneath each signature. Signature by child over 12 but under 18 years also requires signature by parent
Signature of patient Signature of parent or next friend if appropriate	
Signature of personal representative where patient has died	

First response to application for hospital records

	Name of Patient Our ref Your ref	
1	Date of receipt of patient's application	
2	We intend that copy medical records will be dispatched within 6 weeks of that date	YES/NO
3	We require pre-payment of photocopying charges	YES/NO

4	If estimate of photocopying charges requested or pre-payment required the amount will be	£ /notified to you
5	The cost of x-ray and scan films will be	£ /notified to you
6	If there is any problem, we shall write to you within those 6 weeks	YES/NO
7	Any other information	
	Please address further correspondence to	
	Signed	
	Direct telephone number	
	Direct fax number	
	Dated	

Second response enclosing patient's hospital medical records

Name of Patient Our ref Your ref		Address
1	NAME OF PATIENT: We confirm that the enclosed copy medical records are all those within the control of the hospital, relevant to the application which you have made to the best of our knowledge and belief, subject to paras 2–5 below	YES/NO
2	Detail of other documents which have not yet been located	
3	Date by when it is expected that these will be supplied	
4	Details of any records which we are not producing	
5	The reasons for not doing so	
6	An invoice for copying and administration charges is attached	YES/NO

	Signed	
	Date	

CHAPTER 4

MEDICAL RECORDS

Edwina Rawson

4.1 SOLICITORS AND MEDICAL RECORDS

The task of obtaining medical records can often be slow, frustrating and occasionally overwhelming. It is often delegated to junior team members. However, the importance of obtaining a full and comprehensive bundle of medical records cannot be overstated. Inevitably in a clinical negligence case the medical records form the basis of the investigation and quantification of the claim. In personal injury cases, they are relevant to quantum.

4.2 GUIDE TO OBTAINING MEDICAL RECORDS

4.2.1 Step 1: Identify and apply for the records

The medical records will usually be applied for at an early stage. The first step is to identify all the sources of relevant medical records. This sounds trite, but it is easy to overlook obtaining records from an important, albeit perhaps less obvious, source. The starting point is to ask the client for details of all the places where he has received treatment for the injury in question, including details of his GP (whether or not he attended his GP in relation to the specific issue). In addition, details of any hospitals where he has had treatment for an unrelated problem should be obtained and considered, as these records may be relevant to establishing that there was no pre-existing medical problem that caused or contributed to the claimant's existing problem and that there was nothing before the incident that would have interfered with his ability to enjoy life and to work in any event.

In some clinical negligence cases, it may be desirable at the early stages to obtain medical records only from one or two sources, usually the hospital that has been accused of negligence and possibly the patient's GP. This may be done in cases where the solicitor wants to make an early decision as to whether the case is worth pursuing before running up costs. The remaining records can be obtained in due course if the solicitor decides to take on the case.

It may be necessary to obtain records that are not medical as such, but which may include some medical information and an insight into how the injury and any pre-existing conditions have impacted on the claimant's life, for example his personnel, occupational health or school records.

The claimant's solicitor should be responsible for obtaining a full and comprehensive set of medical records. Sometimes, the defendant will send a form of authority for the claimant to sign so that copy records can be released to the defendant directly. However this should be resisted. It is not appropriate to involve the medical expert in applying for the records. Further, in *Bennett v Compass Group UK,*[1] Clarke LJ observed that while a defendant has the right to inspect GP and hospital records in a personal injury case (copies of those records having been provided by the claimant), where the defendant applies for an order for the claimant to provide a written authority for release of those records to the defendant:

> 'a judge should think long and hard before making such an order because a defendant should only be allowed to see a claimant's medical records in carefully defined circumstances'

and such an order would be rare. This decision was considered with approval in *OCS Group Ltd v Wells.*[2]

The medical records should be provided within 40 days,[3] but in reality often take longer to arrive. A fee up to a maximum of £50 can be charged.[4]

When the sources of medical records have been identified, the application for copies will need to be made. If treatment has been provided at an NHS hospital, then the application should be made on the Law Society and Department of Health approved standard form. The standard form is annexed to the Pre-action Protocol for the Resolution of Clinical Disputes ('Clinical Negligence Protocol'). Use of the standard form is entirely voluntary, but as the purpose of it is to 'save time and costs for all concerned',[5] it is wise to use it. Failure to do so may well result in the hospital asking for the standard form to be adopted, thereby delaying matters. The standard form also includes a first response for the hospital to use in order to acknowledge receipt of the request and a second response with which they can enclose the copy records.

---

[1] [2002] EWCA Civ 642.

[2] [2008] EWHC 919 (QB).

[3] Data Protection Act ('DPA') 1998, s 7(8) and (10).

[4] Data Protection (Subject Access) (Fees and Miscellaneous Provisions) Regulations 2000, reg 6; Clinical Negligence Protocol, annex B. 'Access to health records, Guidance for heath professionals in the UK' (December 2008) (hereafter 'Access to health records') provides the consent form at App 1.

[5] Clinical Negligence Protocol, annex B.

If treatment has been provided by a GP or privately, then the request is usually made by letter.

The person requesting the medical records must provide a signed form of consent for the records to be released to his solicitor. It is good practice to use the standard form of consent approved by the British Medical Association and The Law Society,[6] although many solicitors devise their own standard wording. For NHS hospital records, the standard form includes a box for the applicant to sign. Alternatively, the solicitor can simply attach a signed form of consent to the standard form.

In relation to the retention of medical records, the Department of Health document 'Records Management: NHS Code of Practice' should be consulted. The British Medical Association advises private practitioners to adopt a similar approach.[7] The retention period varies depending on the nature of the record; for example hospital records should be kept for a minimum of eight years after treatment, GP records for ten years, and records such as children's records, obstetric records and mental health records should be kept for longer. Under the section 'Good Practice Commitments', the Clinical Negligence Protocol states that healthcare providers should 'establish efficient and effective systems of recording and storing patient records, notes, diagnostic reports and x-rays, and to retain these in accordance with Department of Health guidance'.

Objections have been made to providing copies of the x-rays on the basis that these are not medical records, but the argument does not have any merit.[8]

4.2.2 Who can apply

The following is a list of who can apply for medical records, in accordance with the British Medical Association's 'Access to health records, Guidance for health professionals in the UK':[9]

- competent patients can apply for their records or appoint third parties to do so;

- children under the age of 16 must demonstrate an understanding of what is being proposed. However, children aged 12 and over are generally expected to have capacity to give or withhold their consent to the release of their medical records;

---

[6] 'Access to health records' provides the consent form at App 1.
[7] Ibid, 4, and Clinical Negligence Protocol under 'Good Practice Commitments'.
[8] See Clinical Negligence Protocol, Annex B; 'x-rays ... form part of the patient's records', and 'Access to health records', para 2, which includes x-rays as health records.
[9] December 2008.

- parents may have access to their children's records if this is not contrary to a competent child's wishes;

- patients who lack capacity should not automatically be regarded as lacking the capacity to give or withhold consent to disclosure of medical records. Unless unconscious, most people suffering from a mental impairment can make valid decisions about some matters. If a patient can do so, requests for access by relatives or third parties will require patient consent;

- where an adult patient lacks mental capacity and has a deputy or a nominated individual acting on his behalf, that person's consent is required. Where there is no such individual, requests for access should be granted if it is in the best interests of the patient;

- despite the widespread use of the phrase 'next of kin', a next of kin has no right of access to medical records;

- solicitors, provided an appropriate consent is provided;

- where the patient has died, a personal representative or dependent (see below), or a solicitor acting on his behalf.

4.2.3   Step 2: Keep a good record

It is advisable to prepare a table of the places where the applications for medical records have been made, the date the application was submitted, dates of chaser letters and the date when the records were received. Be diligent about keeping it up-to-date, otherwise it may be necessary to trawl through the correspondence files to find out when the applications were sent and chased. Hospitals often do not provide the standard response or any covering letter with the enclosed records meaning that if the solicitor does not keep track of the medical records, at a later date it is not easy to tell when they were received.

4.2.4   Step 3: Ordering and paginating the records and preparing the index

The medical records may be voluminous, illegible, incomplete, poorly photocopied and often out of order. This is despite the British Medical Association's instruction that they 'must be clear, accurate, factual, [and] legible'.[10]

---

[10]   'Access to health records'. In *Prendergast v Sam & Dee Ltd, Kozary and Miller* (1988) *The Times*, 24 March a pharmacist misread a badly handwritten prescription and dispensed the wrong drug to a patient, who took it and suffered brain damage as a result.

There are a number of ways of dealing with the time-consuming task of ordering the records: some solicitors do it themselves; some firms employ people (often nurses) specifically for the task and some firms send the records to be sorted externally by someone who specialises in this, again often a trained nurse. However it is done, the aim is to have a comprehensive, well-organised bundle of records to send to the expert so that he can prepare his report.

The order of the records will vary depending upon whether they are GP or hospital records, and depending upon the treatment that has been provided.

When the records have been put into good order, they should be paginated starting from page 1 at the beginning of each new source.

An index should be prepared, giving the bundle number for each source and listing the categories of records within that source, with the page numbers identified.

Sometimes, it may be necessary to check the original medical records, rather than relying only on the copies. This would be important if there was any suspicion that the medical records had been tampered with, or if important information appeared to be missing. In *Johnson v John and Waltham Forest Health Authority,*[11] the parties were mislead when a hole punch had obliterated the first digit of a date.

Cardiotocography ('CTG') traces should be on continuous paper, and should be insisted upon in cases where they could be of relevance.

4.2.5   Step 4: Reading the medical records

It is best to set aside a block of time to read the medical records and have a medical dictionary to hand (and sometimes even a medication directory[12]). At the same time, it is useful to prepare a chronology of key events and notes. If the records are being prepared externally, a chronology and list of missing records can usually be provided if requested. However, in any event the solicitor will still need to read the records and do the following:

- check that the records are complete;

- check that the copies are good, and that no information is missing from the edges for example;

---

[11]   [1998] MLC 0244, CA.
[12]   For example, the British National Formulary or the Data Sheet Compendium published by the Association of the British Pharmaceutical Industry. These publications list all current and previous medical therapies and medications, giving all their names, their purpose and contraindications.

- analyse the records to identify any pre-existing conditions that may impact on the claim;

- consider which of any pre-existing conditions will need to be commented upon by an independent medical expert;

- consider whether there is any information that is inconsistent with the evidence of the client. If a claimant, for example, says that he attended his GP on a regular basis complaining of chest pain, it will be important to check the GP notes carefully to ascertain whether the notes support the regular attendances and whether the symptoms have been noted. There can sometimes be considerable disparity between the claimant's evidence and what is noted in the records, which can cause considerable difficulty bearing in mind that the claimant has the burden of proof;

- some records are not filed at hospital with the medical records, and may not have been provided, for example, physiotherapy and psychotherapy medical records. Requests for missing records will need to be made;

- consider whether there may be other relevant material such as photographs, surgical videos, or relevant hospital policies;

- consider whether there are any sensitive issues in the records, such as reference to a termination of a pregnancy or a sexually-transmitted disease and whether these are relevant to the case. The solicitor needs to be aware that he could be liable for breach of Art 8 of the European Convention on Human Rights (see below), and particular care needs to be taken before releasing records to the claimant's employer; and

- highlight any sensitive records to the client and ensure that the client is content for the records to be disclosed to the defendant and medical expert(s).

When the claimant's solicitor has a full set of sorted and paginated records and the client is content for copies to be released, copies should be provided to the defendant at a charge of about 25p per copy.

When the medical expert is instructed, the claimant's solicitor should ask him to identify any records that are missing. If there are any records that are missing, these should be requested from the relevant source.

4.2.6   Step 5: Updating the records

The client may be having ongoing treatment while the case is progressing and after the initial batch of copy medical records have been received.

Applications should be made every so often for updated records. Again, the starting point is to ask the client for details of the places where he has had treatment since the last updates were obtained. When making the applications, it is helpful to indicate the dates upon which the records that have already been provided end. This is to assist the hospital/GP practice to identify from when the records need to be copied, as their own records may not reveal this easily.

All applications for updates can be done by letter, as there is usually no need to resend the Clinical Negligence Protocol application for NHS hospital treatment. If there has been a considerable time lapse between the applications, it may be necessary to send an up-to-date signed patient consent form for the records to be released to the solicitor.

Again, keep a record of when the applications for updates were sent, dates of any chasers and dates of receipt.

When the updated records have been received, these will need to be sorted and added to the existing bundles. Pagination and the index will need to be revised, and usually the new records can be added by modifying the existing pagination, for example 23a, 23b, 23c, rather than repaginating the entire section. Copies of the new paginated pages and a revised index need to be circulated to the experts and defendant with instruction on where to insert them in their existing bundles. The experts need to be asked whether there is anything in the new records that changes their opinion.

4.3 STATUTORY FRAMEWORK

A patient's entitlement to access their medical records is contained mainly in two statutes: the Data Protection Act 1998 ('DPA 1998') and the Access to Health Records Act 1990 ('AHRA 1990'), although the Freedom of Information Act 2000 ('FIA 2000') may be relevant in some cases.

The DPA 1998 applies to all medical records, irrespective of the date, for patients who are living (the DPA does not apply to deceased patients). The AHRA 1990 applies to medical records of deceased patients and only to records dating from 1 November 1991. There is no statutory entitlement to medical records predating 1 November 1991 for deceased patients under the AHRA 1990. However, the Clinical Negligence Protocol provides that it is the Department of Health's policy that patients be permitted to see what has been written about them and that healthcare providers should allow patients access to all their records, not only those falling within the AHRA.

Requests for copy medical records that fall outside the AHRA 1990 and DPA 1998 can be made under the FIA 2000, which provides access to non-personal as well as personal data, and applies retrospectively. There is no residual common law right of access to medical records, and access can be refused if it is in the best interests of the patient.[13]

It is not necessary to give reasons for making the request for medical records. In most cases, the request will be made by a solicitor on the patient's behalf and it is generally thought that solicitors are likely to be provided with a more comprehensive set of records than the patient (probably because they know what to ask for).

4.3.1   Access to Health Records Act 1990

As mentioned, the AHRA 1990 applies to medical records of deceased patients, and only to records from 1 November 1991.

Section 1(1) AHRA 1990 defines a heath record as consisting of 'information relating to the physical or mental health of an individual' that 'has been made by or on behalf of a health professional in connection with the care' of the individual.

The right of access to health records is enshrined in s 3 AHRA 1990, which provides that a request can be made by the patient's personal representative and any person who may have a claim arising out of a patient's death,[14] ie a deceased's dependents. The applicant is entitled to inspect the records or be provided with copies.[15]

The person making the application is given the right to an explanation of the records, where the records are expressed in terms that are not intelligible.[16]

Section 3(4) provides that a fee can be charged for the copy records, as limited by regulations made under the DPA 1998 (see below).[17]

Section 4 AHRA 1990 provides for instances where access can be wholly excluded, namely if the record includes a note, made at the patient's request, that he did not wish access to be given.

Section 5 provides for instances where access can be partially excluded, namely, where the information is likely to cause serious harm to the

---

[13]   *R v Mid Glamorgan Family Health Services Ex p Martin* [1995] 1 WLR 110, CA, request for medical records did not fall within the AHRA 1990 or the DPA 1984 because all of the records had been made before 1991.

[14]   Section 3(1)(f).

[15]   Sections 3(2)(a) and (c).

[16]   Section 3(3).

[17]   A fee can only be charged where access is given to record(s) which have not been made after the beginning of the period of 40 days immediately preceding the date of the application under s 3(4)(a).

physical or mental health of an individual, or where the record contains information that identifies an individual other than the patient or where the record predates the Act.

The British Medical Association is of the opinion that no information other than that which is directly relevant to the claim should be disclosed to the personal representative or dependant.[18] However, this limitation does not appear to be in the Act.

A fee for copying and posting can be charged and copies should be usually provided within 40 days.[19] There are provisions for the application to court if the medical records holder fails to comply with the request.[20] The application for the records to be disclosed under the Act would be made under Civil Procedure Rules ('CPR') 31.16 and 31.17.

4.3.2 Data Protection Act 1998

The DPA 1998 came into force on 1 March 2000 and, as mentioned, applies to all medical records, regardless of date, for patients who are living.

The Act applies to a wide variety of situations. A patient is referred to as a 'data subject', the holder of the records is a 'data controller' and the medical records are 'information constituting [any] personal data'.[21] A health record is defined as 'any record which consists of information relating to the physical or mental health or condition of an individual, and which has been made by or on behalf of a health professional in connection with the care of that individual'.[22] Medical records are also 'sensitive personal data' under the Act because they relate to the patient's physical or mental health or condition.[23]

Section 69 of the Act provides a full and comprehensive definition of health professional, which covers all aspects of medical practice, including osteopaths, pharmacists and chiropractors, as well as doctors and dentists.

The right of access to medical records is enshrined in s 7 of the Act and includes the right to have the information communicated in an intelligible form. Section 8 obliges the data controller to provide a copy of the information, unless to do so is not possible or would involve

---

[18] 'Access to health records'.
[19] Sections 3(4)(a) and (5)(b).
[20] Section 8.
[21] Sections 1 and 7.
[22] Section 68.
[23] Section 2(e).

disproportionate effort. Where the information is expressed in terms that are not intelligible without explanation, the copy must be accompanied by an explanation of those terms.

Again, a fee for copying and posting can be charged, and copies should be provided within 40 days.[24] Section 7(9) provides for an application to the court if the medical records holder fails to comply with the request. Such an application would be made under CPR 31.16 and 31.17.

As the DPA 1998 is of wide application, further provisions have been introduced that deal specifically with medical records, namely the Data (Subject Access Modification) (Health) Order ('D(SAM)(H)O') 2000 and the Data Protection (Subject Access Fees and Miscellaneous Provisions) Regulations ('DP(SAFMP)R') 2000.

The D(SAM)(H)O Order 2000 provides exceptions to the patient's right to access health records under s 7 DPA 1998. Broadly, art 5 of the order provides that there is no right to access where:

- disclosure would be likely to cause serious harm to the physical or mental health of the data subject or any other person;

- an application for records is made on behalf of a child by a person with parental responsibility or by a deputy on behalf of a person incapable of managing his own affairs, but the information had been provided in the expectation that it would not be disclosed to the person making the request;

- the records had been obtained as a result of an investigation to which the data subject consented on the basis that the information would not be disclosed; or

- the data subject has expressly indicated that the information should not be disclosed.

As mentioned, copies of the records can be refused if complying with the request would involve 'disproportionate effort'. The Data Protection Act 1998 does not define 'disproportionate effort' but the British Medical Association does not expect there to be any circumstances in which it would not be possible to supply copies and instructs that the provider should consider more than cost when determining whether a request falls into this category. Factors may include the length of time it would take to deal with the request and whether additional staff would be required to assist.

---

[24]   Section 7(10).

It is likely that there would need to be very compelling reasons for copies of medical records to be refused. In *KH v Slovakia*,[25] the European Court of Human Rights upheld a request by a number of women for copies of their medical records, rather than just permission to view them and make handwritten notes, in a case where they thought they had been sterilised without consent. The European Court found that refusing to provide copies breached Art 8 of the European Convention on Human Rights ('ECHR'), the right to respect for private and family life, and Art 6, the right to a fair trial, as the complainants needed copies to have effective exercise of their right of access to a court.

4.3.3   Freedom of Information Act 2000

As mentioned, the FIA 2000 may be used in cases that fall outside the AHRA 1990 and the DPA 1998. This is wider than both the AHRA and the DPA, as public authorities are obliged to provide access to non-personal as well as personal data. However, where a person is a data subject within the meaning of s 7 of the DPA, the request will be dealt with under that Act, not the FIA; nor will the FIA apply if compliance with the requests would contravene the provisions of the DPA.[26]

4.4   CHARGING FOR COPY MEDICAL RECORDS

The Data Protection (Subject Access Fees and Miscellaneous Provisions) Regulations 2000 provides for a maximum charge of £50 for copy records. This is a maximum fee and covers all costs associated with labour, copying, postage and other forms of delivery.

Charges must be proportionate and justifiable, and should reflect the actual costs incurred. They should not result in a profit for the data controller. There should be no difference in the charge whether the request is made by a patient or solicitor. In *Madden & Finucane v Causeway Health and Social Services Trust*[27] in Northern Ireland, the hospital tried to charge £41.13 including VAT for copies of the claimant's medical records, which it routinely charged where the request was made by a solicitor rather than the £10 plus copying costs under the Access to Health Records (Northern Ireland) Order 1993. The court did not allow the higher charge. The 1993 Order, which was closely based on the AHRA 1990, provided no right to charge a higher amount where litigation was intended.

Hospitals may seek to charge an additional copy fee for copying x-rays. The Clinical Negligence Protocol provides that additional charges for

---

[25]   (2009) 49 EHRR 34.
[26]   Section 40.
[27]   [1997] NI 20.

copying x-rays are permissible and that if there are a large number, the records officer should check with the patient/solicitor before arranging copying.

Reasonable copying charges for the medical records and x-rays and the costs of having the records ordered externally are usually claimed from the defendant as a disbursement. Charges by medical reporting agencies for supplying medical reports and records are recoverable as disbursements, provided they are reasonable, including under the fixed costs regime.[28]

4.5   MEDICAL RECORDS AND LIMITATION PERIODS

The medical records are crucial when considering proceedings under s 14 and/or s 33 of the Limitation Act ('LA') 1980. Under s 14, if a client states that he had knowledge that the injury was significant and attributable in whole or part to the defendant's treatment, the records should be checked very carefully to ascertain whether there is anything contradicting this or upon which an argument for earlier constructive knowledge could be based. In *Mirza v Birmingham Health Authority*[29] it was held that a case based on surgery performed in 1976 was not statute-barred because the claimant did not acquire knowledge under s 14 of the LA 1980 until he had obtained an expert opinion in 1998 after disclosure of relevant medical records in 1997. In *Harris v Newcastle upon Tyne*[30] the defendant refused to provide copies of the patient's medical records on the basis that the claim was statute-barred. The patient had undergone eye surgery in 1961 and 1965, and did not investigate a claim for medical negligence until 1987. The Court of Appeal ordered disclosure of the records, stating that the court could take into account a limitation defence in the context of the case, but that was not a reason to refuse disclosure. Material might also emerge on disclosure which would be relevant for the court exercising its discretion under s 33 of the 1980 Act.

4.6   PRE-ACTION PROTOCOLS

The CPR 1998 contain a number of pre-action protocols, including in relation to personal injury claims, the resolution of clinical disputes, disease and illness claims, and for low value personal injury claims in road traffic accidents. These should be followed, unless there are very good reasons not to do so. The protocols have a consistent theme of encouraging co-operation between the parties and early exchange of information.

---

[28]   CPR 45.10(2); *(1) Woollard (2) Woollard v Fowler*, SCCO Ref: 050071.
[29]   (unreported) 31 July 2001, QBD.
[30]   [1989] 1 WLR 96.

The Clinical Negligence Protocol 'encourages a climate of openness when something has gone wrong'. Objectives of the protocol specifically include 'to ensure that sufficient information is disclosed by both parties to enable each to understand the other's perspective and case, and to encourage early resolution'; 'to ensure that all relevant medical records are provided to patients or their appointed representatives on request, to a realistic timetable by any healthcare provider'; and 'to ensure that relevant records that are not in the healthcare providers' possession are made available to them by patients and their advisers at an appropriate stage'. As mentioned above, the protocol includes forms for applying for the medical records and for the hospital's responses.

Under the section 'Letter of Claim', the protocol provides that the letter of claim should refer to any relevant documents, including medical records and, if possible, enclose copies of any that are not already in the potential defendant's possession.

In the Pre-action Protocol for Disease and Illness Claims ('Disease and Illness Protocol'), the notes of guidance include that the 'cards on the table' approach advocated by the Personal Injury Protocol is equally appropriate to disease claims. The spirit of that protocol, and of the Clinical Negligence Protocol, is followed here, in accordance with the sense of the justice reforms. The specific objectives of the Disease and Illness Protocol include 'to ensure that sufficient information is disclosed by both parties to enable each to understand the other's perspective and case, and to encourage early resolution'; 'to ensure that all relevant records including health and personnel records are provided to employees (past or present) or their appointed representatives promptly on request...' and 'to ensure that relevant records which are in the claimant's possession are made available to the employers or their insurers by claimants or their advisers at an appropriate stage'. Under the section 'Letter of Claim', it provides that 'the letter of claim should identify any relevant documents, including health records not already in the defendant's possession, eg any relevant general practitioner records ... death certificate, post-mortem report, or inquest depositions'.

In the other pre-action protocols, the medical records will be relevant to quantum rather than liability. However, the general tenor of the protocols should result in solicitors providing proposed defendants with medical records in support of injuries as early as possible.

4.7   INCIDENT REPORTS AND OTHER DOCUMENTS

Often, in addition to the medical records, it will be important to have access to other documents that may include highly relevant information in relation to the patient's treatment, such as incident reports, internal investigation reports and management and risk assessment reports. These documents may well provide information that can make or break a case.

The Clinical Negligence Protocol provides that reports on an adverse incident and reports on the patient for risk management and audit purposes *may* form part of the records, with the exception of any specific record or report made 'solely or mainly in connection with a potential or actual claim'.

The British Medical Association provides a much wider definition of a health record, in 'Access to health records, Guidance for health professionals in the UK 2008'. It states:

> 'notes made during consultations, correspondence between health professionals such as referral and discharge letters, results of tests and their interpretation, x-ray films, videotapes, audiotapes, photographs, and tissue samples taken for diagnostic purposes. They may also include internal memoranda, reports written for third parties such as insurance companies, as well as theatre lists, booking-in registers and clinical audit data, if the patient is identifiable from these.'

However, such a comprehensive array of medical records is not disclosed routinely, and a specific request may have to be made. The list above is a useful reference if the hospital is objecting to disclosing any of the items listed.

If there is a report from an internal investigation, the solicitor will certainly need to take all possible steps to obtain this. It will also be the solicitor's responsibility to ask the other side whether there has in fact been an investigation as this information may not be made known.

The disclosure of the internal investigation report may be followed by an admission of liability. If not, it is likely to include important information that may not be evident from other documents. It may also shed light on the extent to which the injuries have been caused by the negligence. The internal investigation report should be regarded by the solicitor in a medical negligence case as of equal importance to the medical records.

The defendant or proposed defendant may object to providing a copy of the investigation report on the basis that it is privileged. The courts have had to find a balance between respecting privilege and the revelation of the report in the interests of public safety. The test adopted by the House of Lords in *Waugh v British Railways Board*[31] is to ascertain the *dominant purpose* of the report at the time it was created. If the dominant purpose was the avoidance of future accidents, it will not be privileged even if a subsidiary purpose was use in any expected litigation. It was recognised that the report probably contained the best evidence as to the cause of the accident and this should only be overridden if the dominant purpose of

---

[31]   [1980] AC 521; [1979] 2 All ER 1169, HL.

the report's preparation was for its submission for legal advice and that, at most, such purpose was only equal to the purpose of ensuring the safety on the railways.

In *Lask v Gloucester Health Authority*[32] a hospital accident report had been prepared as required by an NHS circular. The circular made it clear that hospital accident reports had a dual function, to assist in litigation and to prevent repetition of the accident. The Court of Appeal held that the report was not privileged as the prevention of accidents must in a hospital be of at least equal importance to litigation. On this basis, it will be difficult for a hospital to refuse disclosure of accident/incident reports.

Documents that had been disclosed by an NHS trust to the Health Service Ombudsman were sought by the claimant's solicitor in *R (on the application of Kay) v Health Service Commissioner.*[33] The Court of Appeal held that although blanket disclosure of all the documents provided to the Health Service Ombudsman would not be appropriate, the Ombudsman needed to give proper consideration to the more tailored request for specific categories of documents arising from reading the Ombudsman's preliminary report. The initial request for full disclosure was deemed to have been extreme and a fishing expedition.

Records relating to a complaint will not be privileged if at the time the complaint is made, legal proceedings are not anticipated. In *Hewlett Parker v St Georges Health Care NHS Trust*[34] the court on appeal ordered disclosure of an NHS complaints file.

In fatal accident cases, other documents that should be obtained include the death certificate and post-mortem reports. It is also helpful to attend the inquest to take a note of the hearing, or it is possible to get a transcript of the evidence at the inquest (although this can be quite expensive, so obtain a quote first).

4.8   MISSING AND INCONSISTENT MEDICAL RECORDS

On occasion there may be medical records that the defendant has destroyed or lost. This is a significant hurdle for the claimant because, as mentioned, he has the burden of proof. The onus is on him. However, the courts are willing to look at all the circumstances of the case and, if appropriate, will draw an inference that lost or shoddy note-taking or record-keeping are reflective of poor practice.

In *Malhotra v Dhawan*[35] the Court of Appeal considered the principle of *omnia praesumuntur contra spoliatorem* that: (1) if the destruction (of

---

[32]   [1991] 2 Med LR 379.
[33]   [2009] EWCA Civ 732.
[34]   (unreported), 20 February 1998; noted in the Medical Law Monitor, July 1998.
[35]   [1997] 8 Med LR 319.

financial records in this case, but arguably relevant to medical records) was deliberate so as to hinder the proof of the case, there would be an inference as to the credibility of the destroyer, enabling the court to disregard his evidence; (2) if the court was undecided as to which of the two parties' evidence to accept, then it should decide in favour of the party who had not destroyed the documents; and (3) if the court had a clear view as to the truth, the judge was not bound to follow the principle.

In *Skelton v Lewisham and North Southwark Health Authority*[36] the anaesthetic notes were well below the standard acceptable at the time, being extremely brief, unsigned, with key events not recorded and, although not causative of injury per se, these were deemed to be indicative of an unexplained carelessness. The court held that it was beyond doubt that there was a peri-operative episode of severe hypotension that went unrecorded. In *Rhodes v Spokes and Farbridge*[37] the patient had a history of hydrocephalus for which she had an intracranial shunt in place. Many years later, she suffered neurological symptoms and attended her GP on a number of occasions. Her GP was found to have been negligent in not making a note of the symptoms she was suffering and for not advising the neurologist (to whom she was eventually referred) of the shunt. Smith J said:

> 'A doctor's contemporaneous record of a consultation should form a reliable evidential base in a case such as this. I regret to say that Dr Farbridge's notes of the plaintiff's attendances do not provide any such firm foundation. They are scanty in the extreme. He rarely recorded her complaints or symptoms; he rarely recorded any observations; usually he noted only the drug he prescribed. These brief entries were sometimes accompanied by a cryptic or occasionally even derogatory comment as to the genuineness of the plaintiff's complaints. The failure to take a proper note is not evidence of a doctor's negligence or of the inadequacy of treatment. But a doctor who fails to keep an adequate note of a consultation lays himself open to a finding that his recollection is faulty and someone else's is correct. After all, a patient has only to remember his or her own case, whereas the doctor has to remember one case out of hundreds which occupied his mind at the material time.'

In *Hammond v West Lancashire Health Authority*[38] the Court of Appeal upheld the criticism made by the trial judge of the defendant's practice of destroying x-rays after three years when it knew that proceedings were being contemplated. The x-rays, which formed part of the medical records, should have been copied and sent with the other medical records. The defendant tried to mount a limitation defence, but the court held that a hospital that showed an obvious indifference to the rights of patients to access their medical records would encounter difficulties in pleading prejudice under s 33 LA 1980.

---

[36] [1998] Lloyd's Rep Med 324.
[37] [1996] 7 Med LR 135.
[38] [1998] Lloyd's Rep Med 146; (1998) 95(14) LSG 23.

It is usually difficult in practice to bring a claim if the claimant's evidence is not supported by the medical records. Claimants often suspect that their doctor has written the notes in a way that is not reflective of the true position with a view to avoiding any potential liability and it can of course happen that medical professionals, with many demands on their time, make errors when making their notes. In *Fifield v Denton Hall*[39] the court reiterated the point that medical records are not evidence of the patient having made the statements contained therein but may be put to the patient as a previous inconsistent statement (hearsay evidence). Despite this, in the absence of other evidence to corroborate the claimant's version of events, a solicitor may be unwilling to take the risk that the claimant will be believed over the notes at trial.

4.9 CONFIDENTIALITY

Obviously, a person's medical records are confidential. As mentioned above, it is important that the claimant's solicitor retains control over applying for copy medical records. According to CPR 31.6 the defendant is only entitled to see the documents which are relevant to the either parties' case, namely those that are relied upon or which adversely affect either parties' case.[40] It is inappropriate for the claimant's solicitor to simply give blanket disclosure of the medical records to the expert or defendant, as to do so could be a breach of confidentiality and violation of Art 6 ECHR, which protects the right to a private and family life, particularly if records are included that were not relevant.[41]

4.10 APPLYING TO COURT FOR RECORDS

As mentioned above, the copy medical records should be provided within 40 days of the request being made. Unfortunately, medical records are often not provided within this timeframe and if they have been provided, there may be other documents that are relevant to the case but which have not been provided (such as an incident report). Accordingly the claimant's solicitor may have to make an application to court for an order that copies are provided. Defendants can also make applications for medical records.

As mentioned, the medical records are crucial to resolve liability issues in a clinical negligence case and in relation to quantum in all personal injury cases. The claimant has the onus of proving his claim for losses arising out of the injury and, in relation to future losses, especially loss of earnings, the vast majority, if not all, of the claimant's medical records will be relevant to establishing that the claimant would have been able to work until retirement and did not have any significant pre-existing conditions.

---

[39] [2006] EWCA Civ 169, [2006] Lloyd's Rep Med 251.
[40] *Bennett v Compass* [2002] EWCA Civ 642.
[41] *Cornelius v De Taranto* [2001] EWCA Civ 1511.

It is possible to make applications for copy medical records before court proceedings have commenced and also against non-parties.

Section 33 of the Senior Court Act ('SCA') 1981 provides 'Powers of High Court exercisable before commencement of action'. Section 33(2) states that a person who appears 'likely to be a party to subsequent proceedings', may apply for an order for the disclosure and production of any documents which are 'relevant to an issue arising or likely to arise ...'. Under s 33(2)(b) the court can impose conditions on the production of documents. The court also has other powers including to order inspection and photocopying under s 33(1). There are similar provisions under s 52 of the County Courts Act ('CCA') 1984.

An application for disclosure and production of any medical records that are 'relevant to an issue arising or likely to arise' ... against a non-party can be made under s 34 SCA 1981 and s 53 CCA 1984.

The SCA 1981 and the CCA 1984 provide that applications under ss 33(2) and 52(2) respectively be made 'in accordance with rules of court'. CPR 25.4 provides that where a party wishes to make an application for an order under s 33 or s 52, the application must be made in accordance with the general requirements for applications in CPR Part 23. CPR Part 31 deals specifically with disclosure (except for claims on the small claims track).

The most likely application that the claimant will need to make is against the potential defendant before proceedings have been issued to enable the case to be investigated properly. Before proceedings have commenced the application is made under CPR 31.16, which gives a number of conditions that have to be met, as follows:

'(2) The application must be supported by evidence.

(3) The court may make an order under this rule only where-
(a)   the respondent is likely to be a party to subsequent proceedings;
(b)   the applicant is also likely to be a party to those proceedings;
(c)   if proceedings had started, the respondent's duty by way of standard disclosure, set out in rule 31.6, would extend to the documents or classes of documents of which the applicant seeks disclosure; and
(d)   disclosure before proceedings have started is desirable in order to –
       (i)   dispose fairly of the anticipated proceedings;
       (ii)   assist the dispute to be resolved without proceeding; or
       (iii) save costs.'

There is also a right under CPR 31.3 to inspect the original medical records or other documents that have been disclosed.

4.11 CLAIMANTS' APPLICATIONS

The procedure for obtaining medical records is referred to above.

From the claimant's perspective, problems can arise in relation to records that are sought but that contain confidential information relating to another person. In these circumstances, the court has to balance the public and private interests in maintaining the confidentiality of the other person against the private interests of allowing disclosure for a specific purpose. In *R (on the application of S) v Plymouth City Council*[42] the Court of Appeal allowed disclosure of a mother's son's confidential social services file to enable her to respond appropriately to the social services request for guardianship. Although the son's information was confidential and protected by Art 8 ECHR, the right to private and family life, these factors were outweighed by the mother's Art 6 right to a fair trial and the balance was in favour of allowing disclosure.

In some cases, the courts can impose conditions on the disclosure, in order to find the appropriate balance between the conflicting interests. In *Re R (a child)*[43] the Family Division ordered disclosure of medical records under CPR 31.16 to a child's grandmother even though the records included sensitive material about the child's mother and the hospital had concerns about the effect of disclosure on the child. Disclosure would be to the medical expert and solicitors who were bound by confidentiality and disclosure to the grandmother could be limited to what was relevant to the claim. Both the mother and grandmother had parental responsibility for the child and therefore had the right to see his medical records and there was nothing in the DPA 1998 that either prevented or required disclosure. An injustice could result if material supportive of a claim could not be evaluated. Unusually, the court ordered each side to pay its own costs in this case.

4.12 DEFENDANTS' APPLICATIONS

The procedure for obtaining medical records is referred to above.

There have been many cases in which a defendant has made an application to court for disclosure of some or all of the claimant's medical records following resistance by the claimant to make such disclosure usually on grounds of confidentiality and the right to private and family life under Art 8 ECHR. There have been cases going either way and many of the cases are fact-specific. The tension in the cases arises from the competing interests of the claimant's right of confidentiality and Art 8 rights and the defendant's interest in being able to defend claims made by

---

[42]   [2002] EWCA Civ 388.
[43]   [2004] EWHC 2085.

the claimant. If the court does rule that disclosure is appropriate, it can order a stay in the proceedings until the records have been produced.

It is established that the court has power under the general powers of management in the CPR 1998[44] to order the claimant to sign an authority permitting the defendant to obtain his medical records. The Court of Appeal in *Bennett v Compass Group UK & Ireland Ltd*[45] could not say that the judge had been plainly wrong in making the order, but stressed that such an order should rarely be made and that, if it was made, allowing a third party to permit an opposing party to inspect the medical records, the order had to be very clearly and carefully drafted. The defendant was entitled to disclosure of the records under CPR Part 31.

The court will consider many factors when dealing with a request by a defendant for disclosure. These include whether the claim is being made against an employer; the nature of the claims being made, in particular whether there are any future claims; and (as mentioned) whether it is appropriate to make the disclosure subject to conditions.

As mentioned, in relation to future earnings, the claimant has the burden of proving that he was in good health and but for the index event would have been able to work into the future.

In *Dunn v British Coal Corp*[46] a claim was made by a 53-year-old miner, which included loss of earnings until retirement. The claimant had agreed to disclose records relating to his neck only, including any records relating to a pre-existing condition. The defendant issued a summons for a stay in the proceedings until all of the records were produced. The Court of Appeal upheld the stay on the basis that the defendant was entitled to all the medical records, but with a proviso that these would be disclosed to the employer's medical advisers and not the employer. The defendant's expert would then be able to comment on whether the injury at work caused the neck problem. The court noted that the records could be called for at trial and that by making disclosure to the defendant's expert and not the employer, any embarrassing and unrelated conditions would not be disclosed to the employer.

In *Elliott (Janet Denise) v Mem*[47] the claimant made a claim against her employer for repetitive strain injury. There was a query as to whether the claimant had suffered a relevant pre-existing problem. The claimant's form of authority for records to be released included the proviso:

---

[44]   CPR 3.1(2)(m).
[45]   [2002] EWCA Civ 642.
[46]   [1993] ICR 591.
[47]   [1993] CLY 3217.

'I do not consent to the defence consultant photocopying, or by any other method copying my records nor do I consent to the supply of any information from my records by that consultant other than such as is relevant to my claim.'

The defendant's solicitor objected and sought disclosure. The Court of Appeal held that the medical expert should identify which records were relevant and that these should be disclosed to legal advisers, but the indiscriminate disclosure of all of the claimant's medical records to the employer's solicitors would threaten the claimant's legitimate interest in maintaining the confidentiality, without securing any advantage or benefit to the defendant.

In *Hipwood v Gloucester HA*[48] a claim was made against the claimant's employer that she suffered from rhinitis and asthma as a result of her employment. The defendant applied under s 53(2) CCA 1984 for an order requiring the medical practitioner to produce medical records to the defendant's legal advisors. The Court of Appeal held that the defendant was entitled to have the medical records produced not only to the medical advisors but also to their legal advisers. *Dunn* was distinguished on the basis that, in *Hipwood*, the application had been made under s 53 CCA 1984, which could not restrict disclosure to an expert and not to the legal adviser. Also, if there was an issue about the relevance of a medical record, then the court should be asked to adjudicate on the point. It was not appropriate for the medical experts solely to decide relevance as, however eminent, they may not appreciate the legal implications of a record.

In *Rigby v Incumbent Churchwardens of St Peter's Church*[49] the county court rejected the claimant's argument that it was not necessary to disclose a full set of medical records because no claim was being made for future loss of earnings. Access to the entire medical records was necessary because a claim was being made for general damages in respect of a continuing loss of amenity; the absence of a loss of earnings claim was a 'red herring'. In *Catchpole v Young & Co's Brewery plc*[50] the county court ordered that disclosure should be made to the defendant in a case where the injuries appeared to be minor and there was a possibility of degenerative changes in any event in a man of the claimant's age. The defendant had been put on inquiry that the full extent of the claimant's symptoms might not be attributable to the accident. The fact that the defendant's solicitors had not yet instructed a medical expert did not

---

[48]   [1995] ICR 999, as per McCowan and Simon Brown LJJ.
[49]   [1998] CLY 337.
[50]   [2005] CLY 3073.

mean that medical records should not be disclosed, and sight of the records may be necessary for the defendant to formulate questions for the expert.[51]

4.13   TIMING OF REQUEST

A claimant can object to pre-action production of copies of medical records if the defendant's application for them is premature. In *Wells v OCS Group Ltd*[52] the claimant intended to obtain a report from an orthopaedic surgeon, but no examination had taken place for over a year. Faced with no medical report or schedule of loss, the defendant applied for pre-action disclosure of medical records under CPR 31.16. The judge's refusal to order disclosure was upheld on appeal and based upon the following:

- it was not desirable either to dispose fairly of the anticipated proceedings or to assist the dispute being resolved without proceedings;

- the claimant would not know the full details of her medical records, which might contain either embarrassing or disturbing information or information that could cause her to limit or even withdraw her claim;

- before a medical expert had considered the medical records it could not properly be determined what shape or form the particulars of claim would take as to the damages claimed;

- enforced disclosure of private material when the claim had not yet been precisely delineated could, depending on the content of the records, increase contention between the parties and make proceedings more likely and therefore not save costs;

- it could transpire that the medical records were relevant but of no significant value to the proceedings and play no part in their resolution. If that turned out to be the case then private medical records would have been disclosed without the claimant's consent and without having any beneficial effect on the proceedings; and

- it was both safer and more appropriate for such records to be considered by the claimant's medical expert and then the claimant herself before the defendant's representatives consider them.

---

[51]   See further examples: *Steele v Moule Bedford County Court* [1999] CLY 326; *Wickham v Dwyer, Reading County Court* [1995] CLY 4118; *Fenn v Stewart* [1996] CLY 2140; *Irwin v Donaghy* [1996] PIQR P207.
[52]   [2008] EWHC 919 (QB).

It was concluded that a claimant should be prepared to reveal his medical records to the opposition, but only at the appropriate time and to the appropriate people. Such records should not be disclosed before the claimant had had an opportunity of considering them and their affect upon the claim. *Wells* should be cited in cases where the defendant is making demands for medical records to be disclosed before court proceedings have been started.

4.14   APPLICATIONS TO THIRD PARTIES

The procedure for obtaining medical records against third parties is referred to above and such applications can be made by claimants or defendants.

There may be various documents that the defendant may like to be disclosed to ascertain the extent to which they impact on the claim. Common examples are employment and Department of Work and Pension ('DWP') files. In *O'Sullivan v Herdmans*[53] the House of Lords upheld the Court of Appeal's decision to order that the DHSS (now the DWP) disclose the findings of the medical board that had investigated the claimant's condition as it was plainly in the interests of justice that the document should be available to both parties.

It can be a particularly difficult issue if the defendant asks for disclosure of medical records that relate not to the claimant but to someone else, usually a relative. Obviously, the relative's records are confidential and protected by Art 8 ECHR, and it seems that the courts will only order disclosure in exceptional circumstances. In *A v X & B (non party)*[54] the court refused to order disclosure of the medical records of a claimant's sibling, who may have had the same condition, in order to ascertain whether the claimant's psychiatric problems were likely to be genetic. The court held that there was already ample material in the experts' reports that there was a serious issue on causation and that disclosure was not necessary for a fair disposal of the claim. It is suggested that in these circumstances the best approach is to try to get the relative to agree for the records to be disclosed, as it may be difficult for the claimant to prove his case on causation whilst the issue is left in doubt. However, there is a risk, of course, that the records will undermine the case.

4.15   HOSPITALS' DUTY TO PROTECT CONFIDENTIALITY

If acting for defendants, it is important to be aware of the extent of their obligation to protect confidentiality. In *I v Finland*[55] the applicant worked

---

[53]   [1987] 1 WLR 1047.
[54]   [2004] EWHC 447 (QB).
[55]   (20511/03) (2009) 48 EHRR 31.

as a nurse in a hospital. She was HIV-positive and was treated for this condition at the same hospital. She began to suspect that her colleagues were aware of her HIV status and, at that time, any hospital employee could access her hospital records. The European Court of Human Rights held that there had been a breach by the hospital of Art 8 ECHR, which gives a right to respect for private and family life.

4.16   OBLIGATIONS OF EXPERTS TO PROTECT CONFIDENTIALITY

It is also important that experts acting in cases are aware of their duty of confidentiality. In *Cornelius v De Taranto*[56] the Court of Appeal held that a consultant forensic psychiatrist had breached client confidentiality by disclosing a medico-legal report to the claimant's GP and a consultant psychiatrist without the claimant's express consent. It is suggested that this would apply equally to the medical records. In *Lewis v Secretary of State*[57] a medical practitioner applied to court for a declaration that medical records and documents could be disclosed to the Redfern Inquiry into human tissue analysis in the UK nuclear facilities and disclosure was authorised. The public interest in the disclosure of the material sought outweighed the public interest in maintaining the confidentiality of the medical records, provided that proper safeguards were put in place to ensure that no inappropriate information became public.

4.17   OWNERSHIP OF MEDICAL RECORDS

Ownership of medical records is usually as follows:

*   NHS hospital – NHS trust;

*   GP (NHS) – (health authority, usually part of primary care trust);

*   private treatment – consultant or private GP;

*   NHS scans – NHS trust;

*   private scans – patient;

*   NHS dental – primary care trust;

*   private dental – dentist;

*   optician – optician;

*   NHS physiotherapy – NHS trust;

---

[56]   [2001] EWCA Civ 1511.
[57]   [2008] EWHC 2196 (QB).

- private physiotherapy – physiotherapist;

- NHS counselling – either primary care trust or NHS trust;

- private counselling – counsellor.

4.18   CONTENT OF MEDICAL RECORDS

4.18.1   Hospital records

Hospital notes are usually in a soft A4 file divided into sections. The file will vary depending on the patient's medical history, and may include some of the following:

- accident and emergency records;

- antenatal clinical records;

- post-natal ICU notes;

- prescription charts;

- labour clinical records;

- operation notes;

- anaesthetic notes;

- neonatal clinical records; and

- investigation reports (e g haematology, biochemistry, microbiology).

There are various sources of abbreviations and acronyms, for example *Stedman's Medical Abbreviations, Acronyms and Symbols*,[58] which is used by hospitals and GPs.

4.18.2   GP records

Since the latter part of the 1990s, GP notes (except correspondence) are computerised. However they used to be kept in a small brown paper envelope on which was recorded the patient's name, date of birth and successive addresses. These are often referred to as the 'Lloyd George records'. The patient's notes were contained inside the envelope.

GP records may include the following:

---

[58]   Lippincott Williams & Wilkins (eds) *Stedman's Medical Abbreviations, Acronyms and Symbols* (Stedman's, 2008).

- reports of test/investigation results;

- correspondence from hospitals and other sources;

- discharge summaries; and

- computerised records of the information that used to be on the Lloyd George records.

GP notes can be very difficult to comprehend. They may be scant, illegible and/or in code that the GP has devised for himself as opposed to using the standard medical abbreviations provided by the Royal College of General Practitioners. Some use the SOAP system, ie:

- S, subjective (patient complaint);

- O, objective (doctor's findings);

- A, analysis (diagnosis);

- P plan (treatment, advice, referral).

CHAPTER 5

MEDICAL EXAMINATIONS

Laura Elfield

5.1 INTRODUCTION

Medical evidence is central to every clinical negligence and personal injury claim. Not only can it be essential for resolving issues of breach of duty and causation, it is also the basis upon which general damages are assessed and the framework in which claims for financial losses, both past and future, are made. Many claims settle on the basis of the medical evidence, without the need for the expert to give oral evidence and often even before the defendant has put questions to the expert on the report. If a matter proceeds to a contested hearing on the medical evidence, the integrity of the initial examination and report can be critical to success.

This chapter deals with the steps a practitioner can take to help to obtain a supportive medical report, including the choosing and instruction of a suitable medical expert and with preparing both the expert and the claimant for the medical examination. It also covers the issues that arise in relation to medical examinations and in particular the circumstances in which a claimant might be required to attend such an examination and the circumstances in which a claimant might properly so refuse.

5.2 SELECTING AN EXPERT

5.2.1 Finding the expert

An internet search can produce a bewildering array of experts in almost any discipline. It is advisable to select an expert who has been recognised by either the Academy of Experts or the Society of Expert Witnesses. Details of such experts are available in a number of online databases. Such experts will, in general terms, be governed by codes of practice and guidance as to acting as an expert witness, backed by disciplinary procedures. In addition, APIL provides an expert services' directory with a three-tier system of categorization. The first tier covers experts recommended by APIL members. The second covers experts who do not hold an APIL member reference but who are recognised by the Academy of Experts or the Society of Expert Witnesses. The third tier covers experts where recommendation and recognition has not been provided to

APIL. The Law Society also provides a helpful directory of accredited expert witnesses. Many experts will be accredited by a number of bodies.

5.2.2 Choosing the expert

The first step in deciding which doctor to instruct as an expert is to decide which discipline or disciplines are required. The attached appendix provides a glossary of which experts do what and when to use them.

In addition to narrowing the choice of expert by discipline, it is important to consider the expert's qualifications and experience to give the required evidence. Careful scrutiny of an expert's CV is advisable even within disciplines. For example, a consultant orthopaedic surgeon is likely to be the appropriate expert to deal with a bony wrist injury but it may well be possible to find an orthopod who has expertise in hand and wrist injuries. If the claimant instructs a general orthopaedic surgeon only, that expert may well be at a disadvantage if the defendant proceeds to instruct a specialist wrist surgeon.

In addition to selecting an expert according to the level of expertise in a particular discipline, it is suggested that, if at all possible, an expert should be selected who still practises in the relevant area. Hands-on experience and familiarity with the most up-to-date practice is likely to trump medico-legal expertise in an otherwise retired doctor. Consideration should also be given to the expert's split of claimant and defendant work. A balanced split will provide the best appearance of impartiality and avoid handing easy cross-examination points to the defendant.

5.2.3 Proportionality

When selecting the appropriate expert or experts to use, it is important to remember that, since the advent of the Civil Procedure Rules ('CPR'), expert evidence has been placed under the control of the court, both in terms of use and expense. While this issue is dealt with in greater detail in Chapter 6, as a matter of principle it is a good idea to start by considering whether use of a particular expert is proportionate to the issue(s) in the case. Put simply, the cost of a neurologist to report on a few weeks' of headaches is unlikely to be considered within the spirit of the CPR and the cost of the same will almost certainly be disallowed or substantially reduced when a successful claimant's legal team is reimbursed for their disbursements.

Applying this principle in practice, in a low value claim where the claimant has suffered only very minor soft tissue injuries with a swift resolution period, it may be appropriate to appoint a GP to prepare a report. For slightly more serious soft tissue injuries and minor broken bones, a consultant in accident and emergency medicine may be the appropriate expert. While there is no hard-and-fast rule, it is suggested that where any soft tissue or bony injury is likely to take more than 12 months to resolve, the most expedient course is to go straight to a consultant orthopaedic surgeon. If not, you may find your GP or accident and emergency consultant recommending this course in any event. While the court is unlikely in these circumstances to penalise a claimant in costs, it is sensible to attempt to limit the number of experts at the outset. This is particularly important if further experts in different disciplines are likely to be required to deal with other aspects of the injury – for example, a psychiatric condition consequent upon a whiplash injury.

At the other end of the scale, a catastrophic injury case may properly require numerous experts. For example, a road traffic accident leading to loss of a limb and steering wheel damage to the chest is likely to require reports from an orthopaedic surgeon, a plastic surgeon, a prosthetics expert and a consultant physician. There may well be an associated psychiatric injury to be assessed by a psychiatrist or a head injury requiring the instruction of a neurologist or neurosurgeon. This is before consideration is given to non-medical experts such as care or employment consultants. Even here, regard must be had to the principle of proportionality. There may well come a point where further reports on injuries will add little to the award. Where certain injuries are not contentious – for example if the head injury has involved minor damage to the teeth – it may be that other the experts can simply cover this aspect of the injury by way of history in their own reports.

5.2.4 Use of care and employment experts

The use of care and employment experts is outside the scope of this chapter, however, suffice to say that there will be situations where the medical expert will be insufficiently qualified to provide a detailed report in these areas. In particular, in cases involving grievous injury, it may be necessary to obtain a report from an occupational therapist as to any aids and equipment that a claimant might require or from a nursing care expert as to the amount of care required by an immobile claimant at home.

In terms of employment consultants, their use is increasingly limited by the courts due to the availability and admissibility of statistics from the Annual Survey of Hours and Earnings, available in *Facts & Figures* and *Kemp & Kemp*. However, in cases which are fact-sensitive, involving for example, a particular disability or an unusual occupation or local market, use of an employment consultant might well be indicated.

5.2.5 Use of the treating doctor as an expert

A question that often arises is whether or not the claimant's treating doctor should be instructed to provide a report. The starting point is that the expert must be and be seen to be capable of fulfilling a role independent of the interests of the parties. The duties of experts are dealt with in greater detail in Chapter 6, but in general terms it is the duty of an expert to provide independent assistance to the court by way of objective, unbiased opinion in relation to matters within his expertise. Whether or not to use a treating doctor as an expert for the purposes of court proceedings will depend upon whether there is something in the relationship between the doctor and the claimant that might prevent, or appear to prevent, the doctor from complying with their duty to the court.

There are clear instances of situations where use of the treating doctor as expert is best avoided. An example of this is when the treating doctor concerned is a psychiatrist. The relationship between a patient and psychiatrist which involves a particular emphasis on trust, may well be inconsistent with the psychiatrist providing a truly objective view to the court. Equally, in *Wright v Sullivan*,[1] the Court of Appeal held that a clinical case manager, appointed to assist a severely injured person, owed duties to the patient alone and had to make decisions in the best interests of the patient. If called to give evidence, the clinical case manager should therefore be a witness of fact rather than an expert.

Another situation potentially open to criticism is use of the expert as treating doctor. This can arise where the expert recommends a course of treatment to be carried out by himself. While often such a course may be entirely reasonable, it can be open to the charge that the expert is no longer acting in an objective and independent manner. If the treatment is by an expert on the NHS there is clearly less difficulty than when an expensive course of private treatment is recommended.

The above should not be taken to suggest that use of the treating doctor as an expert should always be avoided. Use of the treating doctor as an expert can be appropriate in certain cases. For example, in low value cases where the claimant has fully recovered and where there is no longer an ongoing relationship between the claimant and the treating doctor, use of the treating doctor as an expert may well be an acceptable and cost-effective approach. This might also be the case where the issue upon which the expert is required to give evidence is limited and discrete – for example, a short period of orthopaedic symptoms in a case mainly involving psychiatric injury. At the other end of the scale, if the treating doctor is the only expert able to give evidence about a course of highly specialised treatment, there may be no option but to obtain a report from that doctor.

---

[1]   [2005] EWCA Civ 656.

5.3 GETTING THE BEST OUT OF AN EXPERT

5.3.1 The medico-legal context

Clear and concise instructions to the expert help to lay the foundation for an effective medical report. In order to prepare such instructions, it is helpful to start by remembering that there is likely to be a gap between the medical mindset and that required for the exigencies of the litigation process.

Unless highly experienced in the litigation process, there are likely to be a number of concepts that the expert may find difficult. The most common of these are the standard of proof, causation of damages and the approach to future treatment and complications. The expert may also not understand the role that they are likely to play in the assessment of damages or of the impact that statements made in the medical report may have on such assessment.

Starting with the standard of proof, it is important that the expert understands the concept of the balance of probabilities, namely whether there is a 51 per cent or more chance of something happening. It can help in discussions with the expert to acknowledge that this is an artificial test, albeit one that is essential to the litigation process.

In terms of causation, the starting point is the 'but for' test. The expert will need to distinguish between what would have occurred in the absence of the accident and what has occurred as a result of the accident. In certain claims – broadly speaking, many occupational injury and clinical negligence cases – the appropriate test will instead be whether the defendant's breach has made a 'material contribution' to the injury. It should not be assumed, when instructing the expert, that the expert will know the correct test so it is helpful if the letter of instruction sets this out clearly.

Consideration of causation often involves assessment of whether the accident has caused an exacerbation or acceleration of a pre-existing condition. Such concepts have little place in the course of everyday practice and have little or no significance in terms of treatment and may be unfamiliar and indeed uncomfortable to the expert. Reassurance that the expert is only being asked to deal with such maters on the balance of probabilities can assist. The effect of the acceleration or exacerbation on pain and suffering, employment prospects and the need for assistance should all be addressed. The difference to the claimant between a sudden onset of symptoms caused by an accident and the gradual onset of symptoms that an underlying condition may have caused should be highlighted if appropriate.

Moving on to the approach to future complications and the need for treatment, here a percentage likelihood is required of a particular complication or treatment option being required – for example, osteoarthritis or the need for a hip replacement operation. There may be different percentages applied within these categories – for example, a 55 per cent chance of osteoarthritis developing but only a 20 per cent chance of symptoms being sufficiently serious to warrant operative intervention and an 80 per cent chance of a hip replacement operation being successful. The expert may also be required to comment upon the timeframe within which such eventualities are likely to occur. As the approach here is different to the simple test for causation, this should be expressly drawn to the expert's attention.

Finally, the expert should be invited, in addition to dealing with the effect of the injury on a claimant's pain and suffering, to address explicitly the salient heads of loss in the schedule of special damage. Bearing in mind the weight that the court will give to the expert's evidence in relation to these heads of loss as compared to the claimant's own evidence, it is important that most items of loss are addressed. While medical experts of course cannot give expert evidence about care requirements, employment prospects or travel, aids and equipment, they are likely to be able to indicate in general terms what limitations the injury has on the claimant's everyday living, employment and mobility. It can be helpful therefore to provide the expert with a copy of the schedule of loss. Doing this can also assist the expert in understanding the effect of their opinion on the way that financial loss is calculated. While not the expert's remit, it can be helpful if an expert realises the difference, for example, between an acceleration period of two years and one of ten years to the valuation of the case. This can help to focus the expert's mind on the relevant issues.

5.3.2   Instructions to the expert

With the above section in mind, the letter of instruction to the expert should, firstly, set out some background information in relation to the particular case. Secondly, the letter should provide a checklist of the areas to be addressed by the expert – most likely to be pain and suffering, the impact of the injury on employment, domestic and leisure activities and a prognosis in relation to the injury. Where there is likely to be a causation issue, brief guidance on the approach to be adopted, together with a request for the expert to address any issues of acceleration or exacerbation, should be provided. The instructions should indicate that for future complications the use of percentages would be useful in addressing the degree of chance or future risk. Finally, the expert should be reassured that an opinion is required only on the basis of what is more likely than not, rather than as a matter of certainty.

In terms of any documentation to be included with the expert's instructions, it can be helpful to provide the claimant's medical records in advance of the examination and certainly before the final report is prepared. The schedule of loss, or at the very least details of the heads of loss to be claimed therein, should be provided to the expert for comment. If the history is complicated – as may well be the case for example in an occupational disease case where symptoms have developed over a long period – it may also be helpful to provide the relevant witness statements to the expert. Care should be taken not to include any drafts of witness statements or of the schedule of loss that are not intended to be served on the defendant. Reference to the same in a report may, in certain circumstances, lead to disclosure of the schedule or statements. The Court of Appeal held in *Lucas v Barking, Havering and Redbridge Hospitals NHS Trust*,[2] that the court will only order disclosure of such documents or statements if there are grounds for believing that the statement given in the expert's report about instructions was inaccurate or misleading. However, the argument is best avoided in the first place.

5.3.3 Ensuring that the report is adequate

Once the expert's report has been received, as suggested below at section 5.4.3, one of the most important steps to take, prior to disclosure to the defendant, is to ensure that the claimant is content with the history section of the report. It is better to attempt to make any factual amendments prior to disclosure to the other side. Secondly, if it transpires that the expert has not dealt adequately or at all with the salient issues, it is important to return to the expert to ensure, if at all possible, that the report is amended so that all relevant matters are properly covered. It is nearly always better to address deficiencies in the report prior to disclosure rather than highlighting any shortcomings by having the expert prepare a supplemental report at a later stage. Thirdly, if the expert recommends further tests or investigations prior to coming to a diagnosis or prognosis, a decision will have to be made as to whether it would be helpful to disclose the report to the defendant before or after such tests or investigations have been carried out. If a defendant is to be asked to pay for any tests or investigations, then the defendant will almost certainly require sight of the report in advance of such payment. Fourthly, if the claimant does not appear to be recovering in any event in line with any prognosis, it will be necessary to return to the expert for an updating report at the appropriate stage. Sometimes, this will require returning to a different expert: for example, a GP report may state that, if a whiplash injury has not resolved within 12 months of the accident, an orthopaedic consultant should be instructed.

---

[2]   [2003] EWCA Civ 1102.

5.4   PREPARING THE CLAIMANT FOR THE MEDICAL EXAMINATION

5.4.1   Before the examination

Attending medical examinations can be stressful for claimants and this is particularly likely to be the case where examination involves investigation of personal issues, for example in claims involving psychiatric injury or gynaecological problems. If the claimant is well-prepared for the examination this can improve the prospects of obtaining a supportive medical report from either side's expert.

The claimant needs to be advised to bring some formal identification to the examination. Although basic, advising the claimant to attend the appointment on time can help to get the examination off to the best possible start.

The claimant should be made aware of what topics are likely to be covered during the examination in order to enable the claimant to marshal their thoughts in advance. These will include how the accident or injury happened; details of the injury itself; the primary symptoms suffered; whether symptoms have now resolved or are improving or deteriorating; in what circumstances the injuries cause pain and whether any activities aggravate or diminish the pain; how the injury has affected employment, domestic and other activities; and the claimant's medical history, including prior injuries or accidents and any pre-existing symptoms or conditions.

It is sensible to reassure claimants in low value cases that it is not necessary for them to still be suffering symptoms when examined. This will often be the case and provided they are able to give a clear account of how their symptoms progressed and resolved, the expert will be able to prepare a report.

Perhaps the most important piece of advice to claimants is to be as honest and forthright about their symptoms and history at the examination as possible. A defensive attitude is an unhelpful start. The claimant should be advised to avoid the temptation to exaggerate symptoms in order to impress upon the expert the severity of their symptoms. If an expert is unable to assess the true level of symptoms, then it becomes more difficult for the claimant to prove their case before a judge. Moreover, if a claimant fails, for example, to mention a previous relevant accident or pre-existing medical history, which is subsequently revealed in the medical records, the damage to credibility can impact upon the entire case. On the other hand, if an expert forms a favourable view of a claimant in terms of consistency and credibility, this is often commented upon in a report and can be very helpful to the case.

5.4.2 During the examination

In terms of the examination itself, the claimant should be advised to ensure that they understand each question before answering it. For example, if the expert asks: 'How are your symptoms now?', the claimant should clarify whether the expert means during the examination or at present in general. A claimant may have intermittent symptoms so it is important that they let the expert know that, for example, they were in pain earlier that morning although they are not at the time of the examination.

The expert will often dictate the report in the presence of the claimant and he may be given an opportunity at that stage to comment on its accuracy or anything that strikes the claimant as being relevant. The claimant should be advised to speak up, if necessary, about any inaccuracies or omissions in the dictated report. If a report is prepared by the claimant's expert, the claimant will of course be given a further opportunity to comment upon accuracy once the report has been prepared. However, this opportunity will not be available if the report is being prepared by the defendant's expert and many experts are unwilling, in any event, to amend the history section of their reports if the claimant has agreed to the history as provided or dictated during the examination.

The importance of a providing a consistent history during the examination has been highlighted by the judgment of Buxton LJ in *Denton Hall Legal Services v Fifield*[3] where it was stated that inconsistent statements made in medical reports could be admissible in evidence to attack the credibility of a claimant at trial.

5.4.3 After the examination

Finally, making contact with the claimant after the examination can be helpful, not only in terms of client care but in gathering information about the particular expert or examination. If the claimant states, for example, that the examination with the defendant's expert lasted only ten minutes, this can be useful information for later challenging the report's contents if necessary. In particular the claimant should be asked to verify that the contents of the 'history' section accurately reflects their medical history as the contents of this section will be important in determining which of the claimant's injuries arose from the accident and which were pre-existing. The claimant's feedback can also of course assist in a decision as to whether or not to instruct a particular expert in the future.

---

[3] [2006] EWCA Civ 169.

5.5   UNREASONABLE REFUSAL AND STAYS

5.5.1   The test

Sometimes claimants insist that they are unwilling to undergo a medical examination by the other side's expert or to undergo a particular form of testing, for example MRI scans or skin patch testing. On other occasions, claimants may seek to impose conditions upon attendance at such examinations – for example, that a friend or their own doctor attends. Often such refusal or request may be entirely reasonable. The court does however have the power to stay proceedings until the claimant submits to an examination and indeed can ultimately strike out the proceedings if the claimant refuses unreasonably to undergo any particular examination or test.

The leading cases in this area, namely *Edmeades v Thames Board Mills Ltd*[4], and *Starr v National Coal Board*,[5] long pre-date the CPR and the Human Rights Act 1998 but remain good law. In short, the court has an inherent jurisdiction to grant a stay where the claimant unreasonably refuses to submit to an examination by a doctor instructed by, or to a test suggested by, the defendant if just determination of the cause is not possible in the face of such refusal. Where the effect of the refusal is to deprive the defendant of the expert of his choice, this will normally be treated as preventing just determination of the cause.

The test is a three-fold one: is the request made by the defendant a reasonable one? Is the claimant's refusal reasonable? Balancing, on the one hand, the defendant's need for information against the claimant's reason for refusal, what do the interests of justice require? In *Starr* the claimant refused outright to be examined by a neurologist instructed by the defendant. The Court of Appeal found that the defendant's request was a reasonable one and the claimant was unable to show that he had acted reasonably in refusing to comply. A stay of the proceedings was upheld.

5.5.2   Objection to a particular test

The court has been willing in a number of cases to refuse a stay of proceedings where it has considered that tests requested by the defendant's expert have gone beyond what is reasonable and that has been particularly the case where the requested tests have been lengthy and invasive.

---

[4]   [1969] 2 QB 67.
[5]   [1977] 1 WLR 63.

In *Aspinall v Sterling Mansell Ltd*,[6] the court refused a stay of proceedings where the claimant was unwilling to undergo skin patch testing in an industrial dermatitis case. The tests were invasive and in particular involved a minor but real risk of recrudescence of dermatitis. Notably, the court rejected the defendant's argument that it was necessary to have a statement from the claimant herself setting out her personal objections to testing. It was enough that her legal advisers had made the position clear.

In *Prescott v Bulldog Tools*,[7] the court refused to stay the proceedings where the claimant would not undergo two particular procedures, a polytomography, which involved an x-ray of the inner ear, and electrocochleography, which involved placing a very fine needle in the ear drum. One factor relied upon by the court in refusing the stay was that the tests would take some three to five days to undertake. The court did allow the defendant to undertake calorific testing, a procedure that involved running water into the outer ear canal. This was a test that the claimant had already been subjected to by his own expert. The court however made clear that sometimes even procedures involving a real but minimal risk of short-term injury to the claimant would be considered reasonable by the court, in particular where the defendant offered to compensate the claimant for any consequent injury.

In *Laycock v Lagoe*,[8] the court refused to order a stay where a claimant refused, on what appears to be little evidence indeed, to undergo an MRI scan. The court did warn that the claimant could not complain if the trial judge took into account the refusal to undergo a test that might help to prove his claim.

5.5.3 Objection to particular doctor

Sometimes a claimant will object to being examined by a particular doctor suggested by the defendant. In *Starr v National Coal Board*,[9] the Court of Appeal acknowledged that there may be situations where such an objection would be considered to be reasonable. Scarman LJ stated:[10] 'In some cases it might not be at all difficult to reach a conclusion, without any criticism of the doctor, that the plaintiff was entitled to say: "Not this doctor".' An obvious illustration of such a case would be a female claimant who had an injury which she would prefer to have examined by a female doctor. One can envisage other cases where objection of a very personal character, in no way reflecting upon the competence or character of the doctor, might exist when the plaintiff should say: 'Not this doctor, but another ...'. The Court of Appeal recognised that this would obviously require an examination of the

---

6   [1981] 3 All ER 866.
7   [1981] 3 All ER 869.
8   [1997] PIQR P518.
9   [1977] 1 WLR 63.
10 At p 72A.

claimant's reasons for the objection – something which might take the court into difficult waters, in particular if a claimant was acting on legal advice.

5.5.4   Attendance of a friend

In practical terms, experts tend to have little difficulty with claimants attending medical examinations with a friend or other supportive third party. However, the question arises as to whether or not a claimant is entitled to insist upon the presence of a friend as a condition of attending an examination with the defendant's expert.

In *Hall v Avon Area Health Authority*,[11] the Court of Appeal, gave examples of where the attendance of a third party would be particularly appropriate, such as if the claimant: 'were in a nervous state or confused by a serious head injury, or if the defendant's nominated doctor had a reputation for a fierce examining manner'.

The court will not in every situation however allow the attendance of a friend or third party. In *Whitehead v Avon County Council*[12] the Court of Appeal considered the position where the claimant was refusing to attend an examination by the defendant's psychiatrist unless she could bring a friend to the examination 'for support'. The defendant's expert however indicated that having another person present would detract from the quality of the psychiatric examination. The court considered both the defendant and the claimant's positions to be reasonable but, in striking the balance between the interests of the parties, was prepared to order a stay unless the claimant attended without a friend. The court in this case was influenced by the fact that a psychiatric examination is unlike other medical examinations in that there are no objective symptoms so that the answers given by the claimant are all-important. If the examiner believed that a correct diagnosis was best achieved free from outside observation then the court was prepared to accept this approach. The examining doctor was well-recognised and the request was not eccentric.

5.5.5   Attendance of claimant's own expert

In *Hall v Avon Area Health Authority*,[13] the claimant sought to have her own expert present at the examination by the defendant's consultant. This request was not considered reasonable by the Court of Appeal although it was not ruled out in every case. Interestingly, the Court of Appeal suggested that the claimant's legal advisor might be able to perform the role of protecting a claimant during such an examination equally well.

---

[11]   [1980] 1 All ER 516 at 516F–517A.
[12]   CCRTI 94/0651/F.
[13]   [1980] 1 All ER 516.

5.6 APPENDIX: GLOSSARY OF EXPERTS – WHO DOES WHAT?

- Accident and emergency medicine: best used for minor soft tissue injuries and minor broken bones.

- Anaesthetist: can be useful for chronic pain cases as many anaesthetists act as pain clinicians.

- Audiologist: an expert in the assessment of hearing loss based on production of an audiogram. May also be used for balance (vestibular) disorders.

- Cardiologist: an expert in the heart.

- Dentist: specialist in injuries to and treatment of the teeth.

- Dermatologist: a specialist in the treatment of skin complaints.

- Ear, nose and throat ('ENT') surgeon: specialist in ear, nose and throat cases namely those involving deafness, taste and/or smell. Can be used in industrial deafness, acoustic trauma and head injury cases.

- Endocrinologist: a specialist in diseases of the endocrine glands. Can be used in cases involving diabetes, hormonal problems and/or growth deficiency.

- Gastroenterologist: a specialist in the stomach and intestines. Often used in cases involving food poisoning.

- General practitioner: can be used for minor self-limiting soft tissue injuries.

- General surgeon: often used in hernia cases and in clinical negligence cases involving negligent surgery.

- Gynaecologist: expert in the female reproductive organs, including internal injuries or cases involving damage which might prevent or reduce the risk of conception or childbirth.

- Hand surgeon: expert in the fingers and hands.

- Hepatologist: expert in the liver. Useful in cases involving serious internal injury or where a claimant has been a victim of chronic alcohol abuse and may accordingly have a reduced life expectancy.

- Maxillo-facial surgeon: specialist in mouth, teeth and jaw injuries.

- Neurologist: specialist in diseases of or damage to the nervous system. Often used in cases involving head injury causing brain or nerve damage or injuries affecting balance and cognitive abilities.

- Neuro-psychiatrist/Neuro-psychologist: specialists in psychiatric- or psychological-type symptoms, such as cognitive, emotional or behavioural problems caused by neurological disorders. A neuro-psychologist will often be used where tests are required to establish whether there is evidence of organic impairment of cognitive function.

- Neurosurgeon: specialist in treating disorders of the brain, spinal cord and peripheral nervous system. Can be used to comment on the damage caused by a head or spinal injury, whether or not surgery is required and as to any increased risk of epilepsy.

- Obstetrician: expert in childbirth or can be useful in claims involving birth accidents.

- Ophthalmologist: specialist in the eye, including injuries to and diseases of the eye.

- Orthodontist: specialist in the teeth and restorative dentistry. Useful where guidance is required as to the cost, type and amount of future dental treatment including implants, bridges and dentures.

- Orthopaedic surgeon: expert in soft tissue injuries and broken bones. Perhaps the most often used expert in personal injury claims involving fractures and whiplash injuries.

- Otolaryngologist: specialist in ear, nose and throat disorders, including deafness and smell and taste problems. Can also be used where damage has been caused to vocal chords.

- Otorhinolaryngologist: specialist in diseases of the nose. Useful in cases involving occupational rhinitis or mucous membrane disease.

- Paediatrician: specialist in issues relating to children, including in matters of growth and development as well as birth accident cases.

- Pain relief: useful in cases involving chronic pain syndrome. Often used where there is no longer an orthopaedic explanation for ongoing symptoms.

- Pathologist: expert in the science of bodily tissues including analysis of tissues and fibres for example in occupational disease cases.

- Physician: general or often chest specialist dealing with overall health and internal medicine. Useful in cases where issues of life expectancy arise.

- Plastic surgeon: specialist in scarring and revision surgery.

- Psychiatrist: expert in the diagnosis and treatment of mental illness. In contrast to psychologists, psychiatrists must be qualified doctors and are useful in particular where issues of medication and treatment arise.

- Psychologist: specialist in the treatment of emotional disorders which may or may not amount to a recognized psychiatric illness.

- Rheumatologist: specialist in the soft tissue structures, namely joints and muscles, of the body. Often used in cases involving fibromyalgia, repetitive strain and sometimes chronic pain.

- Urologist: specialist in urinary disorders.

- Vascular surgeon: specialist in the diagnosis and treatment of diseases of the blood vessels such as hand arm vibration syndrome or Raynaud's phenomenon.

CHAPTER 6

EXPERT EVIDENCE

Maria Panteli

6.1 INTRODUCTION

Expert evidence is essential to a personal injury claim, whether it be a claim for personal injury, industrial disease or clinical negligence. It is important that the right experts are identified and instructed. A case can be won or lost on the basis of the expert evidence.

Clear guidance must be provided to the experts as to their duties and what is expected of them in the provision of their medico-legal report and work. It is important that an expert has all the relevant information they may require to enable them to provide their opinion.

6.2 ADMISSIBILITY OF OPINION EVIDENCE

An expert witness is able to give evidence of opinion whereas all other witnesses may only give factual evidence. This exception to the substantive rule of evidence is provided for in s 3(1) of the Civil Evidence Act ('CEA') 1972 which states that: 'where a person is called as a witness in any civil proceedings, his opinion on any relevant matter on which he is qualified to give expert evidence shall be admissible in evidence'. Under s 3(2) CEA, in relation to experts, '... a statement of opinion by him on any relevant matter on which he is not qualified to give expert evidence, if made as a way of conveying relevant facts personally perceived by him, is admissible as evidence of what he perceived'.

6.3 DUTIES OF AN EXPERT

Prior to the introduction of the Civil Procedure Rules ('CPR') Part 35, which provides guidance about the duties and responsibilities of experts, the duties of experts were found in case law. Cresswell J summarised the duties of experts in the *Ikarian Reefer* case:[1]

---

[1] *National Justice Compania Naviera SA v Prudential Assurance Company Ltd 'The Ikarian Reefer'* [1993] 2 Lloyd's Rep 68. See also the case of *Anglo Group plc v Winther Brown & Co Ltd* [2000] 1 WLR 820 in which Toulmin HHJ further clarified the role of the expert witness.

- Expert evidence presented to the court should be, and should be seen to be, the independent product of the expert uninfluenced as to form or content by the exigencies of litigation.

- An expert witness should provide independent assistance to the court by way of objective unbiased opinion in relation to matters within his expertise.

- An expert witness should state the facts or assumptions upon which his opinion is based. He should not omit to consider material facts that could detract from his concluded opinion.

- An expert witness should make it clear when a particular question or issue falls outside his expertise.

- If an expert's opinion is not properly researched because he considers that insufficient data is available, then this must be stated with an indication that the opinion is no more than a provisional one.

- If the expert cannot assert that the report contains the truth, the whole truth and nothing but the truth without some qualification, that qualification should be stated in the report.

- If, after exchange of reports, an expert witness changes his view on a material matter having read the other side's expert's report, or for any other reason, such change of view should be communicated (through legal representatives) to the other side without delay and (where appropriate) to the court.

- Where expert evidence refers to photographs, plans, calculations, analyses, measurements, survey reports, or other similar documents, they must be provided to the opposite party at the same time as the exchange of reports.

6.4   CPR PART 35 AND THE PROTOCOL

Experts are now governed by CPR Part 35, which provides guidance on the instruction of experts. This incorporates the Instruction of Experts to give Evidence in Civil Claims Protocol ('Experts Protocol'), which is annexed to Practice Direction 35. In 2005, the Civil Justice Council consolidated their advice to experts into a single experts protocol. The protocol replaced the existing Code of Guidance for Expert Evidence published by the Academy of Experts.

The protocol and CPR Part 35 apply to any steps taken for the purpose of civil proceedings by experts or those who instruct them. Any advice which the parties do not intend to use for the purpose of litigation is likely to be confidential and the protocol and CPR Part 35 do not apply in these circumstances.[2]

The expert's overriding duty is to the court. It is the duty of experts to help the court on matters within their expertise.[3] This duty overrides any obligation to the person from whom an expert has received instructions or by whom they are paid.[4]

Practice Direction 35 provides guidance on the duties of an expert and helpfully summarises Cresswell J's list of duties.[5] These duties emphasise the need for experts to be independent, objective, to consider all material facts including those that might detract from their opinion, to make clear when an issue falls outside their expertise and when they are unable to reach a definite opinion (for example, because they have insufficient information).

In relation to independence, the protocol helpfully sets out that a useful test of 'independence' is whether the expert would express the same opinion if given the same instructions by an opposing party.[6] Experts should not take it upon themselves to promote the point of view of the party instructing them.

6.5 CONFLICT OF INTEREST

Before instructing an expert, it is important to confirm that there is no potential conflict of interest. In the case of *Toth v Jarman*,[7] a clinical negligence claim against a GP, the Medical Defence Union ('MDU'), who acted for the defendant, instructed an expert to report. The report of the defendant's expert was preferred at trial to the claimant's expert evidence. On appeal, the claimant argued that the defendant's expert had failed to disclose a conflict of interest arising out of the fact that, at the time he prepared his report, he was a member of the MDU's Cases Committee.[8] The Court of Appeal held that, although this information could have been obtained before the trial, it would not have affected the outcome as the doctor had ceased to be a member of the committee some time before the trial. However, the Court of Appeal said that experts' potential conflicts of interests should be disclosed at an early stage in proceedings

---

[2]   *Carlson v Townsend* [2001] 1 WLR 2415; *Jackson v Marley Davenport* [2004] 1 WLR 2926.
[3]   CPR 35.3(1).
[4]   CPR 35.3(2).
[5]   CPR Practice Direction 35 para 2.
[6]   Experts Protocol para 4.2.
[7]   [2006] EWCA Civ 1028.
[8]   The Cases Committee of the MDU is the section of the MDU that takes decisions in relation to the defence of a defendant's claim.

unless it is 'obviously immaterial'. Further, experts might add to the declaration at the end of their report that they had no such conflict.

The Court of Appeal did not define what might be an 'immaterial' conflict of interest. It also did not explain how its decision was consistent with the principles set out in the *Ikarian Reefer* case that expert evidence should be, and be seen to be, the independent product of the expert uninfluenced as to form or content by the exigencies of litigation. It seems strange that the Court of Appeal did not consider the fact that the expert was on the Cases Committee at the time of preparing his report, which was the basis of the defence, to be a material conflict. The fact that he was no longer on the committee at the time of giving evidence at trial appears to miss the point. It might be concluded from *Toth v Jarman* that for a conflict to be material, it would have to compromise the expert's overriding duty to the court to provide an independent and unbiased view.

The safest course of action is to ensure that an expert declares at the outset any potential conflict of interest he might have and this should be communicated to the other side. This would enable the matter to be discussed between the parties or brought to the attention of the court at an early stage. Further, prior to instructing an expert, one should obtain a copy of his curriculum vitae which should provide details of his employment and any activity that could raise a potential conflict of interest. The expert's curriculum vitae should be served with the expert's report so that the other side also has this information.

Despite the invitation expressed by the Court of Appeal in *Toth v Jarman*, the CPR still do not provide for the statement of truth at the end of an expert's report to include any reference to the expert having to confirm that he does not have any conflict of interest. However, the model directions for Clinical Negligence Cases do include such a reference:

'Experts shall, at the time of producing their reports, produce a CV giving details of any employment or activity which raises a possible conflict of interest.'

The model directions are for use in the first Case Management Conference in clinical negligence cases before the Masters in the Royal Courts of Justice, although there is no reason why some of the provisions could not also be applied to clinical negligence cases in the county courts or to some personal injury actions. They can be found on Her Majesty's Court Service website (www.hmcourts-service.gov.uk).[9]

---

[9]   A copy of the Model Directions for Clinical Negligence Cases can be found at the end of this chapter.

6.6 FACTS AND OPINION

It is important that an expert has all the relevant facts on which to base his opinion. In some cases, the facts may be in dispute. If there are a number of factual positions, the expert needs to consider all of them and to provide a view on each factual hypothesis. If there is any dispute about the facts, this will be determined by the court. Therefore, the expert should not express a view in favour of one or other version of the facts unless, as a result of their particular expertise and experience, the expert considers one set of facts as being improbable or less probable. In such a case, he may express that view and should give his reasons for holding it.[10]

6.7 REJECTING EXPERT EVIDENCE

As already noted above, it is for the judge to decide upon the issues of fact. In the case of *Huntley v Simmons*,[11] the Court of Appeal confirmed that issues of fact and assessment in a personal injury claim were for the judge. The expert evidence was only part of the evidence that the judge had to assess with all of the other evidence when making his decision. In Huntley, the claimant argued that he required 24 hours' care and there was no prospect of any improvement in his condition. The claimant's case was supported by his care expert and neuropsychiatric expert. In the joint statement produced following an experts' discussion between the neuropsychiatrists for each side, the neuropsychiatric experts also agreed with the view that there was no prospect of improvement. The judge did not accept either the recommendations of the claimant's or defendant's care experts, which were at opposite ends of the spectrum. The judge also disregarded the joint statement and made his own assessment of the care that would be needed.

It has been held that the judge is entitled 'to consider and to decide questions of primary fact, upon which expert medical opinions are based, such as whether the claimant is honestly or accurately describing sensations or incapacities'.[12]

However, in *Binks v Ikoku*,[13] in relation to the judge rejecting an agreed medical report Brandon LJ said:

> 'I do not go so far as to say that a Judge is bound to accept every line and every word contained in an agreed medical report. There may be reasons why he should not do so. I would, however, say that, if he is going to depart in a significant manner from what appears to be the agreed medical evidence, then he should at least state and explain in his judgment his reasons for doing so. He may have good reasons for doing so, or he may not,

---

[10] Experts Protocol para 13.11.
[11] [2010] EWCA Civ 54.
[12] Ralph Gibson LJ in *Haines v Crest Hotels Ltd* (unreported) 11 October 1990.
[13] (Unreported) 1981 CA No 72.

but if he just makes findings which are inconsistent with the agreed medical evidence and gives no reasons for doing so, then it is impossible for the parties, or an Appellate Court, to know how it is he has proceeded in that way.'

It has also been held that a judge is entitled to reject the evidence of a jointly instructed expert. In *Armstrong v First York*,[14] the Court of Appeal concluded that there was no principle that an expert's evidence must be preferred to that of a claimant. The trial judge found that the claimants in a road traffic accident had been honest and reliable witnesses. He rejected the evidence of the jointly instructed expert that the claimants could not have suffered injuries in the accident.

6.8   CONDITIONAL AND CONTINGENCY FEES

The importance of the independence and objectivity of an expert is further illustrated by the fact that payments that are contingent upon the nature of the expert evidence given in legal proceedings or upon the outcome of the case must not be offered or accepted. To do so would contravene the expert's overriding duty to the court and compromise their independence.[15] However, any agreement to delay the payment of an expert's fees until after the conclusion of the case is permissible provided that the amount of the fee does not depend on the outcome of the case.[16]

6.9   EXPERT WITNESS SUMMONS

There can sometimes be difficulties in securing the presence of an expert at trial. The Experts Protocol provides that experts have an obligation to attend court if called upon to do so and should ensure that those instructing them are aware of their dates to avoid and take all reasonable steps to be available.[17] Experts should normally attend court without the need for the service of witness summonses, but on occasion they may be served to require attendance.[18] Not adhering to a witness summons can be considered contempt of court and can result in imprisonment.

Witness summons are often used by parties as a prior booking system to ensure that over-committed experts give evidence in their trial rather than another. The law relating to such a situation is unclear and there does not appear to be clear guidance that an earlier witness summons takes priority over a later one.

---

[14]   [2005] EWCA Civ 277.
[15]   Experts Protocol para 7.6.
[16]   Experts Protocol para 7.7.
[17]   Experts Protocol para 19.1.
[18]   Experts Protocol para 19.3 and CPR Part 34.

In one case relating to the unavailability of a key expert witness, the judge stated that 'expert doctors who held themselves out as practising in the medico-legal field had to be prepared, so far as was practical, to arrange their diaries to meet the commitments of the court'.[19]

Solicitors are also duty bound by the Experts Protocol to ascertain the availability of experts before trial dates are fixed, to keep experts updated with timetables, to give consideration (where appropriate) to experts giving evidence via a video-link and to inform them immediately if the trial dates are vacated.[20] In *Simon Andrew Matthews v Tarmac Bricks & Tiles Ltd,*[21] it was also said that solicitors have to make 'real efforts ... to see if the time for the expert to give evidence in one court could be made to fit with the other court. Where holiday dates were jeopardised, efforts should be made to see if they could be changed.'

In the case of *Linda Rollinson v Kimberly Clark Ltd,*[22] the defendant's expert was not available to attend on the dates of the fixed trial and the defendant applied to vacate the trial dates, which was refused. It was held that if there had been any doubt whether that expert would be available then a different expert should have been instructed. In his judgment, Judge LJ said that it is not acceptable 'when a trial date is bound to be fairly imminent, for a solicitor to seek to instruct an expert witness without checking and discovering his availability, or proceed to instruct him when there is no reasonable prospect of his being available for another year. The check having been made and the experts' availability in the near future being in doubt, then a different expert should be instructed.'

It seems rather impractical and a waste of costs to have to instruct another expert when your expert will have already reported and you will have based your claim or defence on his report, although the decision reached by the court in the *Rollinson* case seems to be largely to do with the conduct of the defendant's solicitors in instructing a new expert shortly before the listing appointment and not taking into the account the expert's availability to attend trial. However, the case does provide a warning that you should ensure that you have obtained your experts' availability for the trial period and, if there are particular dates on which they are unavailable, obtained detailed reasons for these that can be provided to the court at the listing appointment. Otherwise the court may list the case for a time when key expert witnesses are not available. It is important to inform the expert as soon as possible of the trial window once it is set so that experts can bear this in mind when organising their diaries. The difficulty is that the trial window in clinical negligence cases

---

[19]   *Simon Andrew Matthews v Tarmac Bricks & Tiles Ltd* CA [2000] 54 BMLR 139.
[20]   Experts Protocol para 19.2.
[21]   [2000] 54 BMLR 139.
[22]   [2000] CP Rep 85.

usually covers a period of two to three months and it can be extremely difficult, if not impossible, for an expert to keep all of this period free for a trial.

The guidance in paragraph 35.2.2 of the White Book says that 'difficulties in securing the presence of an expert witness at trial, including where the expert is double-booked with other court work, can sometimes be overcome by cooperation between trial centres at diary manager or designated civil judge level'.

One case indicates that the court has a discretion to take into account other work that experts have to do when considering whether or not to excuse an expert witness from a witness summons.[23] The court has to ask whether the expert's attendance is necessary for justice to be done, although this will provide little comfort to the party whose expert is not available to give oral evidence at the trial.

An expert faced with a witness summons can apply to the court to have the witness summons set aside[24] if they can show that 'the witness summons has not been issued in good faith for the purpose of obtaining relevant evidence and that the witness named is in fact unable to give relevant evidence'.[25]

One potential solution is for the expert witness to give evidence by deposition.[26] This allows for an expert to give evidence before the trial takes place and to be cross-examined by an appointed examiner. However, this is never likely to provide a satisfactory option in a clinical negligence or personal injury case when oral expert evidence is needed.

6.10   FAILURE TO COMPLY WITH THE RULES

Experts should be made aware that any failure by them to comply with the CPRs, court orders or any excessive delay for which they are responsible may result in the parties who instructed them suffering cost penalties and, in some cases, being debarred from relying on that expert's evidence. The effect of this may result in the party losing the entire action. In *Phillips v Symes,*[27] Peter Smith J held that courts may also make orders for costs (under s 51 of the Supreme Court Act 1981) directly against expert witnesses who by their evidence cause significant expense to be incurred and do so in flagrant and reckless disregard of their duties to the court.

---

[23]   *Society of Lloyds v Clementson* LTL 8 May 1996 [1996] CLC 1205.
[24]   CPR 34.3(4).
[25]   See notes at para 34.3.5 of the White Book.
[26]   CPR 34.11.
[27]   [2004] EWHC 2330 (Ch).

6.11   PRE-ACTION PROTOCOLS ('PAPS')

The PAPs promote best practice, including guidance on the use of expert evidence.

In the Interim Report on Access to Justice (June 1995), Lord Woolf wrote:[28]

> 'The subject of expert witnesses has figured prominently throughout the consultative process. Apart from discovery it was the subject which caused the most concern. The comments were not confined to specific classes of litigation. While the criticisms differed in detail depending on the type of proceedings which were being considered, the general thrust was the same. The need to engage experts was a source of excessive expense, delay and, in some cases, increased complexity through the excessive or inappropriate use of experts. Concern was also expressed as to their failure to maintain their independence from the party by whom they had been instructed.'

6.11.1   Instructing experts under the Pre-Action Protocol for Personal Injury Claims ('PI Protocol')

Paragraphs 3.15–3.21 provide guidance on the instruction of experts in claims for personal injuries. The PI Protocol 'encourages the joint selection of, and access to, experts. The report produced is not a joint report for the purposes of CPR Part 35. The protocol promotes the practice of the claimant obtaining a medical report, disclosing it to the defendant who then asks questions and/or agrees it and does not obtain his own report. The protocol provides for nomination of the expert by the claimant in personal injury claims because of the early stage of the proceedings and the particular nature of such claims. If proceedings have to be issued, a medical report must be attached to these proceedings. However, if necessary after proceedings have commenced and with the permission of the court, the parties may obtain further expert reports. It would be for the court to decide whether the costs of more than one expert's report should be recoverable.'[29]

If the parties are unable to agree on the instruction of a mutually acceptable expert,[30] the parties may then instruct experts of their own choice. It is for the court to decide in due course, if proceedings are issued, whether either party has acted unreasonably.[31]

If the second party does not object to an expert nominated, he is not entitled to rely on his own expert evidence within that particular sphere of

---

[28]   Interim Report on Access to Justice (June 2005): ch 23, para 1.
[29]   PI Protocol para 2.14.
[30]   Ibid paras 3.15 and 3.17.
[31]   Ibid para 3.18.

expertise unless the first party agrees, the court so directs or the first party's expert report has been amended and the first party is not prepared to disclose the original report.[32]

Either party may send an agreed expert written questions on the report which are relevant to the issues, through the first party's solicitors. The expert should send the answers to the questions separately and directly to each party.[33]

The cost of a report from an agreed expert will usually be paid by the instructing first party. In relation to the cost of the expert replying to questions, this will usually be borne by the party that asks the questions.[34]

It should be remembered that a jointly *selected* expert is not a jointly *instructed* expert. The case of *Carlson v Townsend*[35] provides authority for the view that, where a medical expert was jointly selected pursuant to the PI Protocol, whilst the PI Protocol itself contemplated and encouraged the disclosure of that expert's report by the claimant, it neither specifically required disclosure in every case nor overrode the substantive law regarding privilege.

In this case, the claimant brought a personal injury claim against the defendant in respect of a back injury that he alleged had been caused as a result of caring for the defendant's disabled adult son. Prior to issuing proceedings, the claimant proposed three orthopaedic surgeons for the purpose of obtaining expert evidence. The defendant objected to one of the experts only. The claimant therefore instructed one of the experts to whom the defendant had not objected. The defendant was of the view that the expert was instructed on a 'joint instruction basis' and that she would be entitled to disclosure of the report once it was completed. However, the claimant did not disclose this report but disclosed a report from an anaesthetist (a specialist in pain relief). The defendant applied for disclosure of the orthopaedic report.

District Judge Dickinson ruled that on a proper construction of the PI Protocol there was no distinction between 'joint selection' and 'joint instruction' of a medical expert and that the orthopaedic expert should be regarded as jointly instructed and so both parties had an equal right to see the report.

The claimant appealed. Geddes HHJ took the contrary view and concluded that only the claimant had instructed the orthopaedic expert and that there had been no waiver of the privilege that ordinarily attaches to a medical report prepared for the purposes of litigation. The PI

---

[32] PI Protocol para 3.19.
[33] Ibid para 3.20.
[34] Ibid para 3.21.
[35] [2001] EWCA Civ 511.

Protocol did not impose a requirement for the expert to be jointly instructed and nothing in the PI Protocol required disclosure of a report merely because it was provided by a 'mutually acceptable expert'.

The defendant appealed and the appeal was heard in the Court of Appeal. In his judgment, Simon Brown LJ set out[36] that although

> 'the Protocol contemplates the voluntary disclosure of the claimant's expert's report (certainly where it has been obtained from "an agreed expert") in the vast majority of cases I have not the least doubt. Such a course plainly reflects the modern and highly desirable "cards on the table" approach and best facilitates settlement of claims ideally before, but failing that after, the issue of proceedings. But that is not to say that the Protocol specifically requires disclosure in every case and still less that its effect is to override the substantive law with regard to privilege.'

Simon Brown LJ dismissed the appeal and gave the following conclusions:[37]

> '1. Although the Protocol plainly encourages and promotes the voluntary disclosure of medical reports, it does not specifically require this.
>
> 2. Withholding Mr Trevett's report [orthopaedic] did not constitute non-compliance with the Protocol although the instruction of Dr Smith [anaesthetist and specialist in spinal pain relief] without first giving the defendant an opportunity to object plainly did.
>
> 3. Paragraphs 2.1 and 2.3 of the Practice Direction on Protocols provide the court with ample and various sanctions – in particular with regard to directions, costs and interest – for non-compliance with a Protocol. In the present case, of course, the claimant has still to obtain the necessary permission from the court to call Dr Smith. The defendant for her part would almost certainly, if she wished, be permitted to call an expert of her choice. The court would, after all, know that one expert at least, Mr Trevett, had reported less favourably to the claimant's cause than Dr Smith.
>
> 4. One sanction not available to the court, however, would be to override the claimant's privilege in Mr Trevett's report.
>
> 5. This appeal in truth could only succeed if Mr O'Brien [counsel for the appellant] established his central contention that, on a true understanding of the Protocol, the defendant's non-objection to a nominated expert of itself transforms that expert, once instructed, into a single joint expert whose report is accordingly available to both parties. This is not an argument I can accept either in principle or upon the scheme or language of the Protocol.'

---

[36]   *Carlson v Townsend* [2001] EWCA Civ 511 per Simon Brown LJ at para 18.

[37]   Ibid per Simon Brown LJ at para 22.

In *Beck v Ministry of Defence*[38] the Court of Appeal went one step further than in *Carlson*. The defendant obtained a report from a psychiatrist but, prior to exchange, applied to the court for permission to obtain a second psychiatric report on the basis that it did not wish to rely on the first report because the psychiatrist had demonstrated that he was not suitable as an expert (and not because the report was favourable to the claimant). It was held that if permission was granted, the court should require disclosure of the first report as a condition of the granting of that permission to avoid 'expert-shopping'. If the application was refused, disclosure would not be ordered because the defendant would have undermined its own expert evidence and therefore may be forced to proceed to trial without any expert evidence.

This decision (in which Simon Brown LJ also gave the lead judgment) does not appear to be consistent with *Carlson*, where the court held that the first report was privileged and would not order its disclosure. This was also the approach taken in *Ramage v BHS Ltd*[39] where the claimant in a personal injury claim had to disclose the first report before she could rely on a second expert's report. Charles Harris HHJ reviewed the authorities and concluded:[40]

> '1. that where a party obtains a medical report for the purposes of litigation it will be privileged;
>
> 2. that party need not disclose the report if it did not want to use it;
>
> 3. however, if he has to seek leave of the court to use another expert, the court may, as a condition of giving leave, require him to disclose the earlier report;
>
> 4. that would require the party to decide whether or not to pay the price for using a second report of waiving privilege in relation to the first;
>
> 5. since expert shopping was to be discouraged, the court will normally make a conditional order of this kind.'

6.11.2 Pre-Action Protocol for the Resolution of Clinical Disputes ('Clinical Negligence Protocol')

The Clinical Disputes Forum ('CDF') is a multi-disciplinary body which was formed in 1997 as a result of Lord Woolf's 'Access to Justice' inquiry. The CDF promoted the Clinical Negligence Protocol to try to achieve a less adversarial and more cost-effective way of resolving disputes about healthcare and medical treatment.

---

[38]   [2003] EWCA Civ 1043.
[39]   [2006] LTL 22/12/06 unreported elsewhere. See also *Hajigeorgiou v Vasiliou* [2005] EWCA Civ 236.
[40]   [2006] LTL 22/12/06 unreported elsewhere at para 26.

Section 4 of the Clinical Negligence Protocol deals with experts. Although the CPRs encourage economy in the use of experts and a less adversarial expert culture, it is recognised that, in clinical negligence disputes, the parties will require flexibility in their approach to expert evidence. Expert evidence is crucial in a claim for clinical negligence and, in contrast to the PI Protocol, this protocol does not attempt to be prescriptive on issues in relation to expert evidence. In most cases, expert evidence will be required for breach of duty, causation, condition, prognosis and quantum. Decisions on whether experts might be instructed jointly and on whether reports might be disclosed sequentially or by mutual exchange, should rest with the parties. Sharing expert evidence may be appropriate on some heads of quantum.[41]

It should be noted that whilst the Clinical Negligence Protocol provides for more flexibility and for decisions to primarily rest with the parties, this is still subject to CPR 35.7, which provides the court with the power to direct that evidence is to be given by a single joint expert, and the court's power to allow or restrict expert evidence on case management.

Paragraph 4.3 of the Clinical Negligence Protocol sets out that obtaining expert evidence will often be an expensive step and may take time, especially in areas of medicine where there are limited numbers of suitable experts. Parties will therefore need to consider carefully how best to obtain any necessary expert help quickly and cost-effectively. Assistance with locating a suitable expert is available from a number of sources, such as the Actions Against Medical Accidents website (www.avma.org.uk) and various other expert databases.

6.11.3   Pre-Action Protocol for Disease and Illness Claims ('Disease and Illness Protocol')

The Disease and Illness Protocol applies to all personal injury claims where the injury is not as a result of an accident but takes the form of an illness or disease.

Paragraph 2.5 sets out that the timetable and the arrangements for disclosing documents and obtaining expert evidence may need to be varied to suit the circumstances of the case.

Section 9 of the Disease and Illness Protocol deals specifically with experts. Paragraph 9.1 sets out that in disease claims, expert opinions will usually be needed on knowledge, fault, causation, condition, prognosis and to assist in valuing aspects of the claim.

As with clinical disputes, the Disease and Illness Protocol recognises that the parties will require flexibility in their approach to expert evidence.

---

[41]   Clinical Negligence Protocol para 4.2.

Decisions on whether experts might be instructed jointly, and on whether reports might be disclosed sequentially or by mutual exchange, should rest with the parties. Sharing expert evidence may be appropriate on various issues including those relating to the value of the claim.[42]

There will be very many occasions where the claimant will need to obtain a medical report before writing the letter of claim. In such cases the defendant will be entitled to obtain their own medical report. In some other instances it may be more appropriate to send the letter of claim before the medical report is obtained. Defendants will usually need to see a medical report before they can reach a view on causation.[43]

Where the parties agree that the nomination of a single expert (that is, a jointly selected expert) is appropriate, the parties should try to agree upon a mutually acceptable expert. The parties are encouraged to agree the instruction of a single expert to deal with discrete areas such as cost of care.[44] If the parties are unable to agree, the parties may then instruct experts of their own. It is for the court to decide subsequently, if proceedings are issued, whether either party had acted unreasonably.[45]

If the second party does not object to an expert nominated, he shall not be entitled to rely on his own expert evidence within that particular specialty unless the first party agrees, the court so directs or the first party's expert report has been amended and the first party is not prepared to disclose the original report.[46]

Either party may send to an agreed expert written questions on the report, relevant to the issues, via the first party's solicitors. The expert should send answers to the questions separately and directly to each party.[47]

The cost of a report from an agreed expert will usually be paid by the instructing first party. The costs of the expert replying to questions will usually be borne by the party that asks the questions.[48]

Where the defendant admits liability in whole or in part, before proceedings are issued, any medical report obtained under this protocol that the claimant or the defendant relies upon should be disclosed to the other party.[49]

---

[42] Diseases and Illness Protocol para 9.2.
[43] Ibid para 9.4.
[44] Ibid para 9.5.
[45] Ibid para 9.7.
[46] Ibid para 9.8.
[47] Ibid para 9.9.
[48] Ibid para 9.10.
[49] Disease and Illness Protocol paragraphs 9.11 and 9.12.

6.12   THE NHS REDRESS SCHEME

The NHS Redress Act 2006 received the Royal Assent on 8 November 2006. The scheme applies to England and Wales and covers only hospital care. Primary care services such as GPs are not covered. The scheme provides for an investigation, an assessment of liability and a remedy. This remedy might include an apology, an explanation or an award of financial compensation up to a maximum of £20,000 (on the basis of the NHS's assessment of potential damages). The scheme is said to be an alternative to civil litigation, although if a patient does not wish to accept the offer of compensation made through the scheme, they still have the option of taking civil legal action.

The scheme provides for the option of joint instruction of independent medical experts to report on the merits of case.[50] This advice is paid for by the scheme authority.[51] It is said that the NHS will consult with the patient as to the identity of the joint expert. However, the final decision as to whether or not to instruct a joint expert will rest with the NHS. This means that a joint expert will not be instructed if the NHS considers it inappropriate.

It remains to be seen how the NHS will select medical experts for the scheme. There is concern that experts who are selected for the 'panel' may have a bias towards supporting the hospital trusts concerned or defendants generally

Although it remains open for the patient in all cases to obtain their own expert medical opinion, they will have to fund the cost of this themselves. This cost will not be recoverable at the conclusion of the matter as it would be in a successful civil claim for compensation. Further, many patients will not be in a financial position to fund such a report and are unlikely to have the resources to be able to identify and instruct an appropriate expert. This means that a patient will have to make his own assessment of the liability issues without expert input when considering the settlement offer. This seems rather unfair when eligibility for the scheme will still be based on the court's definition of negligence.

If a patient does instruct their own expert, a potential difficulty could arise if an expert appointed by the patient disagrees with the opinion of the NHS instructed expert. In such a case, there is no provision in place to resolve the disagreement and the patient may have spent money on obtaining an expert report which is not accepted by the NHS and thus may not result in an offer of compensation.

Since the NHS Redress Act 2006 was passed, very little has been said about its actual implementation in England, where it is not currently in

---

[50]   NHS Redress Act 2006, s 8(4).
[51]   NHS Redress Act 2006, s 8(1)(b).

operation. However, at the time of writing, it is proposed that the scheme will be piloted in Wales in 2011 and, no doubt, lawyers, health bodies and government will be waiting to see how the scheme works in practice and its impact. There is concern about the lack of independent investigation and lack of advice for the complainant. Others contend that giving health organisations the tools to carry out better investigations will result in more people being satisfied with the result. Whilst this is sensible in principle, in practice, this can only be achieved if independence is a key factor of the scheme so that it has credibility. In the current formulation of the scheme, the NHS is effectively investigating itself.

6.13   INSTRUCTIONS TO AN EXPERT

6.13.1   Immunity

Many experts became concerned about their immunity from disciplinary proceedings following the removal from the medical register of Professor Sir Roy Meadow in July 2005.[52] Professor Meadow gave evidence in the murder trial of Sally Clarke, who was wrongly convicted[53] of the murders of her two children, in which it was held that he had misinterpreted statistical evidence. The Court of Appeal held that the fitness to practise panel of the General Medical Council ('GMC') did have the appropriate jurisdiction and, as a result, Professor Meadow was not immune from disciplinary proceedings.

At present, experts giving evidence in civil and criminal trials enjoy immunity from suit in relation to evidence given at trial and in their report.[54] This enables experts to give evidence without fear of repercussions and ensures that further proceedings do not take place based on one set of facts. It also means that it is unlikely that an expert could be sued for damages.

However, this position was recently challenged in the case of *Paul Wynne Jones v Sue Kaney*.[55] The case concerned a claim for damages for Mr Jones for personal injury. Dr Kaney (psychologist) was instructed to give evidence on behalf of Mr Jones. Her initial report suggested that Mr Jones was suffering from PTSD. The defendant's expert disagreed and there was a telephone discussion between the two experts, following which Dr Kaney signed a joint statement agreeing that Mr Jones did not have PTSD and Dr Kaney had found Mr Jones to be deceitful. Dr Kaney stated that she had signed the statement without having read the report of the defendant's expert and despite the fact that it did not reflect what she

---

[52]   *General Medical Council v Meadow* [2006] EWCA Civ 1390.
[53]   The conviction was overturned on appeal.
[54]   *X v Bedfordshire County Council* [1995] 2 AC 633 HL, *Stanton v Callaghan* [2000] 1 QB 75 CA and *Darker v Chief Constable of West Midlands* [2001] 1 AC 435 HL.
[55]   [2010] EWHC 61 (QB).

had agreed during the telephone discussion. The joint statement had a detrimental effect of the claimant's case, which settled for less than it would have done had Dr Kaney not signed it.

Dr Kaney claimed immunity as a defence. Blake J granted Dr Kaney's application for a strike-out of the action on the basis that he was bound by *Stanton v Callaghan*,[56] which provided immunity from suit for expert witnesses on the basis of public policy. Blake J concluded that for an expert to be immune from liability in such circumstances was arguably incompatible with a claimant's ECHR, Art 6 rights:

> 'An expert who negligently prepares for a joint conference, fails to carefully scrutinise the proposed joint statement before signing it, or is persuaded to record entirely unfounded imputations against his instructing party based upon a failure to remember or record the instructions, can cause great damage to a party in civil proceedings. The policy of the CPR, and expedition and economy in the resolution of disputes means that the courts will not lightly permit a party to find another expert to replace one in which he has lost confidence. The Claimant was not so permitted in the present case. Once the damage is done in a careless concession in a joint report, it cannot be undone. The injured party is left with a wrong without a remedy.'

The decision of European Court of Human Rights in *Osman v UK*[57] was raised by Mr Jones. This set out that blanket immunities preventing claimants seeking damages in tort are disproportionate and may be contrary to Art 6 of the European Convention on Human Rights.

Permission was granted for the case to be heard by the Supreme Court. The case was heard on 11 January 2011 by a panel of seven justices; the main issue being the extent to which the existing immunity for experts is proportionate and compatible with Art 6. At the time of writing, judgment had not been released and is expected in the spring of 2011.

6.13.2 Privilege

Until an expert's report is disclosed to the other side, the report and the instructions to the expert are protected by legal professional privilege. A court cannot order its disclosure, although there are some circumstances where this has in fact occurred (for example, where a party in a claim for personal injury has wanted to instruct a second expert).[58]

CPR 31.14(2) sets out that, subject to CPR 35.10(4), a party may apply for an order for inspection of any document mentioned in an expert's report which has not already been disclosed in the proceedings.

---

[56] See fn 54.
[57] 23452/94 [1998] ECHR 101.
[58] See section 6.11.1 – *Carlson v Townsend* [2001] EWCA Civ 511, *Beck v Ministry of Defence* [2003] EWCA Civ 1043 and *Ramage v BHS Ltd* [2006] LTL 22/12/06.

CPR 35.10(3) sets out that the expert's report must state the substance of all material instructions, whether written or oral, on the basis of which the report was written. CPR 35.10(4) goes on to say that the instructions referred to in para (3) shall not be privileged against disclosure but the court will not order disclosure of any specific document or permit any questioning in court other than by the party who instructed the expert unless it is satisfied that there are reasonable grounds to consider the statement of instructions given under para (3) to be inaccurate or incomplete. The purpose of the rule is to ensure that the instructions are transparent and this should usually be achieved without requiring disclosure of the documents or cross-examination of the expert about his instructions.

It may therefore be important to consider what instructions are given to the expert early on in the case when a party is still considering whether he has a claim and, if so, against whom. In these circumstances, the note to para 35.10.3 in the White Book suggests that the expert should be sent fresh instructions once the court has given permission for expert evidence to be obtained.

In *Morris v Bank of India*,[59] an expert's report in a banking dispute failed to identify all the material instructions relied upon – in this case, some witness statements. The court ordered their disclosure under CPR 35.10(4).

In *Salt v Consignia plc*,[60] all of a solicitor's letters of instruction to a medical expert, as far as they were material, were ordered to be disclosed under CPR 35.10(4).

6.13.3 Privilege in earlier reports or drafts of reports

If a party discloses their report, either voluntarily or in accordance with the directions, privilege is waived. However, disclosure of the expert's final report does not waive privilege of earlier drafts of the report or of any previous reports.

In *Lucas v Barking, Havering and Redbridge Hospitals NHS Trust*,[61] the Court of Appeal held that it would only order the disclosure of an earlier medical report and witness statement if there were grounds to believe that the expert's statement in the report about instructions was inaccurate or misleading. Material supplied by an instructing party to an expert as the basis for that expert's report should be considered part of the instructions and therefore subject to CPR 35.10(4). The defendant sought an order under CPR 31.14(2) for the inspection of a witness statement and earlier expert report, which were referred to in the expert's report. The claimant

---

[59]   (unreported) 15 November 2001, ChD.
[60]   [2002] CLY 420.
[61]   [2003] EWCA Civ 1102.

opposed the application on the basis that the documents were part of the instructions provided to the expert and therefore excluded from disclosure by virtue of CPR 35.10(4). The court concluded that the purpose of CPR 35.10(4) was to prevent the compliance with CPR 35.10(3) making such a statement disclosable unless there were grounds for believing that the statement of instructions in the expert's report was 'inaccurate or incomplete'. The application for disclosure of the witness statement and the earlier report was refused.

In *Jackson v Marley Davenport Ltd,*[62] the Court of Appeal held that drafts of an expert's report remained privileged and the court had no power to order their disclosure in the absence of any breach of CPR 35.10(4). It was argued that the first report should have been disclosed under CPR 35.13[63] and that, if an expert's views developed after fresh evidence, his earlier views in the first report were disclosable. It was held that CPR 35.13 did not provide the court with the power to order the disclosure of earlier reports made by experts in preparation of a final report. Where an expert provided a report for legal advisors or for the purposes of a conference, that report was subject to litigation privilege.

In deciding which documents an expert should have access to, it is important to remember that these could be potentially disclosable to the other side. At the stage of sending instructions to an expert, you may wish to make some tactical decisions about what documents to provide as it is likely that you will not have served any documents on the defendant. For example, it may be better to summarise the claimant's evidence in a letter to the expert (which will be privileged) rather than sending the claimant's draft witness statement to the expert. However, one has to ensure that the expert is provided with all of the relevant material at the time of their instruction to ensure that the expert can provide an accurate report setting out their opinion that is based on all of the material facts.

6.14 FINANCIAL FACTORS WHICH MAY IMPACT ON YOUR CHOICE OF EXPERT

6.14.1 Publicly funded cases

The ability to instruct an expert in a publicly funded clinical negligence case may be affected by the cap placed on experts' fees by the Legal Services Commission ('LSC'), which is still currently £200 per hour. The difficulties posed by this have been diminished somewhat by the LSC's introduction of cost limits for each stage of the proceedings that are based on the number of experts instructed. For example, for the investigation stage of a case requiring two experts on liability, a cost limitation of

---

[62] [2004] EWCA Civ 1225.
[63] CPR 35.13 provides that a party who fails to disclose an expert's report may not use the report at trial or call the expert to give oral evidence unless the court gives permission.

£7,500 will be given providing cost-benefit criteria are met. If the claim is unsuccessful and costs are to be paid by the LSC, provided all of the work for that stage has been carried out, the LSC will pay £7,500. It is therefore possible for the claimant's solicitor to use some of their profit costs to meet the shortfall in the expert's fee. Although this could leave very little for the claimant's solicitor's actual profit costs.

The current prescribed hourly rates by the LSC may restrict the choice of expert and could result in less qualified or experienced experts undertaking the work as they may be prepared to work for a lower hourly rate, or an expert may take less time and care to prepare a report.

This could place the claimant's solicitor in direct conflict with his professional obligation to his client. It could lead to a significant reduction in a claimant's access to justice and will lead to many experts either not acting as expert witnesses or refusing to take on claimant work for more profitable defendant work as the defendant is not limited by such a cap on fees.

Even more concerning are the Ministry of Justice's Proposals for the Reform of Legal Aid in England and Wales and the Proposals for civil litigation funding and costs (Jackson LJ's proposals), which at the time of writing are undergoing consultation.[64] The Proposals for the Reform of Legal Aid in England and Wales contain radical and wide-ranging proposals for reform. These include proposals to scrap legal aid for clinical negligence cases apart from certain unspecified 'exceptional' cases. This will mean that many victims of medical accidents will not be able to have access to justice because they cannot afford to pay. The assumption is that victims of medical accidents will be able to fund their claims under Conditional Fee Agreements. However, the proposals for the reform of civil litigation funding and costs will mean that for many these are not viable alternatives.

In relation to expert fees,[65] there are proposals for introducing a new system of fees for expert witnesses. These fees cannot be increased by the court on assessment. It is envisaged that the new rates (and the subsequent new fee structure) will bind the court to prevent expert fees from increasing at the assessment stage. The proposals set out a new fee structure for expert witnesses, made up of fixed fees (for most areas of work), graduated fees (where specific totals are set for particular activities) and a limited number of hourly rates. The plan is to put experts in different bands with a fee structure for each band. This fee will depend

---

[64] For details see: www.justice.gov.uk/consultations. The closing date for responses is 14 February 2011. The Proposals for civil litigation funding and costs contains a package of Jackson LJ's proposals for reforming Conditional Fee Agreements and other aspects of civil litigation funding and costs.

[65] See Chapter 8, Annex H and Annex J of the Proposals for the Reform of Legal Aid in England and Wales.

on the activity to be carried out by the expert; whether it is a routine and one-off activity (such as a GP report) or involves several different activities (such as carrying out an assessment, providing a written report on the results and giving evidence of the results in court).

For the short term, the plans are to codify the benchmark hourly rates currently applied by the LSC and subject to a 10 per cent reduction. The rates would be the maximum allowable for the type of expert charge, unless it is subject to exceptional circumstances. The proposals suggest that exceptional circumstances should be defined as those where: the experts' evidence is key to the client's case; and either the complexity of the material is such that an expert with a high level of seniority is required or the material is of such a specialised and unusual nature that only very few experts are available to provide the necessary evidence. In some cases, the LSC's benchmark rates for experts in London are lower than those paid outside of London. It is said that this is because there is a greater supply of experts in London, which allows more competitive rates to be paid. By way of example, the maximum hourly rate for a neurologist in London is set at £90 (£153 outside London).

6.14.2   Legal expenses insurance

The availability of legal expenses cover, which limits the claimant's ability to be given a conditional fee agreement until the level of the indemnity is reached, can impact on the choice of the expert to be instructed. Many legal expenses insurers require you to use experts from their panel. However, in some cases, the insurer will agree for you to instruct an expert of your choice and you should write to request this. You should set out the name and qualifications of the expert, enclose a copy of their curriculum vitae and explain why it would be appropriate to instruct them.

6.15   DISCUSSIONS BETWEEN EXPERTS

Under CPR 35.12(1) the court may at any stage direct a discussion between experts for the purpose of requiring the experts to identify and discuss the expert issues in the proceedings and, where possible, to reach an agreed opinion on those issues. An experts' discussion is not mandatory unless the court orders one. Parties should therefore consider carefully whether such a discussion will advance the case. For example, there may not be a benefit to having such a discussion if there are no material differences of opinion between the experts or if the view of each side's expert is at the opposite end of the spectrum and the experts are unlikely to alter their views. Paragraph 9.2 of Practice Direction 35 explains that the purpose of discussions between experts is not for the experts to settle cases but to agree and narrow issues. In particular, to identify:

- the extent of the agreement between the experts;

- the points of disagreement and short reasons for any disagreement;

- action, if any, which may be taken to resolve the outstanding points of disagreement;

- any further material issues not raised and the extent to which these issues are agreed.

It is suggested that the appropriate time to consider whether an experts' discussion is likely to be helpful is following the exchange of expert evidence in the relevant field.

Section 9 of Practice Direction 35 and s 18 of the Protocol for the Instruction of Experts to Give Evidence in Civil Claims ('Experts Protocol') give helpful guidance on discussions between experts. The current Model Directions for Clinical Negligence Cases,[66] which apply to clinical negligence cases in the High Court, also provide useful suggestions for experts' discussions, particularly in relation to the drafting of the agenda and the format of the meetings. These directions could be applied to clinical negligence cases in the county courts and to personal injury claims.

The rules do not require the experts to meet in person and the practicalities and timeframe may make this unfeasible. However, in complex clinical negligence claims, if at all possible, a face-to-face meeting is preferred particularly if there is more than one expert for each side taking part in the meeting.

The parties must discuss and if possible agree whether an agenda, which helps the experts focus on the issues to be discussed, is necessary. The agenda must not be in the form of leading questions or hostile in tone.[67] The notes to the Model Clinical Directions for Clinical Negligence cases contain an obligation for parties to prepare the draft agenda jointly with the relevant expert. The direction is as follows:

> 'Unless otherwise agreed by all parties' solicitors, after consulting with the experts, a draft agenda which directs the experts to the remaining issues relevant to the experts' discipline, as identified in the statements of case shall be prepared jointly by the claimant's solicitors and experts and sent to the defendant's solicitors for comment at least 35 days before the agreed date for the expert's discussions.'

---

[66] A copy of the Model Directions for Clinical Negligence Cases can be found at the end of this chapter.
[67] Practice Direction 35 para 9.3.

The notes to these model directions indicate that experts should note that it is part of their overriding duty to the court to ensure that the agenda complies with this direction.

It is preferable for the experts to receive one agreed agenda, although if the parties are unable to agree on this, each party can submit a list of questions to the experts. The notes to the model clinical negligence directions suggest that, where it has been impossible to agree a single agenda, it is of assistance to the experts if the second agenda is consequently numbered to the first. For example, if the first agenda has 16 questions, the second agenda is numbered from 17 onwards. It is submitted that it is helpful if the issues to be covered are formulated as questions to be answered by the experts, which can be answered as 'yes' or 'no', with reasons to be given. This assists with identifying the issues that can be agreed and those that cannot be agreed.

The parties must not instruct experts to avoid reaching agreement on any matter within the experts' competence and experts are not permitted to accept such instructions.[68]

Unless ordered by the court, or agreed by all parties and the experts, neither the parties nor their legal representatives may attend expert discussions.[69] If lawyers do attend, they should not normally intervene except to answer questions put to them by the experts and to advise about the law. Further, the experts may, if they so wish, hold part of their discussions in the absence of the legal representatives.[70]

There are advantages and disadvantages to lawyers attending experts' discussions. It can be said that if lawyers and their clients do not attend, experts are more able to debate their opinion frankly. On the other hand, the presence of lawyers can be helpful to answer questions on legal matters and procedure, to ensure that the agenda is followed and that the experts produce an agreed statement at the conclusion of the meeting.

In *Hubbard v Lambeth, Southwark and Lewisham Health Authority*,[71] the claimant suggested that not allowing lawyers to attend the experts' discussion was a breach of Art 6 of the European Convention on Human Rights. The Court of Appeal held that Art 6 was not engaged because the court's power to order a discussion is discretionary and any agreement reached is not binding on the parties or court. In *Hubbard*, Hale LJ suggested that one possible solution to lawyers attending experts' discussions is to have the discussion chaired by an independent neutral

---

[68] Experts Protocol para 18.6.
[69] Practice Direction 35 para 9.4.
[70] Practice Direction 35 para 9.5.
[71] [2001] EWCA Civ 1455.

person. It is suggested that this is not a practical option given the huge cost that this is likely to incur – the cost of the chair preparing for the discussion and attending.

Following a discussion between the experts, the experts must prepare a statement for the court setting out those issues on which they agree and disagree, with a summary of their reasons for disagreeing.[72] Individual copies of the statements must be signed by the experts at the conclusion of the discussion or as soon thereafter as practicable, and in any event within seven days. Copies of the statements must be provided to the parties within 14 days of signing.[73] Experts do not require the authority of the parties to sign a joint statement.[74] This is to try to prevent some lawyers insisting that they must approve the draft before the expert signs it. If an expert significantly alters an opinion, the joint statement must include a note or addendum by that expert explaining the change of opinion.[75] The content of the discussion between the experts shall not be referred to at the trial unless the parties agree to this.[76]

Where experts reach agreement on an issue during their discussion, the agreement shall not bind the parties unless the parties expressly agree to be bound by the agreement.[77] However, in view of the overriding objective, the parties should give careful consideration before refusing to be bound by such an agreement and be able to explain their refusal should it become relevant to the issue of costs.[78] Further, it could be very difficult for a party unhappy with an agreement reached at an experts' discussion to persuade the court that this agreement should be set aside unless it can be shown that the expert clearly stepped outside his sphere of expertise.

6.16   SINGLE JOINT EXPERTS

CPR 35.7 and 35.8 and para 7 of Practice Direction 35 deal with single joint experts.

6.16.1   Jointly selected

A jointly *selected* expert is different to a jointly *instructed* expert. A jointly selected expert is one who is chosen by both sides. This usually takes the form of one side providing a proposed list of experts and the other side deciding whether to object to any of those named. However, only one

---

[72]   CPR 35.12(3).
[73]   Practice Direction 35 para 9.6.
[74]   Ibid para 9.7.
[75]   Ibid para 9.8.
[76]   CPR 35.12(4).
[77]   CPR 35.12(5).
[78]   Experts Protocol para 18.12.

party instructs the expert. The instructing party is entirely responsible for the expert's fees and can claim legal professional privilege over the report.[79]

6.16.2 Jointly instructed expert

CPR 35.7 provides that where two or more parties wish to submit expert evidence, the court may direct that the evidence on that issue be given by a single joint expert. If the parties cannot agree the single joint expert, the court may select the expert from a list prepared or identified by the relevant parties or direct that the expert be selected in such other manner as the court may direct.

The notes to paragraph 35.7.1 of the White Book explains that 'there is no presumption in favour of the appointment of a single joint expert. The object is to do away with the calling of multiple experts where, given the nature of the issue over which the parties are at odds, that is not justified.' One might consider whether it is appropriate to instruct a single joint expert in a low value claim where the cost of instructing separate experts may be disproportionate.

It is likely that by the time of the case management conference, the parties will have already instructed experts, at least on liability issues. Whilst the court may be of the view that there are advantages to having a single joint expert, this may delay the timetable and increase costs if a new expert has to be agreed and jointly instructed. Further, if parties are unable to reach an agreement as to the identity and/or the actual instructions to go to a joint expert, this may in fact increase the costs of the case significantly. Parties will inevitably go backwards and forwards to try to reach an agreement and this might also result in having to refer the matter back to the court.

Guidance as to what factors the court might take into account when considering whether to order a single joint expert is set out in para 7 of Practice Direction 35. This was introduced in October 2009 following a proposal by the Civil Justice Council. The factors are whether:

- it is proportionate to have separate experts for each party on a particular issue taking into account the amount in dispute, the importance to the parties and the complexity of the issue;

- the instruction of a single joint expert is likely to assist the parties and the court to resolve the issue more speedily and in a more cost-effective way than separately instructed experts;

---

[79] *Carlson v Townsend* [2001] EWCA Civ 511.

- expert evidence is to be given on the issue of liability, causation or quantum;

- the expert evidence falls within a substantially established area of knowledge that is unlikely to be in dispute or there is likely to be a range of expert opinion;

- a party has already instructed an expert on the issue in question and whether or not that was done in compliance with any practice direction or relevant pre-action protocol;

- questions put in accordance with CPR 35.6 are likely to remove the need for the other party to instruct an expert if one party has already instructed an expert;

- questions put to a single joint expert may not conclusively deal with all issues that may require testing prior to trial;

- a conference may be required with the legal representatives, experts and other witnesses that may make instruction of a single joint expert impractical;

- a claim to privilege makes the instruction of any expert as a single joint expert inappropriate.

In a disputed claim for clinical negligence, a single joint expert is unlikely to be appropriate to deal with breach of duty and causation issues. It may also be inappropriate where there is more than one school of thought on an issue.

This issue arose in the case of *Oxley v Penwarden*.[80] At first instance, the judge set out that he could not see a reason for clinical negligence claims to be treated in a different way to others and ordered that the parties should agree a single joint expert as the sole expert on the issue of causation, failing which the court would appoint one. Both parties were opposed to this and agreed that the question of causation required each party to instruct their own expert. On appeal, it was held that this case required the parties to have the opportunity of investigating causation through an expert of their choice and of being able to call that evidence before the court. If there were more than one school of thought on the issue in dispute, the court would effectively decide an essential question on the case without the opportunity for challenge.

In *Simms v Birmingham Health Authority*,[81] a cerebral palsy clinical negligence case, an order for the joint instruction of a neonatologist was overturned.

---

[80]   [2001] CPLR 1; [2001] Lloyd's Rep Med 347.
[81]   [2001] Lloyd's Rep Med 382.

Another situation where a single joint expert is unlikely to be appropriate is where the expert will be required to attend conferences. In *Peet v Mid Kent Healthcare Trust*,[82] it was held that one party to the proceedings could not hold a pre-trial conference with a joint expert in the absence of the other party or its representatives. The claimant in a cerebral palsy clinical negligence claim wanted a single joint non-medical expert to attend a conference with counsel in the absence of the defendant or its representatives. The claimant wished to test the expert evidence in order to determine the strengths and weaknesses of the case and to explain to the expert witness the impact of her evidence. The Master took the view that it was not appropriate for such a conference to take place and that a conference with a single joint expert could not be held unless both parties consented to such a meeting in writing.

This was upheld in the Court of Appeal who made the following points:

- All contact with a single joint expert should be transparent.

- A single joint expert owes an equal duty of openness and confidence to both parties, besides his overriding duty to the court.

- Any report that the expert had prepared had to be regarded as evidence in the case on all issues covered within the report.

- There was no need for that report to be amplified or tested through cross-examination of the expert witness. However, if there was a need for cross-examination, the court had a discretion to allow that to happen either prior to or during the hearing.

- Clarification of the report can be sought by way of questions under CPR 35.6. This process, together with informed reading of the report, should be sufficient to enable advisers with any experience in this area of litigation to judge the likely outcome of the case in the context of the expert's report.

6.16.3   Instructing a joint expert

Guidance on the instruction of a single joint expert is set out in CPR 35.8 and in para 17 of the Experts Protocol.

While any side may give instructions to the expert, it is preferable to agree a set of joint instructions. If this is not possible, each party may give separate instructions or for supplementary instructions to be given by one of the parties. The expert should serve his report on all instructing parties at the same time. The expert should provide a single report even if he has received instructions that contain areas of conflicting fact or allegation. If

---

[82]   [2001] EWCA Civ 1703.

conflicting instructions lead to different opinions, for example, because the instructions require the expert to make different assumptions of fact, the expert will need to set out his views on the basis of each of those factual positions. It is for the court to determine the facts of the case if there is a dispute.

In *Yorke v Katra,*[83] it was held by the Court of Appeal that there was no rule that a party should be bound by the instruction to a joint expert given by the other side. CPR 35.8(1) provides that each party may give instructions to a joint expert.

6.16.4   Expert's fees

CPR 35.8(3), (4) and (5) set out that the court may give directions about the payment of the expert's fees and expenses and the costs of any inspection, examination or experiments that the expert wishes to carry out. Before an expert is instructed, the court may limit the amount that can be paid to the expert by way of fees and expenses and direct that some or all of the relevant parties pay that amount into court. Unless the court otherwise directs, the relevant parties are jointly and severally liable for the payment of the expert's fees and expenses.

6.16.5   Challenging a joint report

One party may be unhappy with the report of the joint expert. In *Daniels v Walker,*[84] it was held that, in a substantial case, where a party was dissatisfied with the joint expert's report, it should be afforded facilities to instruct its own expert provided that the party's reasons for its dissatisfaction were not fanciful. In respect of a modest claim, Lord Woolf was of the opinion that 'it would be disproportionate to obtain a second report in any circumstances. At most what should be allowed is merely to put a question to the expert who has already prepared a report.'

In *Peet,*[85] the Court of Appeal seems to identify a stricter test for allowing a party to obtain his own separate evidence – that 'good reasons' are needed as opposed to reasons which are not fanciful.

In *Popek v National Westminster Bank plc,*[86] it was held that if the claimant wished to challenge the joint expert's report, he should have done so in his written questions. If a single expert is to be subject to cross-examination, he should know in advance what topics are to be covered and where fresh material is to be adduced for his consideration, this should be done in advance of the hearing.

---

[83]   [2003] EWCA Civ 867.
[84]   [2000] 1 WLR 1382.
[85]   *Peet v Mid Kent Healthcare Trust* [2001] EWCA Civ 1703.
[86]   [2002] EWCA Civ 42.

6.17 QUESTIONS TO EXPERTS

CPR 35.6 is a useful provision where using written questions you can clarify points in the expert's report of your opponent or seek information about matters not included in the report provided they are within the expert's expertise. Paragraph 6.1 of Practice Direction 35 provides guidance on written questions to experts.

Following the service of the other side's expert evidence, it is possible to put written questions about an expert's report to their expert. This is also possible in respect of the report of a single joint expert appointed under CPR 35.7.[87] It is important that you consider the defendant's expert report as soon as you receive it and circulate it to your experts for comments because CPR 35.6(2) provides that written questions may be put only once and must be put within 28 days of service of the expert's report. The questions must be proportionate[88] and must be for the purpose of clarification of the report.[89]

However, it is possible that further information may be extracted as a result of these questions and an expert's answers will be treated as part of the expert's report.[90] This may be of benefit or detriment to a party as illustrated by the case of *Mutch v Allen*.[91]

In this case, the defendant asked the claimant's medical expert if the claimant's injuries would have been less severe if he had been wearing a seat belt. The claimant's expert stated that if the claimant had been trapped in the vehicle before release by the emergency services, his failure to wear a seat belt was likely to have been less causative of his injuries than if he had been thrown from the car. The expert was then provided with reports from the emergency teams at the scene of the accident. The expert concluded that the claimant had been thrown from the vehicle thereby seriously causing his injuries. The judge at first instance ordered that this was outside the scope of his instructions and report and was therefore not 'clarification'. The Court of Appeal disagreed and said that the evidence was admissible even though it was of advantage to the defendant on the issue of contributory negligence.

If a party sends written questions directly to an expert, a copy of the questions must at the same time be sent to the other party.[92]

The rules do not specify a time limit by when the expert should provide his response. Disputes about this can be avoided if a timeframe is

---

[87]   CPR 35.6(1).
[88]   CPR 35.6(1).
[89]   CPR 35.6(2)(c).
[90]   CPR 35.6(3).
[91]   [2001] EWCA Civ 76.
[92]   Practice Direction 35 para 6.1.

provided in the directions order at the case management conference. It is suggested that a period of 28 days would be reasonable and in accordance with the spirit of the CPRs.

It should also be noted that where a party has put a written question to an expert instructed by another party and the expert does not answer the question, the court has the power to order that the party who instructed the expert may not rely on the evidence of that expert or may not recover the fees and expenses of that expert from any other party.[93]

The rules are silent on the position of a sanction if there is a failure by a jointly instructed expert to reply. It may be that a judge may consider that the weight to be attached to that expert's evidence is diminished somewhat by this.

In relation to fees, the party instructing the expert must pay any fees charged by the expert for answering questions put under CPR 35.6. This does not affect the decision of the court at the conclusion of the case about who is ultimately to bear the expert's fees.[94]

The case of *Mutch v Allen*[95] also demonstrates the potential difficulty with the rules not specifying what is meant by 'for the purpose only of clarification'. CPR 35.6 does not set out what is meant by clarification of the expert's report and issues may arise as to the scope of the questions which can be put to experts. The provision could be used to ask your opponent's expert a question about a point not covered in the report but within his expertise.

This could lead to the position where the response from your expert to a question from the other side is not helpful to your case, causing difficulties about how you then challenge that evidence. In these circumstances, it may be necessary (subject to the permission of the court) to obtain new expert evidence, although by this stage the other side will be aware of a potential weakness in your case. If you are successful in obtaining permission to instruct a new expert, it is unclear whether the other side would be able to rely on the evidence provided by the previous expert if you are no longer relying on his report and, if they can, the weight that would be attached to it by the trial judge.

It will be a tactical decision as to whether you wish to ask questions about the other side's expert report or wait until trial to cross-examine the expert. A question could alert the other side to a weakness in its case which it may not have considered and which it might try to strengthen. Alternatively, exposing such a weakness may lead to an earlier resolution of the claim.

---

[93]   CPR 35.6(4).
[94]   Practice Direction 35 para 6.2.
[95]   [2001] EWCA CIV 76.

The notes in the White Book at para 35.6.1 provide helpful guidance on what to do if your expert receives questions which he considers go beyond the spirit of the rules. It is suggested that the right approach is 'for the expert to answer the clearly relevant questions, and to only decline to answer the remainder if (1) to do so would clearly be prejudicial to the instructing party's position or (2) the time and cost of replying to the questions is disproportionate'.

It may be helpful to remember that an expert can ask the court for directions under CPR 35.14 and this may provide assistance if the expert received questions which he considered to be onerous or excessive.

6.18   PERSUADING THE COURT TO ALLOW EXPERT EVIDENCE

The ability to rely on expert evidence is subject to the complete control of the court through the exercise of its case management powers. The court's general power to control evidence may be used to exclude evidence that would otherwise be admissible.[96]

CPR 35.1 sets out that expert evidence shall be restricted to that which is reasonably required to resolve the proceedings. CPR 35.4 sets out the court's power to restrict expert evidence. The restrictions set down are as follows:

- A party may not call an expert or put in evidence an expert's report without the court's permission.[97]

- When parties apply for permission, they must identify the field in which expert evidence is required and, where practicable, the name of the proposed expert.[98]

- If permission is granted, it shall be in relation only to the expert named or the field identified.[99]

- Expert evidence is to be given in a written report unless the court directs otherwise.[100]

In relation to timing in obtaining the court's permission, the first opportunity to indicate your wish for expert evidence is on the allocation questionnaire. Parties are asked to state in the allocation questionnaire whether they are seeking to adduce expert evidence and, if so, the name

---

[96]   CPR 32.1.
[97]   CPR 35.4(1).
[98]   CPR 35.4(2).
[99]   CPR 35.4(3).
[100]   CPR 35.5(1).

and field of expertise of the expert. Parties are asked to set out if the case is suitable for a single joint expert in any field.

It should be noted that the model directions for clinical negligence cases do not require the names of the experts to be stated but just the disciplines of the experts.

You should therefore be cautious about revealing the name of your experts early on in the proceedings, particularly if you have not yet sent them instructions or obtained their report. It is submitted that a party should only name an expert if his report has been received, is supportive of the case and you are clear that you will be relying on that report. In all other cases, only the field of expertise should be set out with the name 'to be advised'. If the report of an expert is not supportive, a party may wish to obtain a further report if he feels that this is warranted in the circumstances and will not wish to disclose the report of the previous expert.

In recent years, in clinical negligence cases, the masters of the Queen's Bench Division, following the service of the defence, have of their own motion dispensed with the need to serve an allocation questionnaire and so the first time that permission to rely upon expert evidence will be explored is at the case management conference.

Permission or refusal to rely upon an expert will be given at the case management stage. During the case management conference, the court will explore with the parties the expert evidence required, whether any of the experts can be jointly instructed and if it is necessary for the experts to give oral evidence at trial.

The difficulty is that most parties, particularly the claimant, will require expert evidence early on in the case in order to assess if there is a claim to pursue and to settle the particulars of claim. The position could arise where the court later decides that the evidence from a particular expert is not necessary. The party is then in the position where the cost of obtaining that expert's report will not be recoverable.

A request for permission to rely on expert evidence at any other time will have to be made by way of an application to the court or perhaps at a further case management conference if this is provided for in a directions order.

If the court considers that the evidence would not serve a useful purpose, there is no right under Art 6(1) of the European Convention on Human Rights to obtain expert evidence.[101] However, one possible course of action is to obtain the expert evidence you believe is necessary without the court's permission and then apply to the court for permission to rely on it

---

[101] Article 6 protects the right to a fair trial.

in the hope that the court will then be able to see the value or necessity of that evidence and give permission for it. As already set out above, the danger is, if the court still refuses permission, you will not be able to rely on the report and you may have difficulty in recovering the cost of the report from the other side at the end of the case, even if you are successful.

6.19   ONE EXPERT PER SPECIALISM

The usual position where a single joint expert is not appropriate is that each party has permission to rely on one expert in each particular field. It is often difficult to persuade the court to allow more than one expert per discipline, even in high value claims. This rule can cause difficulties for the claimant as professional witnesses of fact for the defendant will inevitably give expert opinion in the course of their factual witness evidence to justify or explain their actions.

This matter was explored in the case of *ES v Chesterfield and North Derbyshire NHS Trust,*[102] a cerebral palsy case. The Court of Appeal held that it was just and proportionate to allow the claimant to call two expert obstetricians where the defendant would be able to obtain expert evidence from two consultant obstetricians who were witnesses of fact, in addition to an independent expert obstetrician. The claimant argued that there was a significant risk that the view of a single obstetrician on the range of decisions that represented the spectrum of reasonably acceptable clinical choices might not be wholly representative of that of the profession as a whole, particularly when the defence would be relying on evidence from the two obstetricians involved plus an independent expert.

However, this was not the position in the case of *Beaumont v Ministry of Defence.*[103] In this case, it was held that where a defendant obstetrician in a clinical negligence action would rely upon his own expertise when giving factual evidence, in addition to calling an independent expert obstetrician, that was not sufficient to justify granting the claimant permission to call two experts. The claimant argued that it would be inevitable that the defendant obstetrician would rely upon his expertise and the defence would have the advantage of two experts giving evidence.

In the case of *ES*, the allegations of negligence were directed at two medical practitioners and the court had therefore been faced with the potential imbalance of three experts on the side of the defence and one expert for the claimant. There had to be something in the circumstances of the case that made it just to depart from the normal rule and to permit a second expert. When the defendant obstetrician gave evidence, he would inevitably demonstrate and rely upon his experience and expertise and

---

[102]   [2004] Lloyd's Rep Med 90.
[103]   [2009] EWHC 1258 (QB).

that might carry weight with the trial judge. However, that would be so in most cases involving allegations of professional negligence. The defendant obstetrician was not of such exceptional eminence or expertise as to justify a departure from the normal rule.

In the case of *Kirkman v Euro Exide Corporation (CMP Batteries Ltd)*,[104] a personal injury action, the Court of Appeal found that the judge had erred in refusing to allow the evidence of the surgeon who had treated the claimant on the basis that this would allow the claimant to have two expert witnesses compared to the defendant's one expert. The surgeon's statement was merely evidence of fact about what he would have done in hypothetical circumstances and was not an expert opinion on what most competent surgeons would have done in the same situation. The correctness or accuracy of his advice was not in issue. The Court of Appeal held that the desirability of equality of expert evidence was not an absolute rule and this case was an instance where it should have given way in the interests of justice.

6.20 APPENDIX: MODEL DIRECTIONS FOR CLINICAL NEGLIGENCE CASES (2010)[105]

Introductory note

These are the Model Directions for use in the first Case Management Conference in clinical negligence cases before the Masters.

A draft order in Word format, adopting the Model Directions as necessary, is to be provided by e-mail to the Master at least 2 days before the hearing.

Although there are no radical changes from the 2007 directions, **parties are requested to use the form of order at the end of this document.**

The e-mail addresses of the Masters are:

master.yoxall@judiciary.gsi.gov.uk

master.roberts@judiciary.gsi.gov.uk

The Model Directions allow the court and the parties to be flexible. For example, sequential exchange of quantum statements (say, with schedule and counter-schedule of loss) may be appropriate. The sequential exchange of expert evidence on breach of duty and causation may sometimes be appropriate.

It would be helpful if dates appeared in **bold** type.

---

[104] [2007] EWCA Civ 66.
[105] Before Master Yoxall and Master Roberts.

Please note: Solicitors must ensure that the claimant is accurately described in the title to the order: for example, 'JOHN SMITH (a child and protected party by his mother and Litigation Friend, JOAN SMITH). It is never permissible to refer to such a claimant as 'JOHN SMITH'.

The order should make it clear that it is made pursuant to a Case Management Conference or an application or both.

Note the important change to the direction relating to experts and their role in the preparation of Agendas.

THE MODEL DIRECTIONS

The annotations in italics are to assist the parties and are not part of the Model Directions and need not appear in the order.

A draft order – without the annotations – appears at the end of this document. Parties are requested to adopt this draft.

Allocation

1. The case do remain on the Multi-track.

Allocation: The order states that 'the case do remain on the Multi-track'. Allocation will usually have already been dealt with on allocation questionnaires.

Preservation of Evidence

2. The defendant do retain and preserve safely the original clinical notes relating to the action pending the trial. The defendant do give facilities for inspection by the claimant, the claimant's legal advisers and experts of the said original notes upon 7 days written notice to do so.

Maintenance of records and reports

3. Legible copies of the medical (and educational) records of the claimant / deceased / claimant's mother are to be placed in a separate paginated bundle at the earliest opportunity by the claimant's solicitors and kept up to date. All references to medical notes in any report are to be made by reference to the pages in that bundle.

Amendments

The following is suggested:

Permission to claimant / defendant to amend the Particulars of Claim / Defence in terms of the draft initialed by the Master [or the draft served on   /   /09]; the defendant to serve an amended defence by   /   /09. Costs of and occasioned by the amendments to be borne by (usually, the party seeking permission to amend). [Where no draft is available, but the form of the amendments is not contentious] (Party wishing to amend) to serve draft amended [Statement of Case]

by   /   /09. If no objection to the draft amendments, response to
be served by   /   /09, if objection is taken to the draft, permission
to restore.

Judgment

The following is suggested:

There be judgment for the Claimant with damages to be assessed.

Or

There be judgment for the Claimant for   % of the damages as are
assessed (or agreed by the parties) as due on a full liability basis.

Split Trial

[An order 'That there be a split trial' is inappropriate. The following is
suggested.]

4. A preliminary issue shall be tried between the claimant and the defendant
as to whether or not the defendant is liable to the claimant by reason of the
matters alleged in the Particulars of Claim and, if so, whether or not any of
the injuries pleaded were caused thereby; if any such injuries were so caused,
the extent of the same.

Disclosure

5. There be standard disclosure [on the preliminary issue] [limited to
quantum] by list by   2010. Any initial request for inspection or copy
documents is to be made within 7 to 14 days of service of the lists.

Factual Evidence

6. Signed and dated witness statements of fact in respect of breach of duty
and causation [and quantum] shall be simultaneously exchanged
by   2010. Civil Evidence Act notices are to be served by the same date.
The witness statements of all concerned with the treatment and care of the
claimant at the time of the matters alleged against the defendant shall be
served under this paragraph.

7. Signed and dated witness statements of fact in respect of quantum,
condition and prognosis shall be served by   2010 (claimant)
and   2010 (defendant). Civil Evidence Act notices are to be served by
the same date.

Expert Evidence

A. Single Joint Experts.

8. Each party has permission to rely on the evidence of a single joint expert
in the following fields: [state the disciplines]. The experts are to be instructed

by   2010 and the joint expert is to provide his report by   2010. In case of difficulty, the parties have permission to restore before the Master.

If the parties are unable to agree on the identity of the expert to be instructed, the parties to restore the CMC before the Master. At such hearing the parties are to provide details of the CVs, availability and the estimated fee of the expert they propose and reasoned objections to any other proposed.

B. Separate Experts.

9. In respect of breach of duty and causation, each party has permission to rely on the evidence of an expert in the following fields: [state the disciplines]; permission being given to call the said experts on matters remaining in issue.

The reports of the said experts are to be simultaneously exchanged by   2010.

10. In respect of quantum, condition and prognosis, each party ([where there are several defendants] the defendants acting jointly, unless otherwise directed) has permission to rely on the evidence of an expert in the following fields: [state the disciplines]; permission being given to call the said experts on matters remaining in issue.

The reports of the said experts are to be served by:

Claimant: 2010

Defendant(s):   2010

Literature and CVs

11. Any unpublished literature upon which any expert witness proposes to rely shall be served at the same time as service of his report together with a list of published literature. Any supplementary literature upon which any expert witness proposes to rely shall be notified to all other parties at least one month before trial. No expert witness shall rely upon any publications that have not been disclosed in accordance with this direction without the permission of the trial judge on such terms as to costs as he deems fit.

12. Experts shall, at the time of producing their reports, produce a CV giving details of any employment or activity which raises a possible conflict of interest.

Experts' Discussions

13. **Unless otherwise agreed by all parties' solicitors, after consulting with the experts**, the experts of like discipline for the parties shall discuss the case on a without prejudice basis by   2010. (Usually 8 weeks after the exchange of reports).

Discussions between experts are not mandatory. The parties should consider, with their expert, whether there is likely to be any useful purpose in holding a discussion and should be prepared to agree that no discussion is in fact needed.

(a) The purpose of the discussions is to identify:

   (i)   The extent of the agreement between the experts;
   (ii)   The points of disagreement and short reasons for disagreement;
   (iii) Action, if any, which may be taken to resolve the outstanding points of disagreement;
   (iv)   Any further material points not raised in the agenda and the extent to which these issues are agreed;

(b) **Unless otherwise agreed by all parties' solicitors, after consulting with the experts,** a draft agenda which directs the experts to the remaining issues relevant to the experts' discipline, as identified in the statements of case shall be prepared jointly by the claimant's solicitors and experts and sent to the defendant's solicitors for comment at least 35 days before the agreed date for the experts' discussions;

   Claimants' solicitors and counsel should note the obligation to prepare the draft agenda jointly with the relevant expert. Experts should note that it is part of their overriding duty to the court to ensure that the agenda complies with the following direction.

   The use of agendas is not mandatory. Solicitors should consult with the experts to ensure that agendas are necessary and, if used, are reasonable in scope. The agenda should assist the experts and should not be in the form of leading questions or hostile in tone. An agenda must include a list of the outstanding issues in the preamble.

   [Note: The preamble should state: the Standard of proof: the Bolam test: remind the experts not to attempt to determine factual issues: remind them not to stray outside their field of expertise and indicate the form of the joint statement. It will also be helpful to provide a comprehensive list of the materials which each expert has seen, perhaps in the form of an agreed supplementary bundle (it is assumed that experts will have been provided with the medical notes bundle)]

(c) The defendants shall within 21 days of receipt agree the agenda, or propose amendments;

(d) Seven days thereafter all solicitors shall use their best endeavours to agree the agenda. Points of disagreement should be on matters of real substance and not semantics or on matters the experts could resolve of their own accord at the discussion. In default of agreement, both versions shall be considered at the discussions. agendas, when used, shall be provided to the experts not less than 7 days before the date fixed for discussions.

[Where it has been impossible to agree a single agenda, it is of assistance to the experts if the second agenda is consecutively numbered to the first, ie if the first agenda has 16 questions in it, the second agenda is numbered from 17 onwards]

14. **Unless otherwise ordered by the court, or unless agreed by all parties, including the experts,** neither the parties nor their legal representatives may attend such discussions. If the legal representatives do attend, they should not normally intervene in the discussion, except to answer questions put to

them by the experts or to advise on the law; and the experts may if they so wish hold part of their discussions in the absence of the legal representatives.

15. A signed joint statement shall be prepared by the experts dealing with (a) (i) – (iv) above. Individual copies of such statements shall be signed by the experts at the conclusion of the discussion, or as soon thereafter as practicable and provided to the parties' solicitors within **7 days** of the discussions.

16. Experts give their own opinions to assist the court and should attend discussions on the basis that they have full authority to sign the joint statement. The experts should not require the authorisation of solicitor or counsel before signing a joint statement.

[Note: This does not affect Rule 35.12 which provides that where experts reach agreement on an issue during their discussions, the agreement shall not bind the parties unless the parties expressly agree to be bound by the agreement]

17. If an expert radically alters his or her opinion, the joint statement should include a note or addendum by that expert explaining the change of opinion.

Schedules and periodical payments

18. Claimant do serve a final schedule of loss and damage costed to the date of trial by   2010.

19. The Defendant do serve a counter-schedule by   2010.

20. The parties do set out their respective positions on the periodical payment of damages in the schedule and counter-schedule of loss. [or, The periodical payment of damages is not appropriate to this case.]

Periodical Payments. Parties should, at the first CMC, be prepared to give their provisional view as to whether the case is one in which the periodical payment of damages might be appropriate.

Schedules. Parties are encouraged to exchange schedules in a form which enables the counter schedule to be based on the claimant's schedule ie by delivering a disk with the hard copy, or by sending it as an e-mail attachment.]

Trial Directions

21. The Claimant's Solicitors do by   2010 apply to the Clerk of the Lists in London / [the Listing Officer in the venue] for a listing appointment for a trial period for hearing within the trial window and give notice of the appointment to the defendant. Pre-trial check lists to be filed as directed by the Clerk of the Lists.

Mode of trial: Judge alone; London; Category **[Usually]** B; time estimate days.

Trial window:

[Certified fit for High Court Judge if available].

Trial Directions

The claimant will usually be directed to apply to the Clerk of the Lists for a listing appointment no later than 6 weeks after the CMC.

The Clerk of the Lists, in order to maintain the necessary degree of flexibility for listing, will give a 'trial period' rather than a fixed date, but, in order to accommodate the parties' need for certainty as to dates for experts to attend, will, if an approach is made closer to the beginning of the trial period, confirm the date for the trial to begin as the first day of the trial period.

The trial period will usually be directed to begin at least 2 clear months after the last event besides ADR – this is to allow for ADR.

In relatively modest claims (in term of quantum), the Master may direct:

'If the parties reach agreement upon breach of duty and causation, the parties are to immediately restore the case before the Master so that alternative directions on the assessment of damages may be given.'

22. Parties do agree the contents of the trial bundle and exchange skeleton arguments not less than 7 days before the hearing. Claimant to lodge the skeleton arguments and the Trial bundle under PD 39.3.

Trial Bundles

Note: the object is to ensure that all the relevant material is provided at one time to the Clerk of the Lists to pass to the trial judge. The PD sets out both the contents of the bundle and the time when it must be lodged.

Alternative Dispute Resolution

23. The parties shall by   2010 [a date usually about 3 months before the trial window opens] consider whether the case is capable of resolution by ADR. If any party considers that the case is unsuitable for resolution by ADR, that party shall be prepared to justify that decision at the conclusion of the trial, should the trial judge consider that such means of resolution were appropriate, when he is considering the appropriate costs order to make.

24. Such means of ADR as shall be adopted shall be concluded not less than 35 days prior to the trial.

25. The party considering the case unsuitable for ADR shall, not less than 28 days before the commencement of the trial, file with the court a Witness Statement, without prejudice save as to costs, giving the reasons upon which they rely for saying that the case was unsuitable. The Witness Statement shall not be disclosed to the trial Judge until the conclusion of the case.

['ADR' includes 'round table' conferences, at which the parties attempt to define and narrow the issues in the case, including those to which expert evidence is directed; early neutral evaluation; mediation; and arbitration. The object is to try to reduce the number of cases settled 'at the door of the Court', which are wasteful both of costs and judicial time.]

Further CMC etc

26. There be a further CMC on   2010 at am/pm; Room 106/109; time estimate 30 minutes. This hearing may be vacated by consent provided that all directions have been complied with; no further directions are required; and the Master is given reasonable notice.

27. Permission to restore.

[**Note**: A party may request the restoration of a CMC or application by letter or e-mail to the assigned Master. If possible the Master should be provided with an agreed list of dates to avoid. Where the application is urgent and the time estimate is no more than 30 minutes, the Master will endeavour to list a hearing at 10.00am as soon as possible. Applications estimated to take more than 30 minutes should be applied for as private room appointments in the usual way.]

[Both Masters are willing, in appropriate cases, to hear applications by telephone link, provided sufficient notice is given **directly to the Master concerned** and the relevant papers are provided in advance. E-mails are an acceptable means of communication, provided that they are copied to all parties.]

[NOTE: The court file in cases proceeding before the Masters will not routinely be placed before the Master. Parties wishing for it to be produced should notify the Case Management Section **five clear days** in advance of the appointment. In all other cases parties should bring with them copies of any filed documents upon which they intend to rely.]

28. Costs in case [Or other costs order sought].

29. Claimant to draw and file the order by   2010 and serve the defendant (or claimant to serve sealed order by   2010).

Dated the

DRAFT ORDER

IN THE HIGH
COURT OF JUSTICE
QUEEN'S BENCH
DIVISION

Claim No. HQ09X0zzzz

MASTER [YOXALL / ROBERTS]

BETWEEN

ABC

Claimant

And

DEF NHS TRUST

Defendant

ORDER

UPON a Case Management Conference

[AND UPON the Claimant's / Defendant's application issued on   2010]

AND UPON hearing solicitor/counsel for the Claimant and solicitor/counsel for the Defendant

IT IS ORDERED that

1. The case do remain on the Multi-track.

2. The Defendant do retain and preserve safely the original clinical notes relating to the action pending the trial. The Defendant do give facilities for inspection by the Claimant, the Claimant's legal advisers and experts of the said original notes upon 7 days written notice to do so.

3. Legible copies of the medical (and educational) records of the Claimant / Deceased / Claimant's Mother are to be placed in a separate paginated bundle at the earliest opportunity by the Claimant's Solicitors and kept up to date. All references to medical notes in any report are to be made by reference to the pages in that bundle.

4. A preliminary issue shall be tried between the Claimant and the Defendant as to whether or not the Defendant is liable to the Claimant by reason of the matters alleged in the Particulars of Claim and, if so, whether or not any of the injuries pleaded were caused thereby; if any such injuries were so caused, the extent of the same.

5. There be standard disclosure [on the preliminary issue] [limited to quantum] by list by   2010. Any initial request for inspection or copy documents is to be made within 7/14 days of service of the lists.

6. Signed and dated witness statements of fact in respect of breach of duty and causation [and quantum] shall be simultaneously exchanged by   2010. Civil Evidence Act notices are to be served by the same date. The witness statements of all concerned with the treatment and care of the Claimant at the time of the matters alleged against the Defendant shall be served under this paragraph.

7. Signed and dated witness statements of fact in respect of quantum, condition and prognosis shall be served by   2010   (Claimant) and   2010   (Defendant). Civil Evidence Act notices are to be served by the same date.

8. Each party has permission to rely on the evidence of a single joint expert in the following fields: [state the disciplines]. The experts are to be instructed by   2010 and the joint expert is to provide his report by   2010. In case of difficulty, the parties have permission to restore before the Master.

9. In respect of breach of duty and causation, each party has permission to rely on the evidence of an expert in the following fields: [state the disciplines]; permission being given to call the said experts on matters remaining in issue. The reports of the said experts are to be simultaneously exchanged by   2010.

10. In respect of quantum, condition and prognosis, each party ([where there are several defendants] the Defendants acting jointly, unless otherwise directed) has permission to rely on the evidence of an expert in the following fields: [state the disciplines]; permission being given to call the said experts on matters remaining in issue. The reports of the said experts are to be served by:

Claimant: 2010

Defendant(s):   2010.

11. Any unpublished literature upon which any expert witness proposes to rely shall be served at the same time as service of his report together with a list of published literature. Any supplementary literature upon which any expert witness proposes to rely shall be notified to all other parties at least one month before trial. No expert witness shall rely upon any publications that have not been disclosed in accordance with this direction without the permission of the trial judge on such terms as to costs as he deems fit.

12. Experts shall, at the time of producing their reports, produce a CV giving details of any employment or activity which raises a possible conflict of interest.

13. Unless otherwise agreed by all parties' solicitors, after consulting with the experts, the experts of like discipline for the parties shall discuss the case on a without prejudice basis by   2010.

Discussions between experts are not mandatory. The parties should consider, with their expert, whether there is likely to be any useful purpose in holding a discussion and should be prepared to agree that no discussion is in fact needed.

(a)   The purpose of the discussions is to identify:
      (i)   The extent of the agreement between the experts;
      (ii)   The points of disagreement and short reasons for disagreement;
      (iii) Action, if any, which may be taken to resolve the outstanding points of disagreement;
      (iv)   Any further material points not raised in the Agenda and the extent to which these issues are agreed;

(b)   **Unless otherwise agreed by all parties' solicitors, after consulting with the experts,** a draft Agenda which directs the experts to the remaining issues relevant to the experts' discipline, as identified in the statements of case shall be prepared jointly by the Claimant's solicitors and experts and sent to the Defendant's solicitors for comment at least 35 days before the agreed date for the experts' discussions;

The use of agendas is not mandatory. Solicitors should consult with the experts to ensure that agendas are necessary and, if used, are reasonable in scope. The agenda should assist the experts and should not be in the form of leading questions or hostile in tone. An agenda must include a list of the outstanding issues in the preamble.

(c)   The Defendants shall within 21 days of receipt agree the Agenda, or propose amendments;

(d)   Seven days thereafter all solicitors shall use their best endeavours to agree the Agenda. Points of disagreement should be on matters of real substance and not semantics or on matters the experts could resolve of their own accord at the discussion. In default of agreement, both versions shall be considered at the discussions. Agendas, when used, shall be provided to the experts not less than 7 days before the date fixed for discussions.

14. **Unless otherwise ordered by the Court, or unless agreed by all parties, including the experts**, neither the parties nor their legal representatives may attend such discussions. If the legal representatives do attend, they should not normally intervene in the discussion, except to answer questions put to them by the experts or to advise on the law; and the experts may if they so wish hold part of their discussions in the absence of the legal representatives.

15. A signed joint statement shall be prepared by the experts dealing with (a) (i) – (iv) above. Individual copies of such statements shall be signed by the experts at the conclusion of the discussion, or as soon thereafter as practicable and provided to the parties' solicitors within **7 days** of the discussions.

16. Experts give their own opinions to assist the court and should attend discussions on the basis that they have full authority to sign the joint

statement. The experts should not require the authorisation of solicitor or counsel before signing a joint statement.

17. If an expert radically alters his or her opinion, the joint statement should include a note or addendum by that expert explaining the change of opinion.

18. Claimant do serve a final Schedule of loss and damage costed to the date of trial by   2010.

19. The Defendant do serve a Counter-Schedule by   2010.

20. The parties do set out their respective positions on the periodical payment of damages in the Schedule and Counter-Schedule of loss.

21. The Claimant's Solicitors do by   2010 apply to the Clerk of the Lists in London / [the Listing Officer in the venue] for a listing appointment for a trial period for hearing within the trial window and give notice of the appointment to the Defendant. Pre-trial check lists to be filed as directed by the Clerk of the Lists.

Mode of trial: Judge alone; London; Category [Usually] B; time estimate days.

Trial window:

[Certified fit for High Court Judge if available].

22. Parties do agree the contents of the trial bundle and exchange skeleton arguments not less than 7 days before the hearing. Claimant to lodge the skeleton arguments and the Trial bundle under PD 39.3

23. The parties shall by   2010 [a date usually about 3 months before the trial window opens] consider whether the case is capable of resolution by ADR. If any party considers that the case is unsuitable for resolution by ADR, that party shall be prepared to justify that decision at the conclusion of the trial, should the trial judge consider that such means of resolution were appropriate, when he is considering the appropriate costs order to make.

24. Such means of ADR as shall be adopted shall be concluded not less than 35 days prior to the trial.

25. The party considering the case unsuitable for ADR shall, not less than 28 days before the commencement of the trial, file with the Court a Witness Statement, without prejudice save as to costs, giving the reasons upon which they rely for saying that the case was unsuitable. The Witness Statement shall not be disclosed to the trial Judge until the conclusion of the case.

26. There be a further CMC on   2010 at am/pm; Room 106/109; time estimate 30 minutes. This hearing may be vacated by consent provided that

all directions have been complied with; no further directions are required; and the Master is given reasonable notice.

27. Permission to restore.

28. Costs in case [Or other costs order sought].

29. Claimant to draw and file the order by   2010 and serve the
Defendant (or Claimant to serve sealed order by   2010).

Dated the

CHAPTER 7

WITNESS EVIDENCE

Philip Jones

Witness evidence is the key to any case. This chapter looks at the control that the court has over the admissibility and content of that evidence and how it is to be placed before the court.

7.1 ADMISSIBILITY AND RELEVANCE

Prior to the arrival of the Civil Procedure Rules it was far from clear whether or not a judge had a discretion to exclude evidence that was both relevant and admissible. The position has been made clear by CPR 32.1, which enables the court to control the evidence by giving directions as to the issues on which evidence is required, the nature of the evidence required and the way in which the evidence is to be placed before the court. To make the position even clearer, CPR 32.1(2) contains an express power to exclude evidence that would otherwise be admissible. In addition, the court is given the power to limit cross-examination[1] – which could be achieved either by limiting the issues on which cross-examination is to be permitted or by imposing a time limit. The judge's discretion in these matters is a broad one and would not lightly be interfered with on appeal.[2]

The court's powers under these provisions need to be exercised in accordance with the overriding objective and, in relation particularly to the exclusionary power, the exercise needs to be consistent with the right to a fair trial under Art 6(1) of the European Convention on Human Rights. In this regard, the domestic courts are allowed considerable latitude in determining the admissibility and relevance of the evidence before them.[3]

Categories of evidence that are generally inadmissible are as follows:

- evidence rendered inadmissible on grounds of public policy (including evidence that is privileged: see below);

- irrelevant evidence;

---

[1]   CPR 32.1(3).
[2]   *Watson v Chief Constable of Cleveland Police* [2001] EWCA Civ 1547.
[3]   *Mantovanelli v France* (1977) 24 EHRR 370.

- opinion evidence other than permitted expert evidence;[4]

- evidence of good character;

- evidence of bad character that is rendered inadmissible by s 4 of the Rehabilitation of Offenders Act 1974 (ie spent convictions).[5]

If it is intended to object to the admissibility of another party's evidence, this could be done either by way of an interim application or at trial. Provided that the issues have been fully formulated and it is sufficiently clear that the evidence is inadmissible or will never appear to be relevant or sufficiently helpful to make it right to allow it be adduced, an interim application would be unobjectionable.[6] However, the court will be astute to see that increased costs and delays are not caused by ill-conceived applications to strike out parts of witness statements. Further, there will always be an argument that it is the trial judge who will have the best grasp of the issues and will therefore be best placed to rule on admissibility of a piece of evidence.[7]

7.2   COMPETENCE AND COMPELLABILITY

The old common law rules that prohibited evidence from parties to the action, such as spouses and persons without religious belief, were swept away by the Victorians in a succession of Evidence Acts. For many years therefore the key principle has been that any person may be a competent witness, subject to a number of well-established exceptions. The categories of potential witnesses who are not competent are:

- children who are not able to appreciate the obligation to speak the truth;[8]

- persons who are mentally incapable of testifying;

---

[4]   It should be noted that some forms of lay opinion evidence are unobjectionable. A witness may give opinion evidence as to someone's identity or age and, in an RTA claim, clearly a witness will be permitted to give an estimate of the speed of the vehicles involved.

[5]   The court does however retain a discretion to allow evidence of a spent conviction where justice cannot be done in the case without referring to it: s 7(3) of the Rehabilitation of Offenders Act. A spent conviction can be allowed in evidence in such circumstances as being relevant to credit and not just as going directly to an issue in the case: *Lomas v Metropolitan Police Comr* [1997] QB 813.

[6]   See *Wilkinson v West Coast Capital* [2005] EWHC 1606 (Ch).

[7]   *Stroude v Beazer Homes Ltd* [2005] EWCA Civ 265.

[8]   A child who, in the opinion of the court, does not understand the nature of an oath may still give evidence if the court considers that he understands that it is his duty to speak the truth and he has sufficient understanding to justify his evidence being heard: s 96 Children Act 1989.

- persons who are temporarily rendered incapable (eg by illness or intoxication) of giving a rational account of events;

- persons who do not appreciate the nature of and obligation imposed by an oath or affirmation.

Older cases indicate that a witness who was deaf and dumb and unable properly to communicate was considered to be an incompetent witness. It is difficult to see that this potential category has much relevance in the modern world.

If there is doubt as to the mental competence of a witness to give evidence, the issue may be determined by the judge on a preliminary enquiry as to fitness (see *Spittle v Walton*[9]).

The overwhelming majority of competent witnesses will also be compellable. Those who are not are generally protected by diplomatic or similar status. Thus, neither the monarch nor the head of any other state is compellable. Foreign diplomats, consular officials and staff members of various international organisations are similarly protected.[10] Members of Parliament are also immune during a parliamentary session.

7.3 COMPELLING ATTENDANCE: WITNESS SUMMONSES

A witness summons under CPR 34.2 may be issued by the court in order to require a witness to attend and give evidence or to produce documents to the court. The summons must be in the relevant practice form (N20) and must be issued by the court where the case is proceeding or the court where the hearing in question will be held.[11] Each witness will require a separate witness summons.[12] Although CPR 34.2(1) states the purposes of the witness summons in the alternative, Practice Direction 34A makes it clear that a witness can be summoned both to give evidence and to produce documents.[13] If a witness is being required to produce documents, it is vital that the documents are identified with sufficient certainty to leave no real doubt in the mind of the witness as to what the summons requires him to do.[14]

---

[9]   (1871) LR 11 EQ 420.
[10] See the State Immunity Act 1978, Diplomatic Privileges Act 1964, Consular Relations Act 1968 and the International Organisations Act 1968.
[11] CPR 34.2(2) and 34.3(3).
[12] CPR 34.2(3).
[13] PD 34A para 1.1.
[14] *Tajik Aluminium Plant v Hydro Aluminium AS* [2006] 1 WLR 767.

7.3.1 Witness summons and disclosure

There is a potential overlap between the power to compel a witness to attend and produce documents under CPR 34.2 and the power to order disclosure against a non-party under CPR 31.17. The witness summons procedure is more cumbersome and likely to be considerably more expensive once the costs of the additional hearing at which the documents are produced have been factored in. Despite the absence of any express provision to this effect, it seems that the respondent to a witness summons may be entitled to the costs of collating preparing and producing the documents in answer to the summons.[15] From this point of view therefore the witness summons procedure holds no advantage over non-party disclosure. However, it is possible to see circumstances in which the witness summons procedure would clearly be preferable. If the evidence required from the non-party is more than just documentary evidence, serving a witness summons enables the party to obtain that additional oral evidence. Moreover, if it appears that there is a challenge to the authenticity of the documents sought from the non-party, using the witness summons procedure would enable the documents both to be produced and to be formally proved at the same time.

7.3.2 Permission to issue a witness summons

In certain circumstances, the court's permission will be required to issue a witness summons. These are:

- where the summons is sought less than seven days before trial;

- where the witness's attendance is sought to give evidence or produce documents on any date except that fixed for the trial;

- where the witness's attendance is sought to give evidence or to produce documents at any hearing except the trial.[16]

7.3.3 Setting aside or varying a witness summons

The court has the power to set aside or to vary a witness summons issued under Part 34. The grounds on which the court has exercised this power have included the following:

- oppression, such as where the witness summons relates to documents, disclosure of which has already been refused[17] or where disclosure is prohibited by public interest immunity;[18]

---

[15] *Individual Homes Ltd v Macbream Investments Ltd* (2002) *The Times*, 14 November.
[16] CPR 34.3(2).
[17] *Steele v Savory* [1891] WN 195.
[18] *Bookbinder v Tebbit (No 2)* [1992] 1 WLR 217.

- where the summons seeks evidence that is irrelevant or the issue of the summons amounts to a fishing expedition or is speculative;[19]

- where production of the documents is not necessary for the fair disposal of the matter or to save costs – including where the documents can be obtained by other means (such as non-party disclosure).[20]

7.3.4   Issue and service of the witness summons

The party seeking the issue of the witness summons must file with the court two copies of the summons in form N20.[21] One copy will then be retained on the court file, the other served. Any mistake in the name or address of the person named in the witness summons can be corrected prior to service but the amended summons must be resealed and marked as 'Amended and Re-Sealed'.[22]

The court will serve the witness summons itself, unless the party seeking the summons has indicated in writing at the time of applying for the summons that he wishes to serve it himself.[23] If the court is to serve the summons, the party seeking its issue must deposit with the court office the conduct money required by CPR 34.7.[24]

In general the witness summons will be effective to compel attendance only if it is served on the witness at least seven days before the date on which the attendance of the witness is required, although the court has power to abridge that period.[25] If a witness summons is served in accordance with the provisions of Part 34, it binds the witness to attend until the conclusion of the hearing at which his attendance has been required.[26] If the hearing is adjourned the witness will be under a continuing obligation to attend, unless released by the judge and no further summons would therefore be required for the resumed hearing. Failure to attend in accordance with the witness summons is punishable as a contempt of court.

Under CPR 34.7 at the time of service of the witness summons the witness must be offered or paid: (1) a sum reasonably sufficient to cover his expenses in travelling to and from the court, and (2) compensation for loss of time as specified in Practice Direction 34A. The Practice Direction

---

[19]   *Senior v Holdsworth ex p Independent Television News Ltd* [1976] QB 23; *South Tyneside BC v Wickes Building Supplies Ltd* [2004] EWHC 2428 (Comm), Gross J.
[20]   *South Tyneside BC v Wickes Building Supplies Lid,* above.
[21]   PD 34A para 1.2.
[22]   PD 34A paras 1.3 and 1.4.
[23]   CPR 34.6(1) and PD 34A para 3.4(1).
[24]   CPR 34.6(2) and PD 34A(2).
[25]   CPR 34.5(1) and (2).
[26]   CPR 34.5(3).

makes it clear that the compensation for loss of time is based on the sums payable to witnesses attending the Crown Court.[27]

7.4   WITNESSES AT TRIAL

As pointed out by CPR 32.2, the general rule is that any fact needing to be proved by witness evidence is to be proved at trial by oral evidence given in public. This is bolstered by the requirement in CPR 32.5(1) that if a party has served a witness statement and he wishes to rely on the evidence of the witness who made the statement, he must call the witness to give oral evidence unless the court orders otherwise or he seeks to put the statement in as hearsay evidence.

Well before the trial, the court would have given directions for the service on the other parties of any witness statements containing the evidence relied on in relation to any issues of fact to be decided at trial.[28] A failure to serve such witness statements (or a witness summary) by the deadline imposed by the court may result in the evidence being excluded from the trial. In order to be able to rely upon that evidence the court's permission would be required.[29]

When the witness comes to give evidence at the trial (assuming that the procedural hurdles referred to above have been overcome), his statement will usually stand as his evidence in chief, unless the court orders otherwise.[30] This makes it clear that the court retains a discretion to hear live evidence in chief from the witness. This power is sometimes exercised by a judge who wishes to hear the claimant's account of the accident in his own words or where there is a particularly important conflict of fact on which the judge might want to hear live evidence in chief from each side. In addition to this power, the court may also give permission to the witness to amplify his witness statement or to give live evidence in relation to matters arising since the statement was served – but permission can only be given where the judge considers that there is a 'good reason' not to confine the witness to the contents of his statement.[31]

If the witness, when giving his evidence in chief, has not referred to his witness statement or one of his witness statements (if more than one), he may nonetheless be cross-examined on that statement, even if he had not formally introduced it in evidence.[32]

---

[27]   PD 34A para 3.3 and see the Costs in Criminal Cases (General) Regulations 1986 and the 'Guide to Allowances under Part V of the Costs in Criminal Cases (General) Regulations', which was last issued in 2005.

[28]   CPR 32.4(2).

[29]   CPR 32.10.

[30]   CPR 32.5(2).

[31]   CPR 32.5(3) and (4).

[32]   CPR 32.11.

7.5 WITNESSES NOT ATTENDING TRIAL

Where a witness is unable to attend a hearing, whether through illness, infirmity or geographical obstacles, there are a number of options to ensure that his evidence might still get before the court. Thus, his evidence might be taken by deposition, received over a video link or admitted under a Civil Evidence Act notice. Of these three methods, the use of a deposition is usually the most expensive and, whilst the witness's evidence will carry the greater weight of having been tested, it does not have the advantage of allowing the judge to see the witness give evidence. In most cases video conferencing will be the preferred method of getting the evidence before the judge. However, because they can be taken well in advance of the trial, depositions continue to be an important tool where the witness (particularly a claimant) is suffering from a fatal condition and not expected to live until the trial date.

7.5.1 Depositions

According to the Court of Appeal in *Barratt v Shaw & Ashton*[33] the primary purpose of the deposition procedure under CPR 34.8 is to introduce into the trial the evidence of a witness whom it would be impossible to bring to court for the trial. It might also be appropriate to order a deposition in relation to evidence that needed to be available before the trial. Depositions can be used to obtain evidence from witnesses in England and Wales or out of the jurisdiction.

7.5.2 Witness within the jurisdiction

An application must be made to the court seeking an order for the witness to be examined prior to the hearing.[34] The court has a broad discretion but the substantial costs of the deposition procedure are likely to be a factor in its deliberations. If the order is made, the witness will be examined on oath, usually by an examiner appointed under CPR 34.15.[35] The examination may also be conducted by a judge or such other person as the court appoints (known as a local special examiner).[36] The order will specify the date, time and place of the examination and may also deal with issues such as the production of necessary documents and service of a witness statement or summary prior to the examination.[37] When the order is served on the witness, he must be offered or paid conduct money covering the cost of his travel and compensation for his loss of time.[38]

---

[33]   [2001] EWCA Civ 137.
[34]   CPR 34.8(1).
[35]   The party who has obtained an order must apply to the Foreign Process Section of the Masters' Secretary's Department at the RCJ for an examiner to be allocated.
[36]   CPR 34.8(3).
[37]   CPR 34.8(4), (5) and (7).
[38]   CPR 34.8(6).

7.5.2.1 Conduct of the examination

When the examination takes place, it is conducted in the same manner as if the witness were giving evidence at trial.[39] Thus, the parties should be represented by their respective trial advocates and the format of examination in chief, cross-examination and re-examination ought to be followed. However, unlike the trial, the hearing need not be in public and can be held in private if the examiner thinks it appropriate[40] – a useful provision if the examination is taking place in the witness's home or in a nursing home or hospital. A further potentially useful provision is that the examiner has the power to conduct an examination of a person not named in the order for examination, if that person and the parties consent.[41]

The examiner is obliged to ensure that the evidence given by the witness being examined is recorded in full.[42] The Practice Direction permits it to be recorded on audio- or videotape but it must also be recorded in writing by the examiner, a shorthand writer or stenographer.[43] If the deposition is not recorded word for word, it must contain as nearly as may be the statement of the witness.[44] If there is an objection to a question or if the witness objects to answering, the examiner must record the question, the nature of and grounds for the objection and any answer given. He must also record his opinion as to the validity of the objection. The court will subsequently rule on the validity of the objection and any related costs issues.[45] Once the examination has taken place the examiner must then serve a copy of the deposition on the party who obtained the order for examination and must also file a copy with the court.[46] That party must then distribute copies of the deposition received from the examiner to each of the other parties to the claim.[47]

The examiner is entitled to be paid a fee for conducting the examination and also to withhold the deposition unless the fee is paid.[48] In the first instance it is for the party obtaining the order for examination to pay the examiner's fees and expenses but the ultimate liability to pay those sums will abide the costs order at the conclusion of the claim.[49]

---

[39] CPR 34.9(1).
[40] CPR 34.9(3).
[41] CPR 34.9(2).
[42] CPR 34.9(4).
[43] PD 34A, para 4.3. The precise requirements as to signature of the deposition, amendments etc are set out in PD 34A, para 4.12.
[44] PD 34A, para 4.4.
[45] PD 34A, para 4.5.
[46] CPR 34.9(5).
[47] CPR 34.9(6).
[48] CPR 34.14(1) and (2). The fee is calculated in accordance with PD 34B.
[49] CPR 34.14(3) and (6).

7.5.2.2 Unco-operative witness

In the event of an unco-operative witness, who either fails to attend the examination or refuses to be sworn or to answer the questions or produce any document, the examiner produces a certificate of the witness's failure or refusal, which is then filed with the court by the party requiring the deposition.[50] The certificate can include the examiner's comments on the conduct of the witness or any person attending the examination.[51] That party can then seek an order from the court compelling the witness's attendance or co-operation and the recalcitrant witness will also be at risk of paying costs.[52]

7.5.2.3 Use of the deposition

Once obtained, there is no obligation on the party to use the deposition at trial. Equally, the ability to use the deposition at trial is not limited to the party who sought it. However, any party who wishes to put the deposition in evidence at the trial must give notice of his intention to do so at least 21 days before the date for the hearing.[53] If the trial judge wishes to hear the evidence contained in the deposition orally (and presumably if the witness has unexpectedly become available), there is a fallback provision that enables the court to require the witness to attend.[54]

CPR 34.12 contains an express limitation on the use of a deposition outside the proceedings in which the deposition was taken – such use being limited to where it is by the witness himself, with his agreement or with the court's permission. However, the rule applies only where the examination relates to the witness's or any other assets and is conducted for the purpose of any hearing other than the trial. That is not to say that there are no limitations on depositions taken in other circumstances. In *Dendron GmbH v University of California*[55] (a case that involved an examination conducted abroad following letters of request) it was held that there was an implied obligation not to use the deposition for collateral purposes without the consent of the court or the consent of the witness. Such use might be permitted in 'special circumstances' and where the use would be just in all the circumstances.

7.5.3 Witness outside the jurisdiction

If the witness is outside the jurisdiction, the procedure for obtaining a deposition differs according to whether or not the witness is in a state to

---

[50] CPR 34.10(1).
[51] PD 34A, para 4.8(2).
[52] CPR 34.10(3) and (4). A wilful refusal to obey the order may be proceeded against as a contempt of court: PD 34A, para 4.11.
[53] CPR 34.11(2) and (3).
[54] CPR 34.11(4).
[55] [2005] 1 WLR 200.

which the Taking of Evidence Regulation[56] applies (a Regulation state).
The Regulation states consist of all the members of the European Union
except Denmark.[57]

7.5.3.1 States where the Taking of Evidence Regulation does not apply

If the witness is to be examined in a non-Regulation state, the High Court
has to issue a letter of request to the judicial authorities of that country,
which requests the authorities to take the evidence of the witness or to
arrange for it to be taken.[58] The High Court can issue a letter of request
in respect of county court proceedings. The application is made to a
master or, in a district registry, to a district judge. The detailed
requirements for the contents of the application are set out in para 5.3 of
Practice Direction A to Part 34. Due to the cost of taking evidence
abroad, the court would usually need to be persuaded that reasonable
attempts had been made to obtain the evidence by other means (including
by video conferencing) and that paying the witness's air fare to attend trial
would not be a cheaper alternative. For the application to succeed, the
court would need to see that the witness was able to give substantial and
relevant evidence and that he was either unwilling or unable to attend
trial. Even then, the application might be refused where the request was
oppressive, the terms of the request were too wide, case management
considerations (such as cost and the fair disposal of the proceedings)
militated against the application, or where the application was made
late.[59]

If an order is made by the High Court, it can also appoint a special
examiner to conduct the examination, if permitted by the law of the
foreign state, whose laws will also govern the manner in which the
examination takes place.[60] Following the making of the order, the party
who has obtained it must file a draft letter of request, statement of issues,
a list of questions to be put to the witness and an undertaking to be
responsible for the Secretary of State's expenses.[61] Where necessary,
translated copies of the documents will also be required.[62]

---

[56]   Council Regulation (EC) No 1206/2001.
[57]   CPR 34.22(b).
[58]   CPR 34.13.
[59]   See *First American Corporation v Zayed* [1999] 1 WLR 1154.
[60]   CPR 34.13(4) and (5). The precise manner in which the examination will take place and,
       in particular, whether or not it might be conducted by a British consular officer, will
       often depend on whether a bilateral convention exists between the UK and the foreign
       country or whether that country is party to a multilateral convention such as the 1970
       Hague Convention on the Taking of Evidence Abroad in Civil or Commercial Matters.
       To determine the requirements in any case, liaison is recommended with the Foreign
       Process Section at the RCJ and the Foreign and Commonwealth Office.
[61]   CPR 34.13(6). The form of the draft letter of request is set out in Annex A to PD34A.
[62]   CPR 34.13(7).

7.5.3.2 *Regulation states*

If the witness to be examined is in another Regulation state, the court is able to order the issue of a request to a designated court in that country.[63] If an order is made, the party who sought it must file a draft request for the taking of evidence (in Form A attached to the Taking of Evidence Regulation), where necessary a translation of the form, an undertaking to be responsible for the foreign court's costs in relation to experts, translators or special procedures and communications technology, and an undertaking to be responsible for the expenses of the home court.[64] No translation has to be filed if English is an official language of the Regulation state concerned or if it has indicated under the Regulation that it will accept English.[65] If the evidence can be taken directly in the Regulation state (in accordance with the provisions of Art 17 of the Regulation), the home court can make an order for the submission of a request in accordance with that article, in which case the documents to be filed by the applicant are those specified in CPR 34.23(6).

7.5.4 Video conferencing

Where a witness is unable to attend a hearing the courts are generally amenable to receiving that evidence by way of video link or similar means. This is expressly permitted by CPR 32.3, which gives the court a broad and unfettered discretion to permit such an arrangement where required by considerations of justice and where its use is likely to be beneficial to the efficient fair and economic disposal of the litigation. It does however have to be accepted that receiving the witness's evidence over a video link is not ideal. As the guidance under the CPR points out (see below), the mere convenience of video conferencing should not be allowed to dictate its use and there is a disadvantage in the reduction of control that the court is able to exercise over the witness.

If video conferencing is desirable in any particular case, many courts now have the necessary facilities available. The witness may not have such easy access to suitable video-conferencing facilities and will often have to attend a commercial video-conferencing suite. If the court does not have suitable video-conferencing equipment, it is frequently possible to find commercially-available facilities close to the court to which the hearing can be shifted. If full video-conferencing facilities are not available to the witness, the court might consider use of Skype or equivalent software to enable a link with the witness at home.

With the appropriate technology fairly easily accessible, most of the problems with taking evidence over video links are practical. Annex 3 to PD 32 contains video-conferencing (VCF) guidance, which is intended to

---

[63] CPR 34.23(1) and (2).
[64] CPR 34.23(3).
[65] CPR 34.23(4).

assist with the practicalities but also points out that some foreign countries may object to persons within their jurisdiction giving evidence by VCF to a court in England or Wales. If there is any doubt as to the politics of the situation, the arranging party is encouraged to seek guidance from the Foreign and Commonwealth Office (International Legal Matters Unit, Consular Division).

In order to use VCF in the course of a hearing, the court's permission has to be obtained. Before seeking that permission, the applicant should liaise with the court staff and enquire about the availability of the necessary equipment. If permission is given, the court will normally direct that the applicant is responsible for ensuring that all arrangements are made to enable the VCF transmission.

The practicalities that the arranging party will need to bear in mind include the following:

- time zone differences between the local site (where the judge is) and the remote site;

- whether the witness requires an interpreter and, if so, whether the interpreter will be at the local site or remote site;

- the cost of hiring a VCF suite or necessary equipment (usually to be met in the first instance by the arranging party);

- compatibility of the equipment at the two sites – technical information will have to be obtained and exchanged in order to ensure this;

- the judge and parties at the local site should be able to see all those present in the room at the remote site;

- public access to the local site (if it is not in the courtroom), bearing in mind that the VCF hearing remains part of the trial;

- delivery of the necessary bundle or papers to the witness in sufficient time for the VCF hearing;

- if additional documents might need to be referred to in the course of the witness's evidence, considering how such documents might be transmitted to the remote site;

- determining how the witness is to take the oath and ensuring that, if required, the necessary holy book is available at the remote site;

- determining whether or not the law of the country in which the witness is situated requires the oath or affirmation to be taken in accordance with local custom and, if so, making appropriate arrangements;

- the requirement, if the local site is a VCF studio or conference room, to try to arrange for the royal coat of arms to be placed above the judge's seat.

7.5.5 Civil Evidence Act notices

The Civil Evidence Act 1995 ('the Act') removed all remaining obstacles to the admission of hearsay evidence[66] in civil proceedings and the technicalities that went with it. However, the appropriate mechanism for introducing hearsay evidence should be complied with. A failure to comply with the rules on hearsay evidence does not render the evidence inadmissible but may be taken into account by the court when considering costs and its case management powers and as a matter affecting the weight to be given to the evidence.[67]

Where the evidence relied on is contained in a witness statement and the witness is not being called to give oral evidence, the party seeking to rely on that evidence complies with the machinery under the Act by serving the statement on the other parties to the claim and at the same time informing those parties that the witness will not called to give oral evidence and of the reason why the witness will not be called.[68] If the hearsay evidence is to be given by a witness who is being called to give oral evidence, mere service of the witness's statement containing that evidence is enough to comply with the Act.

In the case of hearsay evidence that is not contained in a statement as considered above, the party seeking to rely upon it must serve a hearsay notice in accordance with CPR 33.2(3). The notice must identify the hearsay evidence, state that the party serving the notice proposes to rely on the hearsay evidence at trial and give the reason why the witness will not be called. That notice must be served no later than the latest date for service of the witness statements.[69] If the hearsay evidence is contained in a document, the party seeking to rely on it must serve a copy of the document on any party who requests it.[70]

---

[66] As defined in s 1(2) of the Civil Evidence Act 1995 and CPR 33.1, hearsay evidence consists of a statement made otherwise than by a person while giving oral evidence in proceedings which is tendered as evidence of the matters stated.
[67] Section 2(4) Civil Evidence Act 1995.
[68] CPR 33.2(1) and (2).
[69] CPR 33.2(4)(a).
[70] CPR 33.2(4)(b).

Hearsay notices are not required in a number of situations specified in CPR 33.3. The situation of most relevance to personal injury litigation is where the evidence is to be adduced at a hearing other than a trial. Oddly and somewhat unnecessarily, the rule also specifies that a hearsay notice is not required where the witness statement that is to be used at trial does not contain hearsay evidence. The requirement for a hearsay notice may also be excluded by a practice direction but no such practice direction has yet been made.

Whether or not the machinery under the Act has been complied with in respect of a hearsay statement, the court will be obliged to evaluate the weight to be placed on the statement. In performing that task, s 4 of the Act requires the court to have regard to any circumstances from which any inference can reasonably be drawn as to the reliability or otherwise of the evidence. In addition to the service or non-service of a hearsay notice, the section contains a non-exhaustive list of the factors to which the court might have regard, as follows:

(1)　whether it would have been reasonable and practicable for the party by whom the evidence was adduced to have produced the maker of the original statement as a witness;

(2)　whether the original statement was made contemporaneously with the occurrence or existence of the matters stated;

(3)　whether the evidence involves multiple hearsay;

(4)　whether any person involved has any motive to conceal or misrepresent matters;

(5)　whether the original statement was an edited account or was made in collaboration with another or for a particular purpose;

(6)　whether the circumstances in which the evidence is admitted as hearsay are such as to suggest an attempt to prevent proper evaluation of its weight.

Where it is proposed to adduce hearsay evidence against a party but it is not proposed to call the maker of the statement to give oral evidence, s 3 of the Act gives the court a discretion to permit that party to call the maker of the statement to be cross-examined. This power is put into effect by CPR 33.4, which provides that an application for permission to cross-examine the witness must be made no more than 14 days after the date on which the hearsay notice was served.[71] It should be noted that the rule refers specifically to cross-examination on the contents of the statement, thus limiting the ambit of permissible cross-examination under this rule. The rule does not specify the consequences if permission is given

---

[71]　CPR 33.4(2).

to cross-examine the witness but the witness does not then attend court. However, the court has a wide discretion under CPR 32.1 to exclude relevant and admissible evidence and the exclusion of the witness's evidence would be the likeliest outcome of a refusal to co-operate in this way.[72]

If a party to the claim wishes to mount an attack on the credibility of a witness who gives hearsay evidence but is not being called to give oral evidence, he may do so but must give notice of his intention to do so not more than 14 days after service on him of the hearsay notice.[73]

7.5.6   Use of statement of absent witness

Where a witness statement has been served by a party but the witness is neither called to give evidence at trial nor is his statement put in as hearsay evidence, any other party to the claim may seek to put that witness statement in as hearsay evidence.[74] This is subject to the court's discretion as to whether to permit the other party to rely on the statement in this way.[75] If the other party does put the statement in, the party who first obtained and served that statement is able then to apply under CPR 33.4 to cross-examine the witness.[76]

7.6   PROCEEDINGS OTHER THAN TRIALS

The converse to the requirement that at trial facts are to be proved by oral evidence is that written evidence will generally suffice at hearings that are not trials.[77] Thus on interim applications a party can rely on written evidence contained in a witness statement, another statement of case or the application notice, provided that the evidence is properly verified.[78] This is subject to the power of the court, rarely exercised, to require the person giving the evidence to attend to be cross-examined.[79] Failure to attend as required by such an order would exclude reliance on that evidence without the court's permission.[80]

---

[72]   See *Polanski v Conde Nast Publications Ltd* [2004] 1 WLR 387.
[73]   CPR 33.5.
[74]   CPR 32.5(5).
[75]   *McPhilemy v The Times Newspapers Ltd (No 2)* [2000] 1 WLR 1732.
[76]   *Douglas v Hello! Ltd* [2003] EWCA Civ 332.
[77]   CPR 32.2(1)(b) and 32.6(1).
[78]   CPR 32.6(2).
[79]   CPR 32.7(1).
[80]   CPR 32.7(2).

7.7   FORM AND CONTENT OF WITNESS STATEMENTS ETC

The evidence that it is intended that a witness should give to the court might be set out in a witness statement, witness summary or an affidavit. The last of those three is now virtually redundant in personal injury litigation.[81] As to the first two, one or other of them will be required in every personal injury claim and CPR Part 32 contains some detailed requirements as to their form and content.

CPR 32.4(1) defines a witness statement as: '... a written statement signed by a person which contains the evidence which that person would be allowed to give orally'. What this definition makes clear is that only admissible evidence will be permitted in a witness statement. Thus, impermissible statements of opinion, legal arguments, evidence that is privileged and irrelevant or scandalous evidence should be excluded. Hearsay evidence is of course permitted but those parts of the statement that do contain hearsay evidence should be clearly identified. To this end, the Practice Direction requires the witness both to indicate which of the statements in the witness statement are within his own knowledge and which are matters of information or belief and to identify the source of his information or belief.[82] The witness statement should be expressed in the first person and, so far as possible, should be in the witness's own words.[83] It is recommended that the statement should follow the chronological sequence of events, with each paragraph dealing with a distinct portion of the subject.[84] In drafting the witness statement, it should be remembered that the statement is intended to stand as the witness's evidence in chief when called to give evidence.[85] It is accordingly important that the statement should deal with each point on which the witness's evidence is required. Whilst it is possible to expand on the statement when the witness takes the stand, this is dependent on the judge permitting it and it would be risky to assume that permission would always or lightly be given.

The Queen's Bench Guide (at para 7.10.4) contains the following guidance as to the matters to be borne in mind when considering the content of witness statements:

(1)   a witness statement must contain the truth, the whole truth and nothing but the truth on the issues it covers;

---

[81]   CPR 32.15 permits affidavit evidence to be used but limits the recoverability of the additional costs of using an affidavit. The detailed provisions as to the form of an affidavit are contained in PD 32, paras 2–16.

[82]   PD 32, para 18.2.

[83]   PD 32, para 18.1.

[84]   PD 32, para 19.2.

[85]   CPR 32.5(2).

(2) those issues should consist only of the issues on which the party serving the witness statement wishes that witness to give evidence in chief and should not include commentary on the trial bundle or other matters which may arise during the trial or may have arisen during the proceedings;

(3) a witness statement should be as concise as the circumstances allow; inadmissible or irrelevant material should not be included;

(4) the cost of preparation of an over-elaborate witness statement may not be allowed.

7.7.1 Form of witness statements

CPR 32.8 requires a witness statement to comply with the requirements of Practice Direction 32. Failure to comply might lead to the exclusion of the evidence in the statement and the disallowance of the costs of preparing the statement.[86] Paragraph 17 of the Practice Direction deals with the heading and para 17.2 set out the requirement to give in the top right-hand corner the details identifying the statement and its exhibits. Paragraph 18 of the Practice Direction specifies how the witness should be identified and described and (in sub-paras 18.3–18.6) gives detailed instructions as to how exhibits are to be dealt with. Requirements for the physical presentation of the witness statement are contained in para 19 of the Practice Direction, which also specifies how numbers should be dealt with and how documents should be referred to.

7.7.2 Verification

A witness statement is a statement of case that is required to be verified in accordance with CPR 22.1. The form of a statement of truth for a witness statement is: 'I believe that the facts stated in this witness statement are true.'[87]

A witness who verifies a witness statement containing a false statement without an honest belief in the truth of that statement is liable to proceedings for contempt of court.[88] Such proceedings can only be brought by the Attorney General or with the court's permission.[89] If it is alleged that a witness has knowingly put forward a false statement, the allegation must be referred to the court dealing with the matter in which the statement was made. That court can then exercise any of its powers under the CPR, initiate contempt proceedings or direct the party making the allegation to refer the matter to the Attorney General.[90]

---

[86] PD 32, para 25.1.
[87] PD 32, paras 20.1 and 20.2.
[88] CPR 32.14.
[89] CPR 32.14(2).
[90] PD 32, para 28.

7.7.3 Alterations

If a party discovers that a witness statement, which they have served, is incorrect they must inform the other parties immediately.[91] Any alteration to a witness statement must be initialled by the witness – failure to do so might render the statement inadmissible, since an altered statement that has not been initialled can be used only with the court's permission.[92]

7.7.4 Foreign language statements

Where a witness statement in English has been made by a witness who does not speak English, it should be made clear that the statement had been read back to the witness in his own language (identifying the person by whom this was done) and that the witness agreed the contents of the statement. Where the court has directed that a witness statement in a foreign language should be filed, the party seeking to rely on it must have it translated and must file the foreign language witness statement with the court. In addition, the translator of the statement must file an affidavit verifying the translation and exhibiting both the foreign language statement and the translation.[93]

7.7.5 Witness summaries

Although in all cases the court will require the parties to serve witness statements of the witnesses they intend to call, it is not always possible to obtain a statement from an intended witness. In such circumstances, the party seeking to call that witness at trial may make a without notice application to serve a witness summary in place of a witness statement.[94]

The witness summary should contain either a summary of the evidence that it is anticipated the witness will give or, if that evidence is not known, a summary of the matters about which it is proposed to question the witness.[95] The witness summary must contain the name and address of the proposed witness, unless the court orders otherwise.[96] Importantly, the witness summary must be served prior to the deadline by which a witness statement would have to have been served.[97] So far as practicable the witness summary should comply with various of the provisions applicable to witness statements.[98]

---

[91] Queen's Bench Guide, para 7.10.4(6).

[92] PD 32, para 22.

[93] PD 32, para 23.2.

[94] CPR 32.9.

[95] CPR 32.9(2).

[96] CPR 32.9(3).

[97] CPR 32.9(4).

[98] CPR 32.9(5). The relevant provisions are CPR 32.4 (requirement to serve witness statements for use at trial), CPR 32.5(3) (amplifying witness statements) and CPR 32.8 (form of witness statements).

7.8 USE OF WITNESS STATEMENT FOR COLLATERAL PURPOSE

A witness statement may be used only for the purpose of the proceedings in which it is served.[99] Use of the statement by either party for a purpose collateral to the claim is therefore prohibited. There are exceptions to this prohibition where the witness gives consent in writing to some other use of the statement, the court gives permission for such use or the statement has been put in evidence at a public hearing.[100]

7.9 PRIVILEGE AND IMMUNITY

There are a number of grounds on which a witness can refuse to give evidence or to answer questions asked of him. The most important of those grounds are as follows:

- where the evidence sought is protected by legal professional privilege, public interest immunity or the privilege attached to without prejudice communications;

- where the privilege against self-incrimination applies – thus the witness might refuse to answer any question if to do so would tend to expose him or his spouse or civil partner to criminal proceedings for an offence or the recovery of a penalty;

- where there is a statutory prohibition on disclosure of information.[101]

A witness has immunity from civil proceedings in respect of his evidence given in the claim and also in respect of his evidence prepared for the claim, which includes the contents of his witness statement prior to his giving that evidence at trial. The policy reason for this immunity is that potential witnesses should not be put off by the possibility that they might be sued in respect of things said during the course of proceedings.[102]

---

[99] CPR 32.12(1).

[100] CPR 32.12(2).

[101] Examples of such statutory prohibitions include restrictions in relation to adopted children under the Adoption Agencies Regulations 1983, to census information under the Population (Statistics) Act 1938, business information obtained under statutory powers in the Water Resources Act 1991 and information affecting national security under the Atomic Energy Act 1946.

[102] See *Darker (suing as personal representative of Docker) v Chief Constable of the West Midlands Police* [2001] 1 AC 435.

CHAPTER 8

VIDEO AND OTHER EVIDENCE

Esther Pounder

8.1 VIDEO EVIDENCE

Many personal injury claims involve some symptoms that are not readily visible to anyone other than the claimant. If the effects of an injury include functional difficulties or brain injury it can be very difficult to assess these objectively. It is, of course, difficult to invent a catastrophic injury and therefore such cases are thankfully rare. However some degree of exaggeration is often alleged in personal injury cases at all levels of seriousness. Sorting where the truth lies is difficult and time-consuming but vitally important if those who are genuinely suffering are to be properly compensated and those abusing the system are to be discovered.

In such a context covert video surveillance has come to play a central role. Given that such evidence can reveal the malingerers and exaggerators of injury in such a precise and compelling way it is no surprise that it has become such a powerful tool in the armoury of defendants and their insurers.

Obtaining video evidence has two main purposes for defendants:

- to show how well the claimant moves/carries out everyday activities when he believes he is unobserved. Can he carry shopping, walk his dog, undertake gardening, paint his fence, drive his car? This can be useful for defendants to show that although the claimant complains of disability this can be put into the context of a tolerably active way of life;

- to identify those claimants who may be deliberately exaggerating the effects of their injury or the extent of their disability.

It must not be forgotten, however, that obtaining video evidence need not be the preserve of suspicious defendants. Claimants can also make use of video evidence as part of their positive case (although this will not usually be on a covert basis). In certain cases it can be a useful and potent means of demonstrating the physical limitations of a claimant in their home environment and day-to-day life, and setting in context the evidence of the claimant's expert doctors and therapists.

8.2   ADMISSIBILITY OF VIDEO EVIDENCE

8.2.1   Excluding or permitting video evidence

In principle in civil proceedings provided that evidence is relevant to a fact in issue, it is admissible unless it is privileged. This remains the case even if the evidence has been obtained illegally (see *Helliwell v Piggott-Sims*[1]). Therefore as technology advances and private investigators find increasingly inventive ways to obtain covert surveillance, claimants face the prospect of such evidence being admissible at trial regardless of how underhand the techniques employed by the investigator were. The Human Rights Act ('HRA') 1998, and the incorporation of the European Convention on Human Rights ('ECHR') into English law changed the landscape, however, creating a new debate as to the admissibility of covert surveillance evidence. Under the HRA two competing rights are engaged. On the one hand there is the claimant's right to privacy under Art 8 of the ECHR, while on the other there is the defendant's right to a fair trial under Art 6, which would be infringed if they were prevented from revealing wrongdoing on the part of a claimant.

In respect of the claimant's Art 8 right to privacy there is, of course, no direct duty on defendants, insurers or private investigators as a result of this right. However there is a duty on the court as a public authority to ensure respect for the right on the basis of Art 8.2. This requires that: 'There shall be no interference by a public authority with the exercise of this right except such as is in accordance with the law and is necessary in a democratic society in the interests of national security.' Accordingly it has been argued that the courts, in order to carry out their duty to protect the right, ought to prevent defendants from relying on evidence that was obtained in breach of the claimant's right to privacy, particularly where it was obtained otherwise than 'in accordance with the law', by reason of some trespass or other tort.

In considering the question of admissibility, therefore, the court is required to conduct a balancing exercise between two competing public interests. On the one hand the interests of the public that in litigation the truth should be revealed; while on the other the interests of the public that the courts should not acquiesce in, let alone encourage, the use of unlawful means to obtain evidence. The balance that the courts have struck is to decide that the court respects each right not by blind enforcement of it but by giving due respect to it in reaching a balance in each case between the two rights, so as to find a fair solution to achieve the overriding duty of the court to achieve justice.

---

[1]   [1980] FSR 356.

In reaching this conclusion the courts have sought guidance in Strasbourg jurisprudence on the ECHR, from cases such as *Schenk v Switzerland*[2] and *Khan v UK*.[3]

A similar approach can also be found in the jurisprudence on the written constitutions of commonwealth countries (many of which are based on the ECHR): see, for example, *Allie Mohammed v The State*.[4] In this case the Privy Council held that the court had a discretion to include or exclude the evidence.

Guidance has also been sought from the approach adopted to similar issues in the criminal context: see, for example, *R v Wright and McGregor*[5] and *R v Loveridge*.[6]

8.2.2   The balancing exercise

The Court of Appeal considered the question of the admissibility of covert video evidence in the context of personal injury cases in *Jones v University of Warwick*.[7] In that case the claimant claimed to have ongoing disabilities as a result of an episode of extensor tenosynovitis caused by an accident for which liability was admitted. Damages of over £135,000 were claimed. Enquiry agents acting on behalf of the defendant obtained video footage of the claimant that contradicted the impression given to the experts as to the level of her disability. What made the evidence objectionable in that case was not the fact that it was covert but the fact that it came from filming the claimant in her own home by enquiry agents who tricked their way in on false pretences.

It was common ground that the enquiry agents were guilty of trespass. The defendant's medical expert was shown the videos and he concluded that they showed the function of the hand to be normal with no ongoing disability, contrary to the impression given in her examination. The claimant's advisors initially did not show the videos to their expert as they objected to their admissibility. By the time the case came to the Court of Appeal, however, the videos had been shown to the claimant's medical expert, who concluded that they showed the claimant on good days and that on other days there was still significant disability. The defendant accepted that since the medical experts had seen the video, if the video could not be admitted in evidence, new experts would have to be instructed and the existence of the recordings concealed from the court and new experts.

---

2   [1991] 13 EHRR 242.
3   (2000) *The Times,* 23 May.
4   [1999] 2 AC 111.
5   [2001] EWCA Crim 1394.
6   [2001] EWCA Crim 1034.
7   [2003] EWCA Civ 151; [2003] PIQR P382.

The Court of Appeal allowed the video evidence to be admitted, Lord Woolf giving the leading judgment concluded that:

> 'The court must try to give effect to what are here the two conflicting public interests. The weight to be attached to each will vary according to the circumstances. The significance of the evidence will differ as will the gravity of the breach of Article 8, according to the facts of the particular case. The decision will depend on all the circumstances. Here, the court cannot ignore the reality of the situation. This is not a case where the conduct of the defendant's insurers is so outrageous that the defence should be struck out. The case, therefore, has to be tried. It would be artificial and undesirable for the actual evidence, which is relevant and admissible, not to be placed before the judge who has the task of trying the case.'

Having allowed the evidence, the court marked its disapproval of the behaviour of the defendant by a costs sanction. Their Lordships considered that it was right for the defendant to pay the costs of determining the admissibility issue before the district judge, circuit judge and Court of Appeal, even though they had succeeded. The problem had arisen as a consequence of the behaviour of the defendant's enquiry agents and, accordingly, the defendants should pay the bill for resolving it. They also provided some more general principles stating, for example, that the trial judge should take account of the defendant's conduct in deciding the appropriate order for costs: they suggested that the costs of the enquiry agents could be disallowed. If the trial judge concluded that there was an innocent explanation for the apparent control of movement by the claimant as shown in the video, they suggested that it might be appropriate to order the defendant to pay the costs on an indemnity basis. Accordingly where a defendant has obtained a video that is of only marginal benefit they may be well advised not to seek to rely on it.

Their Lordships also considered that it had been sensible for the claimant's advisors to withhold the video evidence from the claimant's medical expert until the issue of admissibility had been resolved. In so doing they disagreed with the circuit judge who had been critical of that decision.

One of the considerations for courts embarking on the balancing exercise described in *Jones* is to consider whether the actions of the defendant's agents do in fact amount to a breach of privacy. In *Law Debenture Trust Group v Malley and the Pensions Ombudsman*[8] it was held that covert surveillance was legitimate on appropriate occasions in the investigation of personal injury claims and did not breach Art 8.

---

[8]   (1999) LTL 23 July; (1999) *Independent*, October 25.

8.3 DISCLOSURE OF VIDEO EVIDENCE

8.3.1 Historical context

In addition to allowing defendants to obtain video evidence by whatever means they chose, historically the courts also accepted that a defendant could ambush a plaintiff (as they were then named) at trial with as yet undisclosed evidence, including video evidence. The rationale behind this approach was that plaintiffs would tailor their evidence if they knew what information the defendants had about them.

For an example of this approach see *McGuiness v Kellogg*.[9] The Court of Appeal, including Woolf LJ as its junior member, upheld the first instance decision to exercise the discretion under the Supreme Court Rules to permit the defendant to withhold video evidence of an allegedly malingering plaintiff taken by enquiry agents until the trial of the action, even though a video tape was otherwise a disclosable document under the rules (just as it now is under the Civil Procedure Rules ('CPR') Part 31).

By 1994, however, the tide had turned and defendants were expected to disclose video evidence in advance of the trial: see *Digby v Essex CC*.[10]

Shortly after *Digby* came *Khan v Armaguard*,[11] the leading decision on this new 'cards on the table' approach. In that case it was held that permission to defendants to withhold disclosure of a video until trial should only be granted in the rarest and most exceptional circumstances, and the existence of an allegation of malingering is insufficient.

The effect of this line of authorities is that it would not normally be appropriate to allow video evidence to be withheld in order to allow a claimant to be ambushed at trial.

8.3.2 Current position: CPR Part 31

Pursuant to CPR Part 31 videos are disclosable 'documents'. This is because by virtue of CPR 31.4 a document is defined as anything on which data is recorded. As such, videos are subject to the same rules on privilege, disclosure and admissibility as other evidence. That this is the correct interpretation was confirmed in *Rall v Hume*.[12] It is interesting to note in passing, however, that in the earlier case of *McGuiness v Kellogg* it was common ground that the cinefilm in question was a 'photograph'. If that is correct, this suggests that such evidence falls within CPR 33.6 (see below).

---

9 [1988] 2 All ER 902.
10 [1994] PIQR P53.
11 [1994] 1 WLR 1204.
12 [2001] EWCA Civ 146; [2001] 3 All ER 248.

If a defendant is in possession of a surveillance video at the time of making a list of documents, he should disclose its existence. Once the decision has been made to rely upon it, the defendant must disclose not only its existence, but also its contents.

Disclosure is, of course, a continuing obligation (CPR 31.11) and a video ought to be disclosed when it is received (even though privilege can be claimed for it). If it is not disclosed then the risk is that the court may refuse permission to rely on it (CPR 31.21).

If disclosure is made in accordance with the rules, whether as part of standard or continuing disclosure, the claimant will be deemed to admit the authenticity of the film, unless notice is served that they wish the evidence to be proved at trial. In such circumstances the defendant will be required to demonstrate its authenticity by serving a witness statement from the person who made the film. In many cases, where the video evidence, although covert, does not involve any great intrusion into the claimant's privacy, it will be counter-productive for the claimant to object and it is better to get on with dealing with the contents of the video on its merits rather than making a fuss and thereby appearing to give more weight to the video than the claimant might wish.

If the purpose of the video is not only to show how well the claimant is coping with his supposed injury, but also to allege that the footage is inconsistent with the account given by the claimant to the medical experts about his disability, the question has arisen in the past as to whether this ought to be pleaded as fraud. In *John Edward Cooper v P & O European Ferries (Dover) Ltd*[13] the judge thought that in such circumstances the allegation of fraud or dishonesty should be pleaded expressly. This appears though to have been largely overtaken by the decision of the Court of Appeal in *Kearsley v Klarfeld*.[14] Kearsley concerned a low velocity road traffic accident in which the defendant wished to contend by its orthopaedic expert that the injury as claimed could not have arisen form the impact that it said had occurred. The defendant expressly pleaded fraud. In considering that the claim ought to have been heard by a circuit judge on the multi-track despite its modest quantum, the Court of Appeal nevertheless deprecated the practice of pleading fraud or deliberate fabrication in such circumstances, indicating that it was sufficient to set out fully any facts from which the defence would be inviting the judge to draw the inference that the claimant had not in fact suffered the injuries he asserted.

8.3.3   Timing of disclosure

The best time for a claimant to be served with video evidence is before the service of his statement. Unsurprisingly, however, it is more common for

---

[13]   [1999] 1 Lloyd's Rep 734.
[14]   [2005] EWCA Civ 1510.

claimants to receive video evidence after they have disclosed their witness statements. For defendants the best time to obtain video evidence is around the time of exchange of medical evidence. The footage can then be sent to the defendant's expert. This is useful because it can be used to demonstrate very clearly any discrepancies between how the claimant describes their symptoms to the expert and how they are in reality. It also has an added advantage for defendants because video evidence obtained at this stage can be served after the exchange of medical evidence. By this time the claimant has committed himself as to the extent of his disabilities in his witness statement, but it is not so late as to prejudice the trial date. It can prejudice a defendant's case to obtain video evidence too early and risk not disclosing it for so long that the delay counts against them when seeking permission to rely on it. Accordingly waiting until a fairly late stage before commissioning the evidence can be a neat way of defeating any argument that disclosure has been delayed whilst also ensuring that the claimant has set out their positive case prior to seeing the footage.

8.3.4 Late disclosure

As established in *Khan*, late disclosure is likely to be considered an ambush and, as such, the court will not give permission to rely on the evidence. See for example *Kevin O'Leary v Tunnelcraft*.[15] In that case the defendant was refused permission to rely on surveillance evidence where the court found that the failure to disclose it more than 31 days before the trial amounted to an ambush.

Where late disclosure may impact on the trial date, this too will weigh in the balance against the defendant. However, an application can be made in advance, without notice to the claimant, for permission to withhold disclosure. Nevertheless, except in the most unusual case, the court is likely to insist on a 'cards on the table' approach with early disclosure rather than allowing the claimant to be ambushed in cross-examination.

The leading case on late disclosure is *Rall v Hume*. In that case the claimant had been involved in a road traffic accident for which the defendant had admitted liability. A substantial claim for future loss was submitted on the claimant's behalf, directions were given for disclosure and the matter re-listed for further directions/disposal. Shortly afterwards, the solicitors for the defendant obtained a covert video film containing footage of the claimant's movements. It showed the claimant in the course of her shopping and child-caring activities and travelling by car without any apparent difficulty. The video evidence was not disclosed at that stage as it was clear from the medical evidence that the claimant was going through a continuous process of improvement and it would not be clear before the up-to-date reports were available whether what was shown on the video was at odds with her case as would be advanced at trial. When

---

[15] [2009] EWHC 3438 (QB).

that medical evidence was obtained the video evidence was disclosed. The defendants then obtained and disclosed a further video.

Initially both parties overlooked the need for permission to rely on this evidence prior to the hearing, but in due course the defendant applied to rely on the video evidence. At that hearing the judge refused the application on the basis of it having been made too late, and the defendant appealed. The district judge dismissed the application and on appeal his decision was upheld on the basis that the trial duration estimate would have been insufficient if the whole of the video footage was put in evidence. As such, the application had been made too late. However, on appeal to the Court of Appeal the defendant was allowed to rely upon the evidence and to cross-examine the claimant on it.

The Court of Appeal confirmed that where video evidence was available that undermined a claimant's case to an extent that would substantially reduce the damages to which he was entitled, it would be in the interests of justice to allow the defendant to cross-examine the claimant and his medical advisors on that evidence, so long as it did not amount to trial by ambush. The court considered that by careful case management of the trial, selection of the key extracts of the video to be viewed at trial and advance viewing of the video by all the witnesses, it should be possible for the trial to proceed as planned and so the video evidence could be admitted.

In giving the reasons of the court Potter LJ, with Sedley LJ agreeing, stated:

> 'This was not an ambush case: there had been no deliberate delay in disclosure by the defendant so as to achieve surprise, nor was the delay otherwise culpable, bearing in mind the mutual muddle over the 9 October hearing date. Nor is this the comparatively rare kind of case in which the film has to be independently adduced because what it shows goes beyond what can be established by cross-examination, and where different directions may be needed.'

Potter LJ also considered the application of the CPR and the practicalities of trial preparation in his judgment, stating:

> 'the practical constraints upon such a procedure in terms of Case Management are (1) that showing of a video, or part of it, in court for the purposes of cross-examination requires arrangements to be made for the availability of video equipment in any court where it is not normally to be found and (2) that the whole procedure extends trial time. Hence when fixing a trial date with an estimate of time, it is necessary for the managing judge to make proper allowance for this. It is therefore necessary in the interests of proper case management and the avoidance of wasted court time that the matter be ventilated with the judge managing the case at the first practicable opportunity once a decision has been made by a defendant to rely on video evidence obtained.'

This passage perhaps indicates their Lordships' tacit approval of defendants who wait until after disclosure of documents and exchange of other evidence before deciding whether to put video(s) in evidence. It can, of course, be argued that waiting until the claimant has committed himself in his statement, in his consultation with his own and the defendant's experts and/or in his schedule of loss is reasonable as it is only then that the decision can properly be taken as to whether the video evidence is required.

Similarly in *Uttley v Uttley*[16] it was held that it was acceptable to delay disclosure until after updated witness statements and an updated counter schedule had been served. In that case the defendant obtained significant video evidence but did not disclose it until the claimant had served an up-to-date witness statement and schedule of special damages, which was long overdue and had been frequently requested. On seeing the video, the claimant accepted an earlier payment into court but objected to paying the defendant's costs for a period when the defendant was in possession of the video but had not disclosed it. The court held that the defendant's tactic was reasonable and the usual order for costs should apply.

However, this is a risky tactic for defendants as undue delay in making that decision will very likely be the subject of criticism and may result in the judge refusing to admit the evidence. It is particularly tricky once arrangements for trial have been made. The exception may be where the balance of interests changes at trial. If video evidence was excluded but then a claimant gave evidence that could be flatly contradicted by the video, it might be appropriate to reopen the admissibility of the evidence before the trial judge. In those circumstances even if the trial judge had ruled that the evidence was inadmissible, he may change his view and allow the video to be seen.

8.3.5 Full disclosure

If some video evidence has been disclosed, those acting on behalf of the claimant would be well advised to seek clarification as to whether the defendants have provided all the footage or just the edited highlights to suit their case. Ask whether there is any other video evidence that may be of less assistance to the defendant and more favourable to the claimant. If you suspect that there is more footage than the defendant has disclosed, it can be useful to look at the clock on the screen (if there is one) to see whether sections of time (when the claimant may have been demonstrating difficulty with a particular activity or activities) are missing. Also ask for details of all days on which filming was conducted and details of the duration of filming on each day. You can then check whether that information matches up with the footage that you have been

---

[16] [2002] PIQR P123.

provided with and with your client's instructions as to activities undertaken and places visited on those particular days.

If there are real issues as to whether the footage may be incomplete then it may be necessary to require the person who has taken the film to attend the trial to be cross-examined. If this is to be done then note that objection needs to be taken to the footage as indicated above. In practice this is a rare occurrence and a path to be cautious about going down without a clear idea of what is going to be gained by doing so. Further if the defendant refuses to disclose any additional video evidence then that may be a matter for the court to weigh up in deciding whether permission should be granted for the defendant to rely on the video evidence that it wants to produce, or for the court to draw its own inferences at trial.

8.4   ASSESSING VIDEO EVIDENCE

When acting for the claimant, if such evidence is served by the defendant, it is important to view and consider it dispassionately and carefully. This is best done first without your client present. When watching the film remember to ask yourself whether it reveals things so far removed from your instructions that the claimant may be considered to be fraudulent or is the issue more one of degree of injury and credibility? If you consider that the claimant could be considered to be fraudulent based on the video evidence then discontinuance may be the only option. You should however proceed with caution as alleging fraud is a serious allegation for a defendant to make and they will need substantive evidence to support it.

It is more likely that such video evidence will go towards the claimant's credibility. When you view the video with your client, as you must do, take careful instructions on it and be alive to their reactions to it. People can have good and bad days. Are there sensible explanations for any inconsistencies between what is on the video and the contents of their witness statement and/or what they have told the medical expert(s)? It may be necessary to serve a further statement to explain the contents of the video.

If video footage is permitted to be used at trial, it is important to involve the experts in assessing the impact of such evidence. When acting for the claimant ensure that the expert has seen the video, together with copies of the claimant's statement(s), including in particular any updated statement in response to the video. It may be necessary for the expert to re-examine the claimant and potentially to attend court to give oral evidence in response to the video.

Having considered the evidence with the client and the expert, if appropriate, you should make a reassessment of the value of the claim.

The court will expect to see that both parties have attempted to negotiate as the failure to do so in the face of unhelpful surveillance will very likely sound in costs (see below).

8.5 COSTS

As demonstrated in the case of *Jones v University of Warwick*, substantial costs penalties can follow the wrong decisions of both claimants and defendants in relation to video evidence. In *Ford v GKR Construction Ltd*[17] for example the Court of Appeal dismissed the defendant's appeal against a costs order. This was a case where the claimant was shown through video evidence to be less disabled than she claimed to be. The case involved a road traffic accident in which liability was admitted but quantum remained in dispute. The defendant had made a payment into court of £95,000 in July 1998. An assessment of damages hearing was listed for September 1998 but was adjourned. It was at this stage that the defendant commissioned video evidence of the claimant. The surveillance footage was helpful to the defendant and having been shown the footage the claimant sought to accept the payment into court. However, no agreement as to costs could be reached as the defendant insisted that its costs should be paid after the payment in. When the trial continued in November 1998 the claimant was awarded £85,300. The judge awarded costs in favour of the claimant on the basis that there was no evidence that she was dishonest, albeit that she was more mobile than she was prepared to admit. The defendant appealed and, in dismissing the appeal, Judge LJ commented: 'Sometimes claimants do lie, embellish or fantasise, but if that is to be the defendant's case fairness demands that the claimant should have a reasonable opportunity to deal with those allegations.' It should be noted, however, that costs orders have since been made in other cases even where there was no evidence of deliberate exaggeration (see for example *Uttley v Uttley*[18] and *Islam v Ali*[19]).

Even if the court does not impose any particular sanction, if the video evidence does not in fact show anything that is of great significance, all it will do is increase the claimant's costs that the defendant may end up having to pay. The costs involved in the claimant's solicitor viewing the video, obtaining copies, comparing it with previous statements and medical reports, taking instructions, obtaining the views of experts, considering issues of admissibility, questioning its provenance and completeness and finally responding to the defendant on its contents could outweigh the probative effect of a video that, in fact, reveals very little.

---

[17]   [2001] 1 All ER 802.
[18]   [2002] PIQR P123.
[19]   [2003] EWCA Civ 612.

8.6   DELIBERATE EXAGGERATION

A claimant found to have been intentionally exaggerating their claim
should expect to be penalised in costs, even if ultimately they have been
successful. In *Booth v Britannia Hotels Ltd*[20] the claimant was a
chambermaid who suffered a crush injury to her hand. She claimed that
she had developed symptoms of reflex sympathetic dystrophy which had
the effect of substantially increasing the value of her claim. Video
evidence was disclosed five weeks before the assessment of damages
hearing, following which she was advised to settle her claim for £2,500
(her schedule in its final form claimed £617,000). The costs claimed on the
claimant's behalf were in excess of £80,000 plus VAT. The defendant was
ordered to pay all of the liability costs and 60 per cent of the quantum
costs. Its appeal was successful. Kennedy LJ held:

> 'This case, on the face of it, concerns a claimant pursuing a claim for
> personal injuries which she knows or must be taken to know have not been
> suffered. I see no reason why, even though the video evidence was completed
> and disclosed relatively late, the defendants should be required to bear any
> part of the costs she expended in that unreasonable pursuit.'

In essence a two-stage process is to be undergone when a court is assessing
costs of a claim that was clearly exaggerated. First the court should
consider the costs and disallow entirely those items incurred as a result of
the exaggeration, for example medical evidence. Then the court should
consider making a percentage reduction to the remaining costs to ensure
that the costs were reasonable in the context of the true value of the
claim.

A further demonstration of this principle can be seen in *Painting v
University of Oxford*.[21] In that case the claimant sought damages of
£400,000. The defendant admitted liability and paid into court the sum of
£184,442 shortly before trial. Curiously, it was only after making this
payment in that the defendant then realised it had video surveillance
evidence that significantly undermined the claimant's case. The defendant
applied for permission to withdraw all but £10,000 of the payment into
court. Permission was granted with costs ordered in favour of the
claimant and the assessment of damages hearing was adjourned. The
claimant made no offers and at trial maintained that her claim was worth
in the region of £400,000 (allowing for a 20 per cent deduction for
contributory negligence) on the basis that she was unable to work. At trial
the judge found that the claimant had deliberately exaggerated her injuries
and awarded her £23,331 by way of damages. On the basis that the
claimant had still beaten the payment into court she was awarded all of
her costs.

---

[20]   [2002] EWCA Civ 579.
[21]   [2005] EWCA Civ 161; (2005) *Times*, February 15.

On appeal the Court of Appeal held that although the judge had found that the claimant had exaggerated her injuries he had not given that factor sufficient weight when considering his discretion as to costs. Were it not for the exaggeration the claim would probably have settled. The court should have regard to the conduct of the parties (CPR 44.3(iv)(a)) and whether the claim had been exaggerated (CPR 44.3(v)(d)). While the CPR did not draw a distinction between intentional and unintentional exaggeration, the court should have regard to intentional exaggeration in any assessment of costs. The costs order was set aside. The defendant was ordered to pay the claimant's costs to the date of the payment in, with the claimant paying the defendant's costs thereafter. At para 22 Maurice Kay LJ said:

> '... at no stage did Mrs Painting manifest any willingness to negotiate or put forward a counter-proposal to the Part 36 payment. No one can compel a claimant to take such steps. However, to contest and lose an issue of exaggeration without have made even a counter-proposal is a matter of some significance in this kind of litigation.'

Agreeing, Longmore LJ said:

> '... it is relevant that Mrs Painting herself made no attempt to negotiate, made no offer of her own and made no response to the offers of the University. That would not have mattered in pre-CPR days but, to my mind, it now matters very much. Negotiation is meant to be a two-way street, and a claimant who makes no attempt to negotiate can expect, and should expect, the courts to take that into account when making the appropriate order as to costs.'

Similarly, in *Carver v BAA*[22] the claimant was ordered to pay the defendant's costs in a case where she was found to have exaggerated her claim. Although she was awarded £4,686.26, having rejected a Part 36 offer from the defendant of £3,486, she was ordered to pay the defendant's costs for the period after the relevant period had passed. The Court of Appeal upheld the costs order, emphasising that CPR Part 36, as amended in 2006, permitted a wider review of the circumstances of a case rather than conducting a purely mathematical assessment of who had 'won'. In the circumstances they would not interfere with the judge's exercise of his discretion.

This needs to be contrasted with *Morgan v UPS Ltd (No 2)*,[23] a case where it was held, on the basis of covert video evidence, that the claimant had exaggerated his claim and accordingly had only beaten a Part 36 payment into court by a 'whisker'. The Court of Appeal acknowledged the authorities of *Painting* and *Carver*, but distinguished them on the facts. Their Lordships held that in circumstances such as existed in *Morgan*, where the claimant had been prepared to negotiate realistically in

---

[22] [2008] EWCA Civ 412.
[23] [2008] EWCA Civ 1476.

response to adverse video evidence and where the defendants had persisted in an unmeritorious argument asserting that the claimant had lied in order to undergo a further 'unnecessary' operation, the trial judge had been entitled to exercise his discretion on costs in favour of the claimant.

8.6.1   Contempt of court

Discrepancies between a document verified by a statement of truth and video evidence do not automatically give rise to a contempt of court. What matters is the degree of exaggeration or the circumstances in which the exaggeration is made.

If the court were to conclude that there had been knowing and deliberate falsehood it may amount to contempt of court and the court could impose a penalty. As Coulson J, giving judgment in the case of *Carol Walton v Joanne Kirk*,[24] observed:

> 'Some exaggeration may be natural, even understandable, for the reasons set out by Bell J in Rogers. On the other hand, gross exaggeration and dishonesty will not be tolerated. As Cox J said in her Judgment giving permission to bring the present case, it is in the public interest that personal injury claimants pursue honest claims before the courts and do not significantly exaggerate those claims for financial gain ... Exaggeration of a claim is not, without more, automatic proof of contempt of court. What may matter is the degree of exaggeration (the greater the exaggeration, the less likely it is that the maker had an honest belief in the statement verified by the statement of truth) and/or the circumstances in which any exaggeration is made (a statement to an examining doctor may forgivably focus on the worst aspects of the maker's physical condition, whilst it may be less easy to dismiss criticism of a similar statement made when the maker has been repeatedly asked to specify variations in his or her physical condition, and chosen only to give one side – the worst – of the story).'

8.7   OTHER EVIDENCE

8.7.1   Plans, photographs and other documents

The rules and procedure in relation to witness and expert evidence are dealt with elsewhere in this text. This section simply looks at the other types of documents that parties may wish to rely upon at trial.

By s 13 of the Civil Evidence Act 1995 a 'document' means anything in which information of any description is recorded, and a 'copy', in relation to a document, means anything onto which information recorded in the document has been copied, by whatever means and whether directly or indirectly. This section replaced s 10(1) of the Civil Evidence Act 1968,

---

[24]   [2009] EWHC 703 (QB).

which was a little more descriptive as to the definition of a document. It stated that 'document' included, in addition to a document in writing, (a) any map, plan, graph or drawing; (b) any photograph; (c) any disk, tape, soundtrack or other device in which sounds or other data (not being visual images) are embodied so as to be capable (with or without the aid of some other equipment) of being reproduced there; and (d) any film negative, tape or other device in which one or more visual images are embodied so as to be capable (as aforesaid) of being reproduced therefrom. It is also worth noting that a computer database containing relevant information is considered by the civil courts to be a 'document': see *Derby v Weldon (No 9)*[25] and *Alliance & Leicester Building Society v Ghahremani.*[26]

In civil litigation, provided the civil court rules are followed, the relevant documents are shown to the other side prior to the trial and the judge is satisfied that admitting the evidence will not prejudice a fair trial, admissibility of documents is not usually contentious. This is particularly because, provided the documents have been disclosed in the proper way, they will have been included in the lists of documents exchanged between the parties. If they are asserted on that list to be copies of original documents they will be presumed by the court to be true copies unless authenticity is specifically disputed by the other party.

By CPR 32.19 a party is deemed to admit the authenticity of the documents disclosed to him under CPR Part 31 unless he serves notice that he wishes the documents to be proved at trial.

Section 8 of the Civil Evidence Act 1995 provides that where a statement in a document is admissible, it can be proved by the production of the document itself or by a copy of the document at any number of removes from the original. Further, s 9 provides that any document that is part of the records of a business or public authority is to be received into evidence without further proof being necessary.

In relation to plans, photographs or models, CPR 33.6 provides that notice must be given in advance by a party who intends to rely upon evidence such as a photograph, plan or model that is not part of the witness statements or expert evidence, is not to be given orally at trial or is evidence to which the hearsay provisions of CPR 33.2 apply. If a party gives notice that he intends to rely on such evidence then the other party must be afforded an opportunity to inspect it and to agree to its admission without further proof (CPR 33.6(8)).

---

[25] [1991] 1 WLR 652.
[26] [1992] RVR 198.

CHAPTER 9

PROCEDURAL STEPS

Jennifer Newcomb

9.1 INTRODUCTION

This chapter considers procedural steps that need or might need to be taken both before and during a claim. It moves chronologically: from pre-action disclosure, through to allocation, disclosure and inspection, exchange of witness evidence, service of expert reports and meetings between experts, through to the pre-trial checklist and final preparations before trial. Certain elements of procedure, such as those relating to the disclosure of medical records or expert reports, are dealt with elsewhere in this book.

9.2 PRE-ACTION DISCLOSURE

The Pre-action Protocol for Personal Injury Claims ('PI Protocol') is intended to encourage pre-action contact between parties, in particular, better and earlier exchange of information. If a party considers that the pre-action disclosure by another party is deficient, the party has the option of applying to the court for pre-action disclosure. Consideration must be given to the merits of such an application before it is made: an alternative option available is simply to issue proceedings against the other party, and draw the court's attention to the defendant's pre-action behaviour when the court comes to consider costs. Which route to go down depends on the nature of the disclosure required, the reasons for non-compliance by the other parties and how helpful the disclosure is likely to be once received.

An application to the court for pre-action disclosure is governed by s 33 of the Supreme Court Act ('SCA') 1981 or s 52 of the County Court Act ('CCA') 1984, depending on whether it is issued in the High Court or county court. These sections give the court statutory authority to make the order. The procedure for making the application is dictated by the test set out in Civil Procedure Rules ('CPR') 31.16. CPR 31.16 does not limit any other power that the court may have to order disclosure before proceedings have started.

9.2.1   Why make an application?

A pre-action disclosure order can be useful in making an informed decision about whether to issue proceedings. It is often used tactically by claimants to force a defendant that is dragging its feet on disclosure to comply with the protocol and consider the issues in the case. However, careful consideration should be given to such an application when it is made. If it is made without good reason, or having not been thought through, cost consequences can follow.

9.2.2   The test for pre-action disclosure

The court may make an order for pre-action disclosure only where:

- both the applicant and respondent are likely to be a party to subsequent proceedings (CPR 31.16(3)(a) and (b));

- if proceedings had started, the respondent's duty by way of standard disclosure would extend to the documents or classes of documents of which the applicant seeks disclosure (CPR 31.16(3)(c));

- disclosure before proceedings is desirable either to dispose fairly of the anticipated proceedings or assist the dispute to be resolved without proceedings, or to save costs (CPR 31.16(3)(d)).

These limbs involve both jurisdictional hurdles and discretionary hurdles for the claimant to overcome.

9.2.3   Likely to be a party

Whether a party is 'likely' to be a party to proceedings means 'may well': *Three Rivers DC v Bank of England (Disclosure) (No 1)*.[1] Courts should be hesitant to embark upon any determination of substantive issues during a pre-action disclosure application. However, the applicant must show at least a prima facie case of entitlement to substantive relief: *Mars K Ltd v Waitrose*[2] (a case in which the court refused to make an order because a prima facie case had not been demonstrated). There is no additional requirement to prove that the initiation of proceedings itself is 'likely': *Black v Sumitomo Corpn*,[3] but subsequent proceedings should be properly arguable and have a real prospect of success: *Rose v Lynx Express*.[4]

---

[1]   [2002] EWCA Civ 1182.
[2]   [2004] EWHC 2264 (Ch).
[3]   [2001] EWCA Civ 1819.
[4]   [2004] EWCA Civ 447.

9.2.4 If proceedings had started

'Standard disclosure' is defined at CPR 31.6, and considered below. Parties can only disclose what is reasonably within their control. The test of control regarding disclosure at CPR 31.8 is not specifically referred to in CPR 31.16, so the test to be applied is likely to be that set out in the CCA 1984/SCA 1981: 'those documents in ... possession, custody or power'. In reality, the differences between the tests are unlikely to make any significant practical difference.

A judge will need to understand a case in order to have any idea of what is disclosable in relation to it, so the claimant may need to make representations about his case and who the possible defendants might be (*Black v Sumitomo Corpn*). The documents or classes of documents should be limited to what is strictly necessary (*Snowstar Shipping Co Ltd v Graig Shipping plc*[5]).

9.2.5 Desirability

Whether or not the disclosure is 'desirable' is a discretionary question for the court (*Black v Sumitomo Corporation*). There is no specific test for desirability, and a judge in exercising his discretion will consider all the circumstances of the case. However, case law has given us a fair few indicators of when a court will consider that such disclosure is 'desirable':

- For jurisdictional purposes the court is only permitted to consider the granting of pre-action disclosure where there is a real prospect in principle of such an order being fair to the parties if litigation commenced, or of assisting the parties to avoid litigation, or of saving costs in any event. If there is such a real prospect, then the court should go on to consider the question of discretion, which has to be considered on all the facts and not merely in principle but in detail (*Black v Sumitomo Corpn*[6]).

- If an applicant for pre-action disclosure already possesses enough information to decide whether to plead a claim, it is less likely to be 'desirable' to order it (*Meretz Investments NV v First Penthouse Ltd*[7]).

- The merits of the future claim are relevant to the assessment of desirability.

---

[5]   [2003] EWHC 1367 (Comm).
[6]   As per Rix LJ at para 81.
[7]   [2003] EWHC 2324 (Ch).

- Costs may be cut through pre-action proceedings by avoiding the need to amend at a later stage (*First Gulf Bank v Wachovi Bank National Association*[8]).

- The court will be concerned with the cost of complying with any order (*Black v Sumitomo Corn*).

- An order may be refused if the court is of the opinion that the order is oppressive or would not be in the interests of justice or would be injurious to the public interest (*O'Sullivan v Herdmans Ltd*[9]).

9.2.6   How to make an application

An application for pre-action disclosure should be made pursuant to CPR Part 23 (CPR 25.4). Practice Form N244 should be used. The application must be supported by evidence (CPR 31.16(2)). This evidence can either by included in part C of the application notice or in a separate witness statement. The evidence must be verified by a statement of truth, even if it included in part C of the application notice rather than a separate witness statement (CPR Part 22).

CPR 23.6 requires that the application state what order is being sought and why. Given that judges are likely to form a view of the application on the papers before hearing any oral representations, the better the application and the more defined the disclosure being sought is, the more likely a court will consider it desirable to make an order. Considering the test set out above, the following is a list of information that should be included in the supporting evidence for any application:

- the documents or class of documents being sought;

- the potential subsequent proceedings and why the parties are likely to be parties to the proceedings;

- why it is desirable to have disclosure of the documents before the commencement of proceedings;

- why the documents being sought fall within the definition of 'standard disclosure';

- details of previous requests for disclosure and responses received.

A draft order should be included in the application, and CPR 31.16(4) sets out what information must be included in the order. The order *must* specify the documents or the class of documents which the respondent must disclose and require him, when making disclosure, to specify any of

---

[8]   [2005] EWHC 2827 (Comm).
[9]   [1987] 1 WLR 1047.

those documents which are no longer in his control or in respect of which he claims a right or duty to withhold inspection. An order *may* require the respondent to indicate what has happened to any documents that are no longer in his control and specify the time and place for disclosure and inspection (CPR 31.16(5)). When drafting an order, it is always sensible to include the provisions that a judge *may* include as well as *must* include. If there are numerous documents to be disclosed, attaching a schedule of documents sought to the order might be a more useful way of setting out the order.

The usual rule is that where a court grants an interim remedy before a claim has been commenced, the court should give directions requiring a claim to be commenced (CPR 25.2(3)). An application for pre-action disclosure is specifically excluded from this rule (CPR 25.2(4)). There are obvious reasons for this exception: it may be that once further disclosure is forthcoming, the claimant will make a decision not to pursue a claim against the proposed defendant.

Careful consideration should be given to the description of documents sought in the draft order: this should avoid the need for further applications later in the event of ambiguities being present, or the possibility of a judge dismissing the application because of a lack of particularity in what is sought.

9.2.7   Costs of the application

Costs of such applications must either be agreed or assessed summarily (CPR 48.10). Costs cannot be reserved, or 'in the case', because there is not yet any formal case or any guarantee that a case will be issued in the future.

The general rule is that the court will award the person against whom the order is sought his costs of responding to the application and of complying with any order made (CPR 48.1(2)). However, CPR 48.1(3) states that the court may make a different order, having regard to all the circumstances, including the extent to which it was reasonable for the person against whom the order was sought to oppose the application and whether the parties to the application have complied with any relevant pre-action protocols. Despite the clear rule set out in CPR 48.1(2), claimants are often successful in obtaining their costs of an application in cases where they have been able to demonstrate a failure by the defendant to comply with the pre-action protocol, which is often the basis upon which such claims are made in personal injury cases.

The following cases give some guidance as to the approach judges will take:

- *Bermuda International Securities Ltd v KPMG;*[10]

- *SES Contracting Ltd v UK Coal plc.*[11]

Save in exceptional circumstances, costs incurred by a defendant at the pre-action stage, in responding to issues raised which are subsequently dropped from the claim once commenced, are not costs 'incidental to' proceedings for the purposes of s 51 SCA 1981, and therefore are not recoverable (*McGlinn v Waltham Contractors Ltd*[12]). However, if proceedings are later started, the court is entitled to make an order that a party must pay costs incurred before proceedings have begun (CPR 44.3(6)(d)).

A question recently considered in the county court is whether an application for pre-action disclosure is excluded from the scope of a CFA based on the Law Society's model terms, which covers 'your claim against x for damages and personal injury', and thus whether a claimant has any liability to pay his solicitors any costs relating to a pre-action disclosure application. Most recently, in *Philip Rogers v Enterprise Mouchel,*[13] the court considered it appropriate to adopt a purposive interpretation of the phrase, and concluded that an application for pre-action disclosure was part and parcel of the claim, as a natural consequence of the defendant's failure to comply with the pre-action protocol and therefore did fall within the scope of the CFA.

9.3   TRANSFER OF PROCEEDINGS

There are provisions in the CPR for the automatic transfer of proceedings to a defendant's home court when a number of conditions are met (CPR 26.2). Where the claim is against two or more defendants with different home courts, and the defendant whose defence is filed first is an individual, proceedings are to be transferred to the home court of that defendant (CPR 26.2(5)).

9.4   ALLOCATION

9.4.1   Allocation questionnaires

Once a defendant files a defence the court will serve an allocation questionnaire on each party, unless the court dispenses with the need for a questionnaire, the defendant states in his defence that he has paid the claimant the money owed, and the only claim is for a specific amount of

---

10   [2001] EWCA Civ 269.
11   [2007] EWCA Civ 791.
12   [2005] EWHC 1419, TCC.
13   11 October 2010, Lawtel.

money or the defendant admits part of the claim (CPR 26.3(1)). For more detailed provisions about the allocation questionnaire see CPR 26.3.

The allocation questionnaire has provision for either party to request that the proceedings be stayed while the parties try to settle the case. If such a request is made, or if the court decides of its own initiative that a stay would be appropriate, the court will direct that the proceedings, either in whole or in part, be stayed for one month or for such specified period as it considers appropriate (CPR 26.4(2)). There are also provisions in the CPR for the extension of the stay and for directions to be given at the end of the period if the claimant does not tell the court that settlement has been reached by the end of the stay, including allocating the claim to a track.

9.4.2 Allocation of the claim

Once all defendants have filed their allocation questionnaire, or the period for filing the allocation questionnaires has passed (whichever is sooner), the court will usually allocate the claim to a track (CPR 26.5). The court may order a party to provide further information about his case before deciding to which track to allocate the proceedings or deciding whether the give directions for an allocation hearing to be fixed (CPR 26.5(3)). The court may give any direction it considers appropriate if a party has failed to file an allocation questionnaire (CPR 26.5(5)) or may hold an allocation hearing it is thinks it is necessary (CPR 26.5(4)).

When assessing the financial value of the claim, the court will disregard any amount not in dispute, any claim for interest, costs and any contributory negligence (CPR 26.8(2)). This is an area that parties should be wary of: assessing the claim as a fast-track claim where the majority of damages are agreed may lead to a costs argument at the end of the case regarding only paying fixed small-claim costs.

Once the court has allocated a claim to a track, it will serve notice of allocation on every party (CPR 26.9(1)). At the same time, it will also serve a copy of the allocation questionnaire filed by the other parties and a copy of any further information provided by another party about his case (whether by order or not) (CPR 26.9).

9.4.3 Scope of each track

The small claims track is the normal track for any claim which has a value of not more than £5,000. In personal injury claims, the small claims track is the normal value for any claim for personal injuries where the value of the claim is not more than £5,000, and the value of any claim for damages for personal injuries is not more than £1,000 (CPR 26.6(1)). 'Damages for personal injuries' means damages claimed as compensation for pain, suffering and loss of amenity and does not include any other damages which are claimed (CPR 26.6(2)).

The fast track is the normal track for any claim for which the small claims track is not the normal track and which has a value of not more than £25,000 (CPR 26.6(4)) (although note that if proceedings were issued before 6 April 2009, the limit is £15,000). The fast track is the normal track for these claims only if the court considers that the trial is likely to last for no longer than one day and oral expert evidence at trial will be limited to one expert per party in relation to any expert field and two expert fields (CPR 26.4(5)).

The multi-track is the normal track for any claim for which the small claims track or the fast track is not the normal track (CPR 26.6(6)). Generally, this will mean trials that will last more than a day, involve a higher number of experts than those permitted on the fast track or are worth more than £25,000.

The court will not necessarily allocate a claim to the 'normal' track for that type of claim. When deciding the track for a claim, the court shall have regard to the following matters (CPR 26.8):

• the financial value, if any, of the claim;

• the nature of the remedy sought;

• the likely complexity of the facts, law or evidence;

• the number of parties or likely parties;

• the value of any counterclaim or other additional claim and the complexity of any matters relating to it;

• the amount of oral evidence that may be required;

• the importance of the claim to persons who are not parties to the proceedings;

• the views expressed by the parties; and

• the circumstances of the parties.

The court will not allocate proceedings to a track if the financial value of the claim, assessed by the court under CPR 26.8, exceeds the limit for that track unless all the parties consent to the allocation of the claim to that track (CPR 26.7(3)). The court may subsequently reallocate the claim to a different track (CPR 26.10).

9.5 DISCLOSURE AND INSPECTION OF DOCUMENTS

Once proceedings are issued, the rules about disclosure and inspection of documents in fast track and multi-track cases are set out in Part 31 of the CPR: that part does not apply to small claims. A party discloses a document by stating that the document exists or has existed (CPR 31.2). Subject to some exceptions, once a document has been disclosed to another party, that party has a right to inspect it. A party may not rely on any document which he fails to disclose or in respect of which he fails to permit inspection unless the court gives permission (CPR 31.21). Below we examine disclosure and inspection in turn.

9.5.1 Standard disclosure

As stated above, disclosure is not the physical act of handing a document to another party; rather, it is a statement that a document exists. The phrase 'document' is very wide: it means anything in which information of any description is recorded, and 'copy', in relation to a document, means anything onto which information has been copied, by whatever means and whether directly or indirectly (CPR 31.4). Clearly then, the phrase 'document' is far reaching, encompassing all manner of items, including papers, audio recordings, film, maps, plans, computer files and hard disks on computers.

Standard disclosure requires a party to disclose three categories of document: those upon which he relies; those that adversely affect his own case, adversely affect another party's case or support another party's case; and documents that he is required to disclose by a relevant practice direction (CPR 31.6). An order for disclosure made by a court is an order for standard disclosure, unless the court directs otherwise (CPR 31.5). Usually, an order is made for disclosure at the first case management hearing, or if there is no case management hearing, after the filing of defence and allocation questionnaires, but before witness statements are served. For claims on the fast track, the court may direct less than standard disclosure (CPR Practice Direction 28, para 3.6(1)(c)). Factors the court is likely to consider include the amount of relevant documentation and the amount of pre-action disclosure that took place.

The CPR spells out the duties that the parties have when dealing with standard disclosure. A party is required to make a reasonable search for documents that undermine their case or assist or undermine the case of another party, as well as documents required to be disclosed as a result of a practice direction. A number of factors are relevant to the question of reasonableness, including the number of documents involved, the nature and complexity of proceedings, the ease and expense of retrieval of any particular document and the significance of any document that is likely to be located during the search (CPR 31.7). If a party takes the view that it would be unreasonable to search for a category or class of documents, he must state this in his disclosure statement and identify the category or class of document. The overriding principle of proportionality should always be borne in mind: it may be reasonable to decide not to search for documents coming into existence before a particular date, or to limit the search to documents in some particular place or places, or to documents falling into particular categories (CPR Practice Direction 31, para 2).

A party's duty to disclose documents is limited to documents that are or have been in his control (CPR 31.8).

Although a party need not disclose more than one copy of a document, a copy that contains a modification, obliteration or other marking or feature on which a party intends to rely or that adversely affects his own case or another party's case or supports another party's case is treated as a separate document (CPR 31.9).

The parties may agree in writing or the court may direct that disclosure or inspection or both shall take place in stages (CPR 31.13).

9.5.2   Electronic disclosure

The CPR now sets out general principles that parties should bear in mind when considering their disclosure obligations in relation to electronic documents.[14] The practice direction only applies to cases that are likely to be allocated to the multi-track, unless the court orders otherwise, and is intended to encourage and assist parties to reach agreement in relation to disclosure of electronic documents in a proportionate and cost-effective manner. For more detail, see Practice Direction 31B and *Goodale v Ministry of Justice*.[15]

9.5.3   Procedure for standard disclosure

Each party must make and serve on every other party a list of documents (CPR 31.10(2)). The list must identify the documents in a convenient order and manner and as concisely as possible (CPR 31.10(3)). The list must indicate those documents in respect of which the party claims a right or duty to withhold inspection; and those documents that are no longer in the party's control (as well as what happened to those documents) (CPR 31.10(4)).

The list should be on Form N265. The Practice Direction suggests that it will normally be necessary to list the documents in date order, to number them consecutively and to give each a concise description (eg letter, claimant to defendant) (CPR Practice Direction 31, para 3.2). Where there is a large number of documents that fall into a particular category

---

[14]   CPR PD 31B.
[15]   [2010] EWHC 1643 (QB).

the disclosing party may list those documents as a category rather than individually (eg 50 bank statements relating to account number x at bank y).

A statement must be included in the list of documents relating to any documents inspection of which a person claims he has a right or duty to withhold (CPR 31.10(4)). The list must include a 'disclosure statement', which is a statement made by the party disclosing the documents dealing with a number of things (CPR 31.10(5) and (6)):

- setting out the extent of the search that has been made to locate documents that he is required to disclose;

- certifying that he understands the duty to disclose documents; and

- certifying that to the best of his knowledge he has carried out that duty.

The disclosure statement should expressly state that the disclosing party believes the extent of the search to have been reasonable in all the circumstances and, in setting out the extent of the search, draw attention to any particular limitations on the extent of the search that were adopted for proportionality reasons and give the reasons why the limitations were adopted (eg the difficulty or expense that a search not subject to those limitations would have entailed or the marginal relevance of categories of documents omitted from the search) (CPR Practice Direction 31, para 4.2).

Where the party making the disclosure statement is a company, firm, association or other organisation, the statement must also identify the person making the statement and explain why he is considered an appropriate person to make the statement (CPR 31.10(7)). Those details must include his name and address and the office or position he holds in the disclosing party or the basis upon which he makes the statement on behalf of the party (CPR Practice Direction 31, para 4.3). However, parties may agree in writing to disclose documents without making a list or to disclose documents without the disclosing party making a disclosure statement (CPR 31.10(8)). A disclosure statement may be made by a person who is not a party where this is permitted by a relevant practice direction (CPR 31.10(9)).

A legal representative for a disclosing party must endeavour to ensure that the person making the disclosure statement (whether the disclosing party or, in a case to which CPR 31.10(7) applies, some other person) understands the duty of disclosure under Part 31 (CPR Practice Direction 31, para 4.4).

Proceedings for contempt of court may be brought against a person if he makes or causes to be made a false disclosure statement without an honest belief in its truth (CPR 31.23).

9.5.4   Applications for specific disclosure or inspection

The court can make an order for specific disclosure or specific inspection. If a party believes that the disclosure of a party has been inadequate, he may make an application for an order for specific disclosure. The application should be made in accordance with CPR Part 23. The court can order a party to disclose documents or classes of documents specified in the order, carry out a search to the extent stated in the order and/or disclose any documents located as a result of that search (CPR 31.12(2)).

9.5.5   Inspection

A party may inspect a document mentioned in a statement of case, witness statement, witness summary or affidavit (CPR 31.14(1)). Subject to rules relating to instructions for an expert's report, a party may apply for an order for inspection of any document mentioned in an expert's report that has not already been disclosed in the proceedings (CPR 31.14(2)).

Where a party has a right to inspect a document, that party must give the party who disclosed the document written notice of his wish to inspect it. Once received, the party who disclosed the document must permit inspection not more than seven days later. If the party wishes to have a copy of the document, a copy can be requested and, if he also undertakes to pay reasonable copying costs, the party who disclosed the document must supply him with a copy not more than seven days after the date on which he received the request (CPR 31.15).

If a party inadvertently allows a privileged document to be inspected, the party who has inspected the document may use it or its contents only with the permission of the court (CPR 31.20).

9.5.6   Exceptions to right to inspection

A party does not have a right to inspect a disclosed document where the document is no longer in control of the party that disclosed it (CPR 31.3(1)). A party is said to have or have had a document in its control if it is or was in his physical possession, he has or has had a right to possession of it; or he has or has had a right to inspect or take copies of it (CPR 31.8).

A party does not have a right to inspect a disclosed document if the party disclosing it has a right or duty to withhold inspection (CPR 31.3(1)). A person may apply, without notice, for an order permitting him to withhold disclosure of a document on the ground that disclosure would damage the public interest (CPR 31.19(1)). The CPR set out detail about how to make such an application which is beyond the scope of this work.

If a party considers that it would be disproportionate to the issues in the case to permit inspection of documents within a category or class of document disclosed, he is not required to permit inspection of documents within that category or class, but he must state in his disclosure statement that inspection of those documents will not be permitted on the grounds that to do so would be disproportionate.

9.5.7 Claim to withhold disclosure/inspection

If the disclosing party wishes to claim that he has a right or duty to withhold a document or part of a document in his list of documents from inspection (CPR 31.19(3)), he must state in writing that he has such a right or duty and the grounds on which he claims that right or duty (CPR Practice Direction 31, para 4.5). The statement should normally be included in the disclosure statement and must indicate the document, or part of a document, to which the claim relates (CPR Practice Direction 31, para 4.6).

9.5.8 Once disclosure has taken place

The rules limit how a party is allowed to use documents that have been disclosed to them. A party to whom a document has been disclosed may use the document only for the purpose of the proceedings in which it is disclosed (CPR 31.22). There are some exceptions to this rule: where the document has been read to or by the court, or referred to, at a hearing that has been held in public, the court gives permission or the party who disclosed the document and the person to whom the document belongs agrees. Even if the document has been read to or by the court or referred to at a hearing that has been held in public, the court may make an order restricting or prohibiting the use of a document (CPR 31.22(2)). An application for such an order may be made by a party or by any person to whom the document belongs.

Any duty of disclosure continues until the proceedings are concluded (CPR 31.11). This means that if documents to which the duty extends come to a party's notice at any time during the proceedings, he must immediately notify every other party. If, after a list of documents has been prepared and served, the existence of further documents to which the order applies comes to the attention of the disclosing party, the party must prepare and serve a supplemental list (CPR Practice Direction 31, para 3.3).

9.5.9   Disclosure applications against non-parties

An application for disclosure against a person who is not party to proceedings is permitted under s 34 of the Supreme Court Act 1981 or s 53 County Court Act 1984. CPR 31.17 deals with this area. Such an order may be made by a court only where the documents of which disclosure is sought are likely to support the case of the applicant or adversely affect the case of one of the other parties to the proceedings and disclosure is necessary in order to dispose fairly of the claim or to save costs (CPR 31.17(3)). An order must specify the documents or the classes of documents that the respondent must disclose and require the respondent, when making disclosure, to specify any of those documents that are no longer in his control or in respect of which he claims a right or duty to withhold inspection (CPR 31.17(4)). Such an order may require the respondent to indicate what has happened to any documents that are no longer in his control and specify the time and place for disclosure and inspection (CPR 31.17(5)).

Many of the phrases used in the section reflect those phrases used in a pre-action disclosure application, the meaning of which have been examined above. CPR 31.17 does not limit any other power that the court may have to order disclosure against a person who is not a party to proceedings.

9.6   EXCHANGE OF WITNESS STATEMENTS

The court will order a party to serve on the other parties any witness statement containing the oral evidence that the party intends to rely on in relation to any issues of fact to be decided at the trial (CPR 32.4(2)). The court may give directions as to the order in which witness statements are to be served and whether or not the witness statements are to be filed (CPR 32.4(3)).

Generally, when witness statements are served will depend on what track the claim is allocated to. On the small claims track, standard directions are that each party shall, at least 14 days before the date fixed for the final hearing, file and serve on every other party copies of all documents on which he intends to rely at the hearing (CPR 27.4(3)), but special directions could be given instead of standard directions (CPR 27.4(1)). However, Part 32 does not apply to small claims (CPR 27.2).

When a case is allocated to the fast track, the court will give directions for the management of the case and set a timetable for the steps to be taken between the giving of the directions and the trial, which includes directions for the service of witness statements (CPR 28.2(1) and 28.3(1)). A typical timetable that the court may give for the preparation of the case would include exchange of witness statements at about 10 weeks from the date of notice of allocation (CPR Practice Direction 28, para 3.12). That exchange will usually be simultaneous.

When a case is allocated to the multi track, under CPR 29.2 the court will give directions for the management of the case and set a timetable for the steps to be taken between the giving of directions and the trial or fix a case management conference or pre-trial review, or both, and give such other directions relating to the management of the case as it sees fit. Under CPR 29.4, if the parties agree proposals for the management of the proceedings (including a proposed trial date or period in which the trial is to take place) and the court considers that the proposals are suitable, it may approve them without a hearing and give directions in the terms proposed. Such directions, whether proposed by the court or parties in the first instance, will specify by when the parties need to exchange their witness statements.

If the court directs that a witness statement is to be filed, it must be filed in the court or division or office/registry of the court or division where the action in which it was or is to be used, is proceeding or will proceed (CPR Practice Direction 32, para 23.1).

9.7 EXCHANGE OF EXPERT EVIDENCE

Chapter 6 deals with expert evidence. Information relating to experts in this chapter is limited to procedural steps for the exchange of expert evidence and meetings between witnesses. Questions relating to disclosure of expert evidence and privilege are also found in Chapter 6.

Where a party has disclosed an expert's report, any party may use that expert's report as evidence at the trial (CPR 35.11).

9.8 MEETINGS OF EXPERTS

The court may, at any stage, direct a discussion between experts for the purpose of requiring the experts to identify and discuss the expert issues in the proceedings; and, where possible, reach an agreed opinion on those issues (CPR 35.12(1)). The court may specify the issues which the experts must discuss (CPR 35.12(2)). The court may direct that following a discussion between the experts they must prepare a statement for the court setting out those issues on which they agree and disagree, with a summary of their reasons for disagreeing (CPR 35.12(3)). The content of the discussion between the experts shall not be referred to at the trial unless the parties agree (CPR 35.12(4)). Where experts reach agreement on an issue during their discussions, the agreement shall not bind the parties unless the parties expressly agree to be bound by the agreement (CPR 35.12(5)).

9.8.1   Agendas

Where experts are to meet, the parties must discuss and if possible agree whether an agenda is necessary, and if so, attempt to agree one that helps the experts to focus on the issues that need to be discussed. The agenda must not be in the form of leading questions or hostile in tone (CPR Practice Direction 35, para 9.3).

9.8.2   Attendance of lawyers

Unless ordered by the court, or agreed by all parties, and the experts, neither the parties nor their legal representatives may attend experts' discussions (CPR Practice Direction 35, para 9.4). If the legal representatives do attend, they should not normally intervene in the discussion except to answer questions put to them by the experts or to advise on the law, and the experts may if they so wish hold part of their discussions in the absence of the legal representatives (CPR Practice Direction 35, para 9.5).

9.9   PRE-TRIAL CHECKLIST

9.9.1   Small claims track

There is no provision in the CPR for pre-trial checklists to be completed on the small claims track.

9.9.2   Fast track

The court will send the parties a pre-trial checklist (listing questionnaire) for completion and return by the date specified in the notice of allocation unless it considers that the claim can proceed to trial without the need for a pre-trial checklist (CPR 28.5(1)). The date specified for filing a pre-trial check list will not be more than eight weeks before the trial date or the beginning of the trial period (CPR 28.5(2)). If no party files the completed pre-trial checklist by the date specified, the court will order that unless a completed pre-trial checklist is filed within seven days from service of that order, the claim, defence and any counterclaim will be struck out without further order of the court (CPR 28.5(3)). If a party files a completed pre-trial checklist but another party does not, a party has failed to give all the information requested by the pre-trial checklist, or the court considers that a hearing is necessary to enable it to decide what directions to give in order to complete preparation of the case for trial, the court may give such directions as it thinks appropriate (CPR 28.5(4)).

As soon as practicable after the date specified for filing a completed pre-trial check list the court will fix the date for the trial (or, if it has already done so, confirm that date), give any directions for the trial, including a trial timetable, which it considers appropriate; and specify any further steps that need to be taken before trial (CPR 28.6(1)). The court will give the parties at least three weeks' notice of the date of the trial unless, in exceptional circumstances, the court directs that shorter notice will be given (CPR 28.6(2)).

9.9.3   Multi track

The court will send the parties a pre-trial checklist for completion and return by the date specified in directions given under CPR 29.2(3) unless it considers that the claim can proceed to trial without the need for a pre-trial checklist (CPR 29.6(1)). Each party must file the completed pre-trial checklist by the date specified by the court (CPR 29.6(2)). If no party files the completed pre-trial checklist by the date specified, the court will order that unless a completed pre-trial checklist is filed within seven days from service of that order, the claim, defence and any counterclaim will be struck out without further order of the court (CPR 29.6(3)). If a party files a completed pre-trial checklist but another party does not, a party has failed to give all the information requested by the pre-trial checklist; or the court considers that a hearing is necessary to enable it to decide what directions to give in order to complete preparation of the case for trial, the court may give such directions as it thinks appropriate (CPR 29.6(4)).

If, on receipt of the parties' pre-trial checklists, the court decides to hold a pre-trial review or to cancel a pre-trial review that has already been fixed, it will serve notice of its decision at least seven days before the date fixed for the hearing or, as the case may be, the cancelled hearing (CPR 29.7).

As soon as practicable after each party has filed a completed pre-trial checklist, the court has held a listing hearing under CPR 29.6(3); or the court has held a pre-trial review under CPR 29.7, the court will do one of three things (CPR 29.8):

- set a timetable for the trial unless a timetable has already been fixed, or the court considers that it would be inappropriate to do so;

- fix the date for the trial or the week within which the trial is to begin (or, if it has already done so, confirm that date); and

- notify the parties of the trial timetable (where one is fixed under this rule) and the date or trial period.

9.10   BUNDLES (CPR PRACTICE DIRECTION 39A, PARA 3.9)

Rules in relation to trial bundles are set out in Practice Direction 39A at para 3. They are lengthy and detailed. The responsibility for the preparation and production of the trial bundle lies with the legal representative who has conduct of the claim on behalf of the claimant, even where it is delegated to another person (CPR Practice Direction 39A para 3.4). It should be paginated continuously throughout and indexed with a description of each document and the page number. Where the total number of pages is more than 100, numbered dividers should be placed at intervals between groups of documents (CPR Practice Direction 39A para 3.5). The bundle should normally be contained in a ring binder or lever arch file. Where more than one bundle is supplied they should be clearly distinguishable (the practice direction suggests by different colours or letters). If there are numerous bundles, a core bundle should be prepared containing the core documents essential to the proceedings, with references to the supplementary documents in the other bundles (CPR Practice Direction 39A para 3.6).

Unless the court orders otherwise, the claimant must file the trial bundle not more than seven days and not less than three days before the start of the trial (CPR 39.5 and Practice Direction 39A para 3.1). Unless the court orders otherwise, the trial bundle should include (CPR Practice Direction 39A para 3.2):

- a copy of the claim form and all statements of case;

- a case summary and/or chronology where appropriate;

- requests for further information and responses to requests;

- all witness statements to be relied on as evidence;

- any witness summaries;

- any notices of intention to rely on hearsay evidence under CPR 32.2;

- any notices of intention to rely on evidence (such as a plan, photograph, etc) under CPR 33.6 which is not contained in a witness statement, affidavit or expert's report, being given orally at trial, or hearsay evidence under CPR 33.2;

- any medical reports and responses to them;

- any experts' reports and responses to them;

- any order giving directions as to the conduct of the trial; and

- any other necessary documents.

The originals of the documents contained in the trial bundle, together with copies of any other court orders should be available at the trial (CPR Practice Direction 39A para 3.3).

CHAPTER 10

THE ROLE OF COUNSEL

Christopher Stephenson

10.1   WHAT IS COUNSEL'S ROLE?

The popular conception of a barrister is as a specialist in advocacy. Given that the overwhelming majority of personal injury claims settle well before a final hearing, is it still the case that a barrister can assist in this area of work? The answer is clearly yes. Whether it be in a low value fast-track case or the most complicated of catastrophic injury or fatal accident claims, the proper use of counsel can not only ensure the best outcome for the client, but also save time and money.

Counsel can be involved to good effect in all stages of the litigation process. In the pre-action stage specialist counsel can be expected to advise on the merits of a case and the evidential hurdles that are faced. Counsel can be relied upon for specialist drafting skills and, once the claim has been issued, for interlocutory advocacy. Counsel should be able to assist in managing the evidence, instructing appropriate experts, drafting the questions to be put to the expert(s) and plotting the tactics of the litigation. Perhaps most importantly of all, counsel can be used to provide an overview of the claim to a solicitor and client to enable successful resolution of the case, either by settlement or at a final hearing.

To obtain the best from counsel, however, the instructing solicitor must be prepared to work in partnership with him. The roles of solicitor and counsel are different but if combined effectively will ensure the best possible result for a client.

Counsel should be able to assist with:

- advisory work (eg advice on merits, evidence, value and points of law, on paper or in conference);

- drafting (eg pleadings, correspondence, applications);

- witness statements (eg drafting, perfecting);

- skeleton arguments;

- negotiation (eg drafting Part 36 offers, appearing at joint settlement meetings);

- advocacy at interlocutory and final hearings;

- appeals (eg advising, drafting the appropriate notices and appearing at the appeal hearing).

10.2   WHO CAN INSTRUCT COUNSEL?

There are now three accepted routes for instructing counsel. The first (and clearly the most used) is direct professional instruction, through a solicitor. Certain licensed professionals can instruct counsel, most frequently accountants, surveyors and the like (licensed access). Finally, the public can instruct a barrister directly if certain requirements are met.

There has in fact never been a rule of law preventing a lay client from instructing a barrister directly. It has only ever been the Bar Council's own regulations that have prevented direct instruction. Recently these regulations have changed. Since July 2004 lay clients have been able to instruct counsel directly (direct professional access), provided that the barrister is registered to accept such instructions. However, a barrister's role when directly instructed is not nearly as wide-ranging as that of a solicitor. For example, a directly instructed barrister cannot issue proceedings on a client's behalf, cannot send letters on his own headed paper on a client's behalf, cannot investigate or collect evidence for use in proceedings or instruct expert witnesses. Therefore, even when instructed directly, counsel's role really remains one of specialist advice and advocacy.

The precise requirements of licensed access and direct professional access are beyond the scope of this chapter. Further information can be found on the Bar Council's website at www.barcouncil.org.uk. The remainder of this chapter will focus on professional instruction by solicitors.

10.3   WHEN TO INVOLVE COUNSEL

It is important to remember that the relationship between solicitor and counsel should be as team members, rather than as individuals. Both have different roles in the process and, if combined together, should ensure the best result for the client.

The first thing for a solicitor to do is decide at what stage of proceedings to instruct a barrister. This will largely depend on the type and complexity of case. However, it is not necessarily right to assume that counsel can only be of value in complicated matters. It may well be that instructing a barrister is a cost-effective way of conducting the litigation. For example, it may ultimately be cheaper to instruct counsel to provide an advice or draft proceedings in a fast-track case. An early advice may well identify issues that will focus the litigation and avoid unnecessary investigation and cost. A pleading drafted by counsel may lead to an early admission of liability or discontinuance of the claim.

In a fast-track claim it might be that the first time counsel is involved is in the drafting of pleadings; in a multi-track claim the first involvement might well be an early advice on the prospects of success, prior to the drafting of proceedings. In a catastrophic injury or fatal accident claim, it is likely to be sensible to involve counsel at an early stage so that the client is assured that his claim is in the hands of an expert 'team' and so that the overall tactical approach to the claim can be planned from the start. In the bigger cases an early conference with counsel is recommended.

10.4   INSTRUCTIONS

It is vital that counsel is properly instructed, because the best results will only be obtained if counsel understands what he is being asked to do. If proper instructions are drafted at the time of first instruction, they form the template of all later instructions and will save the solicitor and counsel time and therefore keep costs to a minimum.

Instructions to counsel should contain the following:

- an index of the enclosures;

- a summary of the client's details: the claimant's date of birth, details of the professional client (eg insurer);

- details of the funding arrangements;

- a summary of the factual background: date and location of the accident, relationship to the defendant (eg employer/employee, occupier/visitor etc);

- an outline of the factual issues;

- a summary of the legal issues with a summary of the solicitors own views;

- a precise request of what the solicitor wants counsel to do (eg advise on liability, quantum, evidence, jurisdiction, limitation etc);

- a timeframe, particularly if there is urgency (eg an impending limitation date); and

- the solicitor's contact details, in particular email address.

The documents provided with the instructions will largely depend upon what counsel is being asked to do. It is strongly recommended that counsel is not sent original documents as they might get lost in the post or counsel may wish to make markings on them. In most personal injury claims counsel should be provided with the following:

- the pleadings, including all court orders;

- the witness evidence;

- the documentary evidence that has been disclosed by the parties;

- relevant medical reports;

- personnel and occupational health files (especially in, but not limited to, employer's liability claims);

- medical records; and

- relevant correspondence.

10.5   DRAFTING

In most personal injury claims counsel will be asked to draft the particulars of claim (or other statement of case). The Civil Procedure Rules ('CPR') set out the basic requirements for the statement of case, but it is important that counsel is provided with all the relevant information to satisfy those requirements.

It goes without saying that the particulars of claim should set out a concise summary of the claimant's case. The pleading should not include evidence but, that said, it is of course vital that the claimant's evidence is summarised so that the defendant and ultimately the court understands the basis upon which the claim is made. So, for example, in a simple tripping case it may be useful to append a photograph of the accident location and the defect complained of.

The basic aim of a pleading is to tell the story of the circumstances leading to the event complained of (the index event), to set out the allegations of the breaches of duty (statutory or common law) that flow from the accident, followed by details of what the breaches have caused (injury, loss and damage). As long as those fundamentals are included in the pleading, there is no right or wrong way to plead a claim. Pleading a claim need not be formulaic and most individuals develop a style of their own.

It is always sensible to ask counsel to draft any pleadings, be that the particulars of claim, the defence, Part 18 requests for further information and/or replies. If there are any concerns about the medical evidence, counsel should be asked to consider the merits of asking questions of the relevant experts, pursuant to CPR Part 35.

10.6   THE ADVICE ON EVIDENCE

One often overlooked exercise is the advice on evidence. Although the vast majority of claims settle before a final hearing, the best way to ensure that the settlement is as advantageous as possible is to approach the claim from the very beginning as though it was to be determined at a trial. Counsel's ultimate purpose is as an advocate and they should therefore approach any claim as though it is going to be determined by a judge at a trial. Any claim is only as good as the evidence called in support of it. The law can only be applied to the facts as they are found to have existed at the date of the event complained of and so it is essential that thought is given to the evidential burden and standard of proof.

One of the most valuable tools is therefore the advice on evidence. Certainly in a high value or complex claim it is essential that counsel is asked to advise on the totality of the evidence: to consider the evidence already obtained and what further evidence is required to make out the claim. This will encompass looking at documentary evidence and both lay witness evidence and expert evidence, as to which see further below.

However, the advice on evidence should not be confined to high value or complicated claims. It is suggested that if any claim is heading towards a final hearing it is prudent to ask counsel to advise on the evidence. The stage that the advice is sought might be different in each case. Sometimes it is important to ask counsel to review the witness evidence before it is exchanged so that any holes can be identified and filled. In other cases it is prudent to ask for an advice on evidence after the witness evidence has been exchanged so that the need for any further evidence can be identified and remedied.

In a fast-track claim such an advice may prove vital. For example in an employer's liability claim there may well be reams of documentary and lay witness evidence but counsel, who has to present the evidence at trial, will be able to identify how that evidence should be marshaled and called at the trial. By way of example, in a case involving a piece of machinery, counsel might advise that photographs or a video are needed to show the judge how the machine was *supposed* to work and what happened to cause the accident.

10.7   COUNSEL AND THE EXPERT EVIDENCE

Counsel should also be closely involved in the gathering and marshaling of expert evidence in a personal injury claim, particularly in a high value or complex claim. The need for expert evidence is not, of course, limited to medico-legal expert evidence; there may be need for expert evidence on the issue of liability (engineers, ergonomists etc) and other expertise on the quantum issues (eg accountants, employment experts, care experts, architects etc).

In high value claims it is essential that counsel is asked to advise on the need for expert evidence at an early stage. In most cases the choice of expert type is not a difficult one, but in a significant number of cases the right choice of expert is vital. Counsel and the solicitor should be encouraged to pool their knowledge of experts, because it may well be that a solicitor has experience of a particular expert that counsel does not have or vice versa. Such knowledge may well make or break a claim, particularly for example in a case where there are likely to be difficult issues of medical causation.

If counsel is involved in the obtaining and consideration of the expert evidence at an early stage then the shape of the evidence is likely to be properly developed. For example, counsel may take the view that an early conference with the expert will assist in identifying the correct issues and focusing the expert's mind on those issues when he comes to report. A pre-trial conference is vital to ensure that the expert is aware of the issues that are likely to be raised in cross-examination and to assist counsel to prepare for cross-examination of the other party's experts. Counsel should be asked to advise on the medical evidence in good time before any final hearing and, ideally, well before the joint report stage. It may be that some carefully considered Part 35 questions will identify the issues more clearly than the main report has done.

In high value claims it will almost always be essential to have a conference with counsel and the experts before the joint report stage, so that the final medical evidence can be considered alongside the other party's evidence in advance of the joint report. It may well be that there is an overlap between different areas of expertise and that one expert's view might be modified or enhanced by hearing what another expert has to say. For example, a care expert might well benefit from hearing from a neurosurgeon how it is anticipated that a claimant's condition might or might not deteriorate in later life. That alone might add a substantial amount to the overall value of the claim and might even lead to the need for further expert evidence (eg an architect to consider the costs of renovations to existing accommodation).

10.8   ADVISING IN CONFERENCE

The conference is a vital tool in personal injury litigation and choosing the right time to have a conference with counsel can often resolve a difficult claim. The relationship between a solicitor and his client is very different from that between counsel and the client. The former is often a more personal relationship, built up from first instruction through to conclusion of the claim. The latter is less personal and counsel will often find it easier to give unpalatable and objective advice than a solicitor might. Counsel will also benefit from an opportunity to assess the credibility of a witness and make a judgment as to what evidence should be called at trial.

When the conference takes place will depend on a number of factors. In cases with a complicated factual background (eg a stress at work claim, a claim involving a complex piece of machinery or an industrial disease claim), it may well be sensible to have a conference early in the case, so that counsel can understand the facts or the process involved in a way that might be difficult to ascertain from a witness statement. At the other end of the spectrum, a conference is often a better way of explaining to a claimant why a Part 36 offer should be accepted than a written advice.

Even in a relatively low value fast-track claim it will usually be advisable to have a conference with counsel and the key witnesses prior to any trial. Counsel will therefore have an opportunity of explaining to the witnesses the process to be expected at the trial and also to test the evidence. As a result, by the date of the actual trial it is likely that the evidence will be enhanced and more accurate: the witnesses' nerves will be better controlled and their minds more focused on the principal issues than if they simply were to walk cold into the witness box.

In a high value or complicated claim it is likely that there will need to be more than one conference in the run up to any trial or settlement. If counsel is involved early, as is recommended, then it is suggested that he should meet the client early in the process. That may be a matter of weeks after the accident. In a fatal accident claim counsel may well be instructed to represent the family of the deceased at an inquest and that process is made all the easier if counsel has met the family in conference prior to the hearing. Solicitors should not be afraid to ask counsel to travel to meet claimants at their homes or in hospital and it should not be assumed that conferences can only take place in counsels' chambers.

10.9   JOINT SETTLEMENT MEETING

Increasingly, parties seek to resolve high value or complicated claims at a meeting attended by all parties, a joint settlement meeting ('JSM'). In fact, courts now encourage parties to attend JSMs either by gentle persuasion or by order. An illustration of this is that some courts (eg Southampton county court and Brighton county court) will make an order that all parties attend a case management conference or pre-trial review with trial counsel with the aim of settling the claim on that day and the judges will actively try to mediate between the parties.

Counsel should be instructed in good time for the JSM because it will usually be necessary to draft a schedule of loss or a counter schedule if this has not already been done. Further, it is likely that there will be evidential issues that are best addressed in good time before the JSM. For example, it may be necessary to ask an expert questions about a particular issue before the claim can be finally valued.

Early instruction will also allow counsel and the solicitor to discuss the tactics to be employed at the JSM in advance of the actual meeting. It is also recommended that there is a conference with the client in advance of the JSM. That might be in the days or weeks before the appointed date of the JSM or it might be scheduled for earlier in the day of the JSM. Either way, it is good practice for the client to have met his counsel before the JSM begins so that tactics can be discussed with the client and up-to-date instructions taken.

It is not common practice to have experts at a JSM. However, there may well be situations in which the process is facilitated by having an expert available by telephone so that arguments raised by the opponent can be readily tested and responded to. Counsel should be asked well in advance of the JSM whether the presence of an expert should be sought.

CHAPTER 11

TRIAL

Rajeev Shetty

11.1 PERSUASIVE AND EVIDENTIAL BURDEN OF PROOF

The concepts of the legal (or persuasive) burden of proof and the evidential burden of proof are easily misunderstood.

The legal burden is an obligation that remains on the party for the duration of the claim. It is an obligation to prove or disprove a fact in issue to the required standard of proof. The standard of proof in a civil case is, of course, the balance of probabilities, which has also been described as proving a matter so that it is more likely than not. There is ample authority for a sliding scale of proof (moving up towards the criminal standard) if the allegations made by the claimant amount to serious misconduct or even criminal conduct but it is hard to see this applying in the context of a negligence/breach of duty case where such heightened allegations do not need to be made to pass the threshold of liability.

In general terms, the legal burden lies upon the party who asserts the affirmative of the issue.[1] In deciding which party asserts the affirmative, consideration must be given to the substance of the issue so that the court must consider whether the allegation is an essential part of a party's case; the proof of that allegation rests on him.

The legal burden of course carries with it a standard of proof. In civil proceedings, it is settled law that the standard is the balance of probabilities or, put another way, the allegation of fact is more likely than not to have happened.

The evidential burden is not in fact a burden of proof but the burden to adduce sufficient evidence to properly raise an issue at court. Generally, the party bearing the persuasive burden will also bear the evidential burden.[2]

---

[1]   See *Phipson on Evidence* (Sweet & Maxwell, 16th revised edition, 2005), ch 6 and *Robins v National Trust Co* [1927] AC 515, 520.

[2]   There may be some doubt as to this practicalities of this following the case of *Donna Egan v Central Manchester & Manchester Children's University Hospitals NHS Trust*

The evidential burden is 'to show, if called upon to do so, that there is sufficient evidence to raise an issue as to the existence or non-existence of a fact in issue, due regard being had to the standard of proof demanded of the party under such obligation'.[3]

In *Sheldrake v DPP*,[4] Lord Bingham described the evidential burden as not being a burden of proof but rather the burden of raising an issue as to the matter in question fit for consideration by the tribunal of fact. The evidential burden can rest on either party, although it usually relates to matters raised by the defence.

If, for example, a defendant is defending the issue of a particular statutory regulation such as reg 4(1)(a) of the Manual Handling Operations Regulations 1992 and it asserts that is was not reasonably practicable to avoid the claimant performing manual handling that involved a risk of injury, then there is an evidential and thereafter persuasive burden to raise the issue of reasonable practicability. That evidence can however come from witnesses for the claimant (in cross-examination) or in the course of the defence case. In practice, the evidential burden may shift back to the claimant to raise issues of what might have been practical (see the case of *Egan* which is summarised in fn 2).

In a highways tripping case under s 41 of the Highways Act 1980, once the claimant has surmounted the legal burden of proving that he suffered an accident as a consequence of an actionable defect on the highway, the evidential and persuasive burden shifts onto the defendant to prove its statutory defence under s 58 of the Highways Act 1980.

A further example would be the case of *Ward v Tesco Stores Ltd*.[5] Following the claimant proving that she slipped on a spillage of yoghurt, the Court of Appeal (Lawton LJ and Megan LJ with Omrod LJ dissenting) held that some explanation should be forthcoming from the defendants to show that the accident did not arise from any want of care on their part and, in the absence of any explanation, the judge may give judgment for the claimant. However such a burden was described as evidential rather than probative.

[2008] EWCA Civ 1424. In this case, the claimant sought damages for breach of statutory duty under the Manual Handling Operations Regulations 1992. The Court of Appeal stated that once it had been shown that the manual handling operation carried some risk of injury, the burden shifted on the defendant to plead and prove that it had taken appropriate steps to reduce that risk to the lowest level reasonably practicable. In practice, if allegations were made by the claimant that there were steps that could have been taken and the employer said there were none, there would be an evidential burden on the claimant to advance the suggestions even though the legal burden would remain on the employer (see para 22 of the judgment of Smith LJ).

3   *Cross and Tapper on Evidence* (OUP, 11th edn, 2007).
4   [2004] UKHL 43.
5   [1976] 1 WLR 810.

11.2 CONFLICT OF EVIDENCE AND FINDINGS OF FACT

Generally speaking there is a duty on the trial judge to decide the issues relevant to his judgment and not evade them. However a line of authorities recognises that there may be exceptional cases where the resolution of the ultimate issue, namely telling the truth, is blocked by an 'intractable evidential tangle'.[6] In such an exceptional case, a trial judge may hold that a claimant and a Part 20 claimant fail to prove either claim. The court's ability to do this was upheld by May LJ in *Morris v London Iron Steel Company*.[7] Of particular relevance to the personal injury practitioner is however the case of *Dorothy Cooper v (1) Floor Cleaning Machines Ltd (2) Dean Crompton*,[8] in which the Court of Appeal stated that it would be rare indeed that a motor accident case will fall into the exceptional category described by May LJ (as he then was) in *Morris*. This case involved a road traffic accident that occurred on the M25 motorway. The trial judge was unable to accept the evidence of either party and concluded that neither had established negligence on the part of the other and therefore dismissed the claim and counterclaim. The second defendant appealed on the grounds that the judge was wrong to have approached the case on this basis that there was one right story and one wrong story. The Court of Appeal stated that it would have been prudent for the judge to have raised with the parties at the end of their submissions that he was provisionally of the view that both claims failed on the basis of a failure to discharge the burden of proof. The Court of Appeal stated that 'what was inescapable was that the accident could not have occurred without at least one of the parties being negligent'. Furthermore it was incumbent upon the judge to analyse the evidence and conclude which account was more likely.[9] The court did refer to the case of *Baker v Market Harborough Industrial Co-Operative Society*,[10] in which the facts were that vehicles met in the middle of the road and there was no witness alive or able to 'tell the tale where there is an inference that both parties are equally to blame'.[11] However in this case there were two diametrically different accounts of how the accident happened.

In *Sewell v Electrolux Ltd*,[12] the Court of Appeal were confronted with an appeal from a recorder's finding that the claimant had failed to prove his case because of conflicting medical evidence. Following an accident at work, the claimant suffered substantial back pain and the issue before the recorder was whether it had been caused by the accident or by a pre-existing condition. Two orthopaedic surgeons gave conflicting opinions. The recorder did not summarise the expert evidence or analyse the strengths and weaknesses and simply announced in relation to this

---

6   Per Sedley LJ in *Ashraf v Akram* (unreported) 22 January 1999.
7   [1987] 2 All ER 496.
8   [2003] EWCA Civ 1649.
9   Per Scott Baker LJ at paras 13 and 15.
10   [1953] 1 WLR 1472.
11   Per Scott Baker at para 19.
12   (1997) *The Times*, 7 November.

issue, that the claimant had failed to discharge the burden of proof. The court held that the recorder had abdicated his duty to make findings and had failed to 'address and resolve the central issue and such of the subsidiary issues as it was necessary to resolve to decide the central issue'.[13]

These authorities were reviewed in the case of *(1) Stephen John Stephens (2) Sheila Dilys Stephens v (1) Charles Cannon (2) Sheila Cannon,*[14] in which Wilson J stated the following principles with regards to findings of fact and resort to the burden of proof:

'(a) The situation in which the court finds itself before it can dispatch a disputed issue by resort to the burden of proof has to be exceptional.

(b) Nevertheless the issue does not have to be of any particular type. A legitimate state of agnosticism can logically arise following enquiry into any type of disputed issue. It may be more likely to arise following an enquiry into, for example, the identity of the aggressor in an unwitnessed fight; but it can arise even after an enquiry, aided by good experts, into, for example, the cause of the sinking of a ship.

(c) The exceptional situation which entitles the court to resort to the burden of proof is that, notwithstanding that it has striven to do so, it cannot reasonably make a finding in relation to a disputed issue.

(d) A court which resorts to the burden of proof must ensure that others can discern that it has striven to make a finding in relation to a disputed issue and can understand the reasons why it has concluded that it cannot do so. The parties must be able to discern the court's endeavour and to understand its reasons in order to be able to perceive why they have won and lost. An appellate court must also be able to do so because otherwise it will not be able to accept that the court below was in the exceptional situation of being entitled to resort to the burden of proof.

(e) In a few cases the fact of the endeavour and the reasons for the conclusion will readily be inferred from the circumstances and so there will be no need for the court to demonstrate the endeavour and to explain the reasons in any detail in its judgment. In most cases, however, a more detailed demonstration and explanation in judgment will be necessary.'

11.3   FUNCTIONS OF THE JUDGE IN RELATION TO EXPERT EVIDENCE

There have been a number of cases decided on the issue of expert evidence. In *Flannery v Halifax Estate Agencies,*[15] the Court of Appeal stated that a judge had to give reasons for preferring the evidence of one

---

[13]   Per Hutchinson LJ.
[14]   [2005] EWCA Civ 222.
[15]   [2000] 1 WLR 377.

expert to another, and that failure to do so may be valid grounds for an appeal and for remitting the case back for a re-trial. It is not sufficient for a court to find favour with one expert because that expert was highly reputable and representative of a responsible body of medical opinion: *Smith v Southampton University Hospital NHS Trust.*[16]

In *(1) Smith (2) Co-Operative Group Ltd v Mark Hammond,*[17] the Court of Appeal was confronted with an appeal arising from (inter alia) the trial judge's rejection of expert evidence on reaction times given by an expert. The judge rejected the evidence on the basis that it did not accord with his own experience. The Court of Appeal allowed the appeal and stated a judge is not bound to accept the expert's evidence if he had good grounds for not doing so but if he was going to reject it he should give reasons for doing so other than simply saying that it did not accord with his own experience. Whilst it was tempting for judges when dealing with matters of everyday experience, to regard their own perceptions and experience as more reliable than the opinions of those who sought to describe such matters in scientific terms, the temptation should be resisted. There had been no satisfactory grounds for rejecting the expert's evidence on the matter, and if the judge had rejected it he had not been entitled to resort to his own experience to provide a basis for a different finding.[18]

11.4 COMMON ISSUES OF BURDEN OF PROOF IN PERSONAL INJURY LITIGATION: NEGLIGENCE, CONTRIBUTORY NEGLIGENCE, CAUSATION, MITIGATION

The claimant alleging negligence or breach of statutory duty has to get his case off the ground by proving the allegation. Proving causation arising out of negligence is also a matter of proof for the claimant.

Once the claimant proves these matters, he either succeeds or the defendant may try and establish a defence of reasonable practicability or a defence such as, for example, *ex turpi causa* or automatism.

Contributory negligence, although not strictly speaking a defence to the action as a whole, is for the defendant to prove. This applies to both the issue of fault and causation. The case of *Dawes v Aldis*[19] affirmed the view that there must be sufficient evidence on which to make a finding of contributory negligence. Put another way there is an evidential and legal burden on the accuser.

---

[16] [2007] EWCA Civ 387.
[17] [2010] EWCA Civ 725.
[18] See para 16 of the judgment of Moore-Bick LJ.
[19] [2007] EWHC 1831 (QB).

In respect of proving or disproving the quantum of damages, the general rule is that the onus of proving that a claimant has failed to mitigate his loss lies upon the defendant.[20]

11.5   RES IPSA LOQUITUR

The Latin maxim of *res ispa loquitur* (the thing speaks for itself) is an evidential presumption. It is used for situations where although there is a legal and evidential burden on the claimant to prove something (in the context of this book, typically negligence), he cannot prove exactly how a certain event occurred. When the circumstances of the accident speak for themselves, the claimant may rely upon the maxim *res ipsa loquitur*. The formulation of the principle can be found usefully summarised in the case of *Scott v London & St Katherine Docks Co*:[21]

> 'There must be reasonable evidence of negligence, but where the thing is shown to be under the management of the defendant or his servants, any accident is such that in the ordinary course of things does not happen if those who have the management use proper care, it affords reasonable evidence, in the absence of explanation by the defendant, that the accident arose from want of care.'

Where all the facts are known or there is another inference other than negligence, the maxim will not apply.

11.6   JUDICIAL NOTICE

Judicial notice is a rule in the law of evidence that allows a fact to be introduced into evidence without formal proof, such as calling a witness. There are two categories. The first category covers those matters that are so notorious or clearly established or susceptible of demonstration by reference to a readily obtainable and authoritative source that evidence of their existence is unnecessary. Secondly there are numerous statutory provisions that provide judicial notice to be given of specific matters.[22]

The reasoning behind judicial notice is that it would be a waste of resources to require a party to prove every fact through evidence.

Judicial notice will be taken of the existence and contents of all public statutes and all Acts of Parliament. Other examples of where judicial notice has been given are as to standards of weight and measure, coin and currency and its relative value, banking and accountancy practices, the meaning of common words, weather and time and medical matters that are within the province or an ordinary member of the public. The court is

---

20   *Garnac Grain Co Inc v HMF Faure & Fairclough Ltd* [1968] AC 1130 at 1140.
21   (1865) 2 H & C 596, 601 per Erle CJ.
22   See *Phipson on Evidence*, ch 3, for a full analysis of the concept.

allowed for example to take judicial notice of the fact that a city such as London is busy in certain areas and at certain times.

11.7 THE CIVIL PROCEDURE RULES AND EVIDENCE AT TRIAL

The Civil Procedure Rules (the CPR) place considerable emphasis on both parties preparing their cases pre-trial with an increased relaxation in respect of evidence at trial.

The CPR provide a comprehensive set of rules to govern and assist the court with regards to evidence during a trial. Parts 32 and 33 are the relevant sections.

11.7.1 Hearings in public – the general rule and exceptions

Whilst CPR 39.2(1) states that the general rule is that 'a hearing is to be in public', CPR 39.2(3) states that a hearing, or any part of it, may be in private if:

(a) publicity would defeat the object of the hearing;

(b) it involves matters of national security;

(c) it involves confidential information (including information relating to personal financial matters) and publicity would damage that confidentiality;

(d) it is necessary to protect the interests of any child or patient;

(e) it is a hearing of an application made without notice and it would be unjust to any respondent for there to be a public hearing;

(f) it involves uncontentious matters arising in the administration of trusts or in the administration of a deceased person's estate; or

(g) the court considers this to be necessary in the interest of justice.

This reflects s 12 of the Administration Act 1960. CPR 39.2(3)(g) gives the court wide discretion. The question of whether evidence should be excluded on the ground of public interest and whether the court should sit in private are distinct. Once it is determined that the immunity attaches, the evidence is excluded as a matter of law and the court has no discretion to admit it on terms that it be heard in private.[23]

---

[23] See *Powell v Chief Constable of North Wales* [1999] EWCA Civ 2097.

CPR 39.2(4) also states that a court may order that the identity of any party or witness must not be disclosed if it considers non-disclosure necessary in order to protect the interests of that party or the witness.

In respect of general principles covering anonymity, the Court of Appeal in *R v Legal Aid Board, ex p Kaim Todner*[24] (pre-CPR) held that the decision was one for the judge based on principles in *Scott v Scott*[25] and A-G v *Leveller Magazine*.[26] Any protection against identification must depend on some exception to the general rule that all proceedings should be conducted in public. Those not involved in proceedings were more likely to be entitled to anonymity than those involved. Protection for a limited period was less of a restriction than blanket protection and would be looked on more favourably.

11.7.2 Admissibility

CPR 32.1(2) gives the court the power to 'exclude evidence that would otherwise be admissible'. Unhelpfully the CPR does not give the court further assistance as to principles to be applied to the exercise of this discretion. It is submitted that the court must regard evidence as admissible unless there is good reason to exclude otherwise admissible evidence. The discretion should be exercised fairly and with due regard to the overriding objective. Relevance to the issue would ultimately be an important consideration for the court.

In *O'Brien v Chief Constable of South Wales*,[27] the House of Lords considered the issue of admissibility of similar fact evidence. After a review of both civil and criminal authorities on the topic, the court stated that the test for admissibility of such evidence is relevance as becoming potentially probative of an issue in the case. Whilst there was no need to insist on the additional requirements for admissibility of such evidence that apply to criminal cases, a judge managing a civil case should keep well in mind (a) the policy considerations found in the Criminal Justice Act 2003 (that deal with bad character) and (b) the need to deal with the case in such a way that was proportionate to what was involved, in a manner that was expeditious and fair.

11.7.3 Proving facts

CPR 32.2(1)(a) provides that facts that need to be proved by the evidence of witnesses should be proved at trial by oral evidence given in public. For claims brought under CPR Part 8, CPR 8.6(1) provides that the case will be heard on the basis of the written evidence only.

---

24 [1999] QB 966, CA.
25 [1913] AC 417.
26 [1979] AC 440.
27 [2005] UKHL 26.

Not every fact needs to be proved by the formal production of evidence. This is where the doctrine of judicial notice comes into play (see above).

11.7.4 Witnesses

The CPR does not set out the order in which witnesses must be called. Typically factual witnesses will be dealt with first by both sides sequentially and then experts of like discipline are called. If there is more than one defendant, there is no set practice as to whether the claimant should cross-examine before or after other defendants have done the same.

11.7.5 Trial bundles

It is good practice where possible to agree the contents of the trial bundle. Under Practice Direction (PD) 39, para 3.9, documents in the trial bundle may be treated as evidence of the facts stated in them even if a notice under the Civil Evidence Act 1995 has not been served. Parties are taken to accept that documents disclosed to them are authentic unless they serve notice that they wish the document to be proved at trial under CPR 32.19. Such notice must be served by the latest date for serving witness statements or within seven days of disclosure of the document.

11.7.6 Examination-in-chief

CPR 32.1(3) provides specific power to limit cross-examination; however there is no equivalent rule to limit examination-in-chief. However the court has general case management powers under CPR 32.1(1) to control the evidence by giving directions.

Generally, under CPR 32.5(2) where a witness is called to give oral evidence, his witness statement shall stand as his evidence-in-chief unless the court orders otherwise. This is in keeping with the requirement set out in CPR 32.1(c), which covers the court's power to give directions as to the way in which evidence is to be placed before the court. The discretion is purely a matter for the trial judge. Typically a judge will consider whether the witnesses' credibility is in issue if, for example, there are allegations of fraud.

Supplemental questions are often asked in practice at trial and the general attitude of the courts is that they should be allowed. However it is in the trial judge's discretion as to whether he wishes to permit supplementary questions intended to elicit evidence not in the witness statement. CPR 32.5(3) states that permission must be sought for supplemental questions to be asked that (a) amplify a witness statement or (b) give evidence of new matters arising since the statement was served on other parties. The relevant rule states that the court will only give permission if it considers that there is 'good reason' not to confine the evidence of the witness to the contents of his witness statement (CPR 32.5(4)).

Examples of such situations may be where a witness needs to point out locations on maps, plans or photographs. It is submitted that it is always good practice for the intention to be notified in advance to the other party before the trial. To do otherwise risks the potential of suggested ambush or prejudice. It is further submitted that if the party had the opportunity to serve a supplemental witness statement dealing with such matters, then this might lead a judge to conclude that there is no good reason to allow further examination-in-chief.

When a witness is called and the witness statement is to stand as evidence-in-chief, the common practice is for the witness to take an oath or affirmation and then confirm his or her identity by way of name and address, then confirm the contents of the witness statement and the signature. It almost goes without saying that any errors in the witness statement should be identified at the outset by counsel inviting the witness to do the same. Counsel will then typically ask for the witness statement to be the witness's examination-in-chief.

If examination-in-chief is taken by questions and answers, there is a bar to leading questions, which suggest the answer within the question (questions such as 'and was it after seeing the car turn right that you decided to cross the road?'). A useful rule of thumb is that typically questions starting with 'When, why, who, what and how' tend not to be leading questions.

At common law there was a rule against a party attempting to discredit his own witness. For example, if a witness refuses to adopt his witness statement or appears to show a hostile attitude towards the claimant despite being his witness, then the claimant may wish to put to him his previous inconsistent statement or ask him about other matters that may undermine him. A judge may allow a party to cross-examine his own witness if that is necessary in the interests of justice. Section 6(3) of the Civil Evidence Act 1995, provides that s 3, 4 or 5 of the Criminal Procedure Act 1865 apply.

11.7.7 Cross-examination

Cross-examination follows examination in chief. Leading questions are permitted (and indeed should be encouraged!). A party is not restricted to cross-examine on matters adduced in chief. Questions must be relevant but oblique questions are common when it comes to matters of credibility.

A witness should be cross-examined on any evidence that is not accepted and that the asking party wishes to challenge.[28] The general rule is that a party should put to his opponent's witnesses as much of his own case as concerns that particular witness. This practice was affirmed in *Deepak Fertilizers Ltd v Davy McKee* Ltd.[29] A judge can conclude that a party is taken to accept a witnesses' account on any issue that he is not challenged about. Witnesses can be recalled at the judge's discretion if counsel fails to cross-examine on relevant matters that require challenge. If a party wishes to challenge a witnesses' testimony in whole or substantially by suggesting that the witness has fabricated his evidence then counsel can sometimes mention to the judge that he does not propose to go over every single point when the attack is on credibility as a whole.

Part of the court taking an active role in case managing under the CPR reforms was reflected in the court's power to limit cross-examination under CPR 32.1(3). This could be limited as to issues or timing. This discretion must not be exercised unreasonably. So in *Hayes v Transco plc*,[30] a decision by the trial judge to restrict cross-examination of an important witness to five more minutes was held to be wrong in principle and unfair to the other party. The trial judge also refused the defendant's application to adduce in evidence a supplementary witness statement of one of their witnesses where it contained a matter relevant to that cross-examination. Indeed it amounted to a serious procedural irregularity within the meaning of CPR 52.11(3)(b). This can be compared to the case of *Three Rivers DC v Bank of England*,[31] where the trial judge ordered that a cross-examination of one of the defendant's witnesses, that was estimated to last 12 weeks, should be limited to seven weeks. The Court of Appeal dismissed the claimant's appeal against the ruling.

CPR 32.11 provides that a witness called to give evidence may be cross-examined on his witness statement, whether or not the statement or any part of it was referred to during the witness's evidence-in-chief.

With regards to medical or expert evidence generally, there should be no need for the report to be amplified or tested by cross-examination at trial.[32]

There is a general rule as to finality when cross-examining on collateral matters. It is submitted that this rule is honoured more in the breach than observance and quite often a party is permitted to use evidence to contradict a matter that is raised by a witness in cross-examination.

---

[28]   *Browne v Dunn* (1894) R 67, HL.
[29]   [2002] EWCA Civ 1396.
[30]   [2003] EWCA Civ 1261.
[31]   [2005] EWCA 889.
[32]   *Peet v Mid Kent Healthcare Trust* [2001] EWCA Civ 1703.

11.7.8　Re-examination

This should be restricted to matter arising out of cross-examination. The rule against leading questions still applies. Counsel sometimes asks questions that are not re-examination with the permission of the judge. This will inevitably lead to permission for the opposing party to cross-examine on the new piece of evidence if necessary.

11.7.9　Submission of no case to answer

At the end of the claimant's case, a defendant may submit that there is no case to answer. If the submission succeeds judgment may be given for the defendant without requiring him to call evidence.

Such submissions are now exceedingly rare. However a defendant can make a submission at the end of the claimant's case. If this submission succeeds then the defendant is entitled to judgment without having to adduce evidence. The test is whether there is no such case for the judge to put to himself whilst wearing his jury hat.[33]

In *Benham Ltd v Kythira Investments Ltd*,[34] Simon Brown LJ (as he then was) said that the test is whether or not, on the evidence adduced by the claimant, the claimant has 'a real prospect of success', but accepted that this test is not altogether clear. His Lordship stated the test could be whether the claimant had 'advanced a prima facie case to answer, a scintilla of evidence in support of the inference for which they contend, sufficient to call for an explanation from the defendant?' His Lordship also stated that the fact that the claimant's case may be weak and unlikely to succeed unless assisted, rather than contradicted, by the defendant's evidence, or by adverse inferences to be drawn from the defendant not calling any evidence, would not allow it to be dismissed on a no-case submission.

There is enormous tactical disadvantage to the defendant in that he is put to his election as to whether to call evidence.[35] The judge has discretion not to put the defendant to his election but this discretion should be rarely used.[36]

---

[33]　*Bentley v Jones Harris & Co* [2001] EWCA Civ 1724.

[34]　[2003] EWCA Civ 1794, CA.

[35]　*Boyce v Wyatt Engineering* [2001] EWCA Civ 692; *Miller v Cawley* (2002) *The Times*, 6 September.

[36]　*Cross and Tapper on Evidence* (OUP, 11th edn, 2007), *Phipson on Evidence* (Sweet & Maxwell, 16th revised edition, 2005).

CHAPTER 12

QUANTUM EVIDENCE

Shahram Sharghy

12.1 HEADS OF DAMAGE

12.1.1 General damages

The term 'general damages' covers a number of heads of loss, and is used as a collective term for damages that are not special damages ie 'non-pecuniary' loss.

The main heads of general damage are:

- pain, suffering and loss of amenity (damages for injuries sustained);

- loss of congenial employment (loss of enjoyment from a particular job or skill set);

- loss of enjoyment (such as a holiday or activity);

- loss of use (such as of a vehicle);

- loss of leisure (such as where more hours have to be worked in a lesser paid job to keep at the same pre-accident earnings level).

Although traditionally items of general damages were not included in the schedule of loss, this is no longer the case in the modern era of Civil Procedure Rules ('CPR') where practitioners are encouraged to set out which items of general damages are being claimed, the value placed on the same, as well as the evidence in support.

12.1.2 Special damages

The fundamental principle in respect of recovery of 'pecuniary' loss is that the claimant should, so far as possible, be put back in the financial position he would have been in 'but for' the wrongdoing of the defendant. In considering the recoverability and assessment of special damages, a practitioner needs to bear in mind the following general principles:

- To be recoverable, the expense/loss claimed must be recognised in law and not be prohibited by reason of illegality or public policy.

- The expense/loss must be the claimant's or, alternatively, must fall into one of the recognised exceptions for claiming on behalf of third parties such as a claim for care and assistance.

- The expense/loss claimed must be attributable to the defendant's wrongdoing.

- The defendant takes his victim as they find them. As long as personal injury was a foreseeable outcome of the defendant's breach of duty, the defendant will remain liable for the claimant's expense/loss notwithstanding the fact that it is out of proportion to the injuries sustained (the 'eggshell skull' principle).

- Both the incurring of the expense/loss in principle and the amount of the same must be 'reasonable' – this is to be judged from the standpoint of the claimant.

- The claimant is entitled to recover only his 'net' loss.

- The expense/loss must actually have been incurred as opposed to being notional or hypothetical, but damages may be recovered for lost opportunities arising between the date of the wrongdoing and the date of trial as long as the lost chance can be said to be 'real' or 'substantial'.

- The claimant may recover a reasonable expense/loss incurred in attempting to mitigate his injury, loss or damage, even if the costs of an attempt to mitigate adds to the overall loss, but the defendant is entitled to the benefit of any successful mitigation.

- Damages may not be recovered for an expense/loss that would have occurred or been incurred in any event.

- The amount recoverable may be reduced by reason of contributory negligence.

- A claimed expense/loss may be reduced where the claimant has been guilty of deliberate exaggeration or malingering.

- Interest will be awarded on past expenses/losses in order to compensate the claimant for being kept out of his money.

While in theory there is an unlimited range of potential expenses/losses which may be claimed, there are a number of defined heads that have been developed over time and that are recognised heads of loss for which evidence will need to be obtained/collected in order to recover the same:

- loss of earnings;

- pension loss;

- medical and treatment expenses;

- medication and prescription charges;

- care and assistance (whether professional or gratuitous);

- aids, equipment and appliances;

- accommodation/housing expenses (either because of a forced move or alteration, extension or adaptation);

- travel and transport expenses;

- damages for destroyed clothing and property;

- inability to perform domestic tasks such as DIY, painting, decorating, gardening, window cleaning and the like;

- increased household bills such as heating, water, gas, electricity costs while the claimant was recuperating from his injuries;

- inability to care for others necessitating payment for professional or other assistance;

- additional holiday costs such as the provision of extra leg room on flights, car hire for transportation and similar additional expenses arising out of the claimant's injuries;

- increased leisure costs;

- costs of education, training and other professional courses.

A schedule of loss does not have to be cumbersome. When a claimant first attends for interview, a practitioner should not only be thinking about proof of liability but also about proof of losses. It is now more important than ever to assess the value of the claim at an early stage because it may well affect the funding of the claim. For example, if a practitioner is considering taking a case on a conditional fee basis, he might think twice if the claim is likely to fall within the small claims track. Alternatively if the value of the claim is high ie over £50,000, it is likely to affect the premium to be paid for ATE insurance to guard against an adverse costs order.

12.2   GATHERING EVIDENCE TO PROVE THE LOSS

12.2.1   The claimant

The primary (and most obvious) source of evidence is the claimant. It is important that when taking a statement from the claimant, he describes life before the accident as well as life afterwards. The claimant should describe the physical and mental anguish he has gone through as a result of the accident. The statement should also set out the difference in his capabilities and enjoyment of life before and after the accident. Within this description the claimant should also be asked to set out his limitations, restrictions and other difficulties that were endured post-accident and that were not present prior to the same. He should be asked to explain the longevity of each limitation and restriction and whether this is continuing, fully recovered, intermittent or activity-related.

The statement should also record the past and future medical treatment, the operations he may have had, visits to his GP, hospital, physiotherapy and any other steps taken to seek treatment for his injuries that have arisen out of the accident.

One of the most common errors that practitioners make is to use the accident questionnaire provided by a claims handling company/agency or indeed the claimant himself as the basis for the statement which is subsequently drafted and served on the defendant and the court. The difficulty with this method of obtaining evidence is that it often lacks detail, is out of date by the time a statement comes to be drafted and notably misses out some of the most important pieces of evidence that are likely to make a difference to the level of damages awarded to the claimant.

Therefore practitioners should (as a matter of good practice) seek to obtain full and detailed instructions from the claimant at an early stage so that they are fully aware of the impact which the accident has had on the claimant's daily life and capabilities. This information can then be reduced to writing in the form of a detailed witness statement that set out the pre- and post-accident situation, which in turn informs the defendant and the court about the pain, suffering and loss of amenity that was suffered by the claimant as a result of the accident, together with specific expenses/losses arising out the same. Another benefit of obtaining a detailed witness statement from the claimant at an early stage is that this document can form part of the instructions to the medical (or other) expert and will allow that expert to provide an opinion on the limitation, restriction and/or other difficulties complained of by the claimant. If the claimant's reported symptoms are able to be corroborated by an expert report this is likely to further strengthen his claim for the damages sought.

The claimant is under an obligation to outline how he feels about the injuries and the continuing effect of the same on his life as well as the impact that this has had on others such as family, friends and work colleagues. If he does not provide this full and detailed description of the impact of the accident on his life, there is a danger that a judge will not have a true and accurate picture and this is likely to lead to the award for damages not truly reflecting the loss he had suffered.

12.2.2 The importance of the first interview

Having received the initial details of the claim via a claims handling agent or other source, the practitioner will need to be tactful at the first interview with the client (whether this is conducted on the phone or in person). One of the main aims of this meeting/discussion is to ascertain the approximate value of the claim without building up the claimant's hopes that he is going to receive a large sum of money. From the claimant's perspective he is really only interested in knowing two things: (1) 'do I have a good claim?' and (2) 'how much will I get?' One usually finds that if a claimant is given figures (however approximate) at the first interview, they find it difficult to revise those figures downwards as evidence is gathered and/or accept changes for the worse in future.

As set out above an initial detailed statement should be taken setting out the injuries the claimant has suffered, how those injuries have affected his life and the expenses and losses that have been incurred to date. In setting about drafting this statement all areas of the claimant's life should be considered such as work, domestic, social and leisure. Particular attention will need to be paid to any losses that are continuing. Efforts should be made to obtain 'tangible' evidence of losses such as photographs of lost or damaged property or goods which are being claimed. This is to avoid any future dispute regarding their recoverability.

12.2.3 Statements from family and friends

Statements in support of the claimant's claim for damages can often assist the claimant in receiving an increase in his award but is all too often overlooked by practitioners. Often claimants may be reluctant to reveal the true impact of the injuries they have sustained in an accident. This could be for a variety of reasons such as the inability to come to terms with the injuries or the change in lifestyle. This reluctance often extends to the medical profession such that medical records/reports may well not provide an accurate diagnosis and prognosis of a claimant's injuries and any ongoing symptoms. However, claimant's can seldom hide the physical and emotional impact of their injuries from family and friends and, as such, the latter class of witness may well be capable of providing a judge with accurate evidence of how a claimant has been affected by the accident and the injuries sustained.

12.2.4   Medical records

Practitioners should obtain a claimant's medical records (GP, hospital, physiotherapy) as soon as practicable. This is important for a number of reasons:

- to identify any relevant medical history or problem;

- to support the claimant's version of events regarding the circumstances in which the injury was sustained including the facts surrounding the accident;

- to indicate the nature and severity of the injuries sustained;

- to detail the nature and extent of any past or ongoing treatment;

- to assess the reasonableness of the care/treatment received;

- to give an indication of how the injuries have affected the claimant and the extent of any ongoing disability;

- to see whether or not the claimant has made any previous claims for personal injury;

- to assist the practitioner in considering the approximate value of the claim;

- to consider the most appropriate field of expertise from which to obtain a medical opinion.

12.2.5   Types of medical records

There are many types of medical records that a practitioner should consider obtaining. The most common categories include:

- ambulance and paramedic records;

- GP notes and records;

- accident and emergency records;

- hospital in-patient and out-patient records;

- psychiatric records;

- counselling/therapy records;

- pain clinic notes and records;

- physiotherapy, osteopathy, chiropractic treatment, acupuncture and any other forms of alternative therapy records;

- dental records;

- optician records;

- rehabilitation records; and

- records relating to private treatment by doctors, surgeons and nurses.

The claimant's medical records and notes may be voluminous and at times illegible. In those circumstances, and where the gravity/value of the case requires it, a practitioner should consider utilising the services of a medical sorting agency who can provide invaluable help and assistance to separate the different records, arrange them in chronological order and advise upon any medical records that may be missing. It is not uncommon for a claimant's medical records to be incomplete. For example some relevant documents may not be kept in the claimant's medical records and are not normally disclosed unless specifically asked for. In many cases it will be necessary to see the original x-rays, CT or MRI scans. In addition a claimant may wish to have sight of adverse outcome/incident reports, and any complaints file or reports from independent reviews/ investigations. These documents are ordinarily disclosable if specifically asked for and would not attract legal professional privilege unless it can be shown that the sole or dominant purpose of the document when it first came into being was for legal advice in actual or contemplated litigation.[1]

The procedure for obtaining a claimant's medical records is relatively simple and standard now. Generally speaking, a claimant has a right to seek access to his medical records under the Access to Health Records Act 1990 or the Data Protection Act 1998. The claimant also has the right to be sent copies of any records for a maximum fee of £50. The record holder must supply the claimant with copies within 40 days of receiving the request for disclosure or payment, whichever is later.

12.2.6 Disclosure of medical records to the defendant

Historically, the defendant to a personal injury claim was entitled to obtain disclosure of the claimant's entire medical records because they were considered to be relevant and necessary to decide the important issues between the parties. That was until the implementation of the

---

[1] *Waugh v British Railways Board* [1980] AC 521.

Human Rights Act 1998, which in turn implemented into UK law Art 8 of the European Convention on Human Rights. In the case of *MS v Sweden*[2] the European Court of Human Rights held that the applicant's medical history and medical records were part of her private life. However, under Art 8(2) the disclosure of the applicant's medical records was justified because it was held to be in accordance with law, was founded on a legitimate aim and necessary in a democratic society. The position may well be different, however, where the other party is not a public authority and therefore cannot rely on Art 8(2).

More recently in the case of *Bennett v Compass Group UK*[3] the Court of Appeal has provided helpful guidance on the issue:

- The combined effect of CPR 31.3, 31.6 and 31.8 mean that the defendant has a right to inspect the claimant's medical records.

- In the ordinary course of events, it will be for the claimant (and/or his legal representatives) to obtain a copy of the medical records, and for the defendant to request inspection of the same, rather than the defendant being granted authority to obtain the records directly from the relevant bodies.

- In exceptional cases, it may be necessary to apply to the court for an order that the defendant be given authority to obtain copies of the claimant's medical records directly, in default of which the claim be stayed. However, care should be taken to ensure that the terms of any such order are clearly and carefully defined in order to protect the claimant's rights, whether under the European Convention of Human Rights or otherwise.

12.2.7   Medical evidence

When instructing a medical expert it is important to choose the expert with the most appropriate qualifications to provide an expert opinion on the diagnosis and prognosis of the claimant's injuries as well as the likely impact that the accident has had on the claimant in terms of limitation, restriction and other difficulties and the likelihood that this may continue into the future. It is generally not advised to seek an opinion from a general practitioner when the claimant has sustained serious injuries such as a fracture, serious soft tissue injury, ligament damage or psychological injury, except for the most minor of travel anxieties that can probably be adequately dealt with by a general practitioner. This is because in each of the circumstances mentioned, it is likely that an orthopaedic surgeon with a specialism in the limb that has been injured or a psychologist/ psychiatrist is required to provide a judge with an authoritative opinion on the medical position of the claimant.

---

[2]   [1997] 3 BHRC 248.
[3]   [2002] EWCA Civ 642.

All too often a practitioner simply relies on the medical agency to provide the 'most suitable' expert for a particular case. It should be borne in mind that the medical agency does not know the circumstances of the accident or the injuries sustained better than the file handler. The choices provided by the medical agency must be scrutinised carefully to ensure that the CV of the medical experts proposed are suitable for the particular case. For example, if the claimant has suffered from a fracture to his ankle with ongoing symptoms, a choice of three orthopaedic experts without a specialism in lower limb injuries may not be appropriate.

It is also important to ensure that the letter of instruction to the medical expert is detailed and focused on the issues that the expert is being asked to provide an opinion on. The following is a short list of factors to ask the medical expert to place in his report:

- the date of birth and age of the claimant;

- accurate details of the accident – the expert would be greatly assisted by the detailed witness statement discussed above;

- a full history of the injuries suffered, the treatment provided, present condition and a prognosis for the future;

- description of the limitation that the accident places on the claimant's working and social life;

- indication whether there is a mental element to the claimant's symptoms, which, depending on its severity, can be investigated by separate psychiatric/psychological evidence;

- confirmation, where appropriate, that there is no past medical history of relevance in relation to the diagnosis and prognosis;

- where there was a relevant pre-existing injury, the likely future course of those symptoms but for the accident and any medical studies and/or papers in support;

- documents that the expert has read, including x-rays, scans, medical reports. The expert should also indicate what further documents he requires before finalising his opinion.

12.2.8   Other helpful documents

In addition to the evidence discussed above, photographs are of great assistance when dealing with a claimant who has a noticeable physical deformity or scarring. However, in order to provide a judge with the assistance that he is likely to need in reviewing a physical deformity or scarring, the practitioner should obtain photographs of the claimant pre- as well as post-accident. In so far as the availability of post-accident photographs is concerned the practitioner should consider obtaining professional photographs so that the physical deformity or scarring can be seen clearly from different angles and distances. Photographs taken by the claimant and/or his family soon after the accident may be of assistance in demonstrating the appearance of the deformity or scarring shortly after the accident. Practitioners should also inform the claimant that he should take additional photographs of the deformity or scarring at regular intervals from the date of the accident until trial in order to illustrate the evolution of the deformity or scarring.

Where a practitioner deals with a claimant who used to be proficient in a particular sport, hobby or had a particular skill set. It is important not only to detail this in the claimant's statement but also obtain any certificates or other document that evidences the claimant's abilities and proficiency.

12.3   DOCUMENTARY PROOF

12.3.1   Receipts, invoices, valuations and estimates

The general rule is that the more evidence that is collated in support of the claim for damages, the more likely it is that it will succeed. When beginning the task of collecting evidence in relation to loss and damage, practitioners should consider the three main heads that are likely to be claimed (1) damages for pain, suffering and loss of amenity, (2) loss of earnings, and (3) costs in respect of the need for services such as care and assistance, medical treatment and DIY. On many occasions the claimant may incur an expense that is recoverable as a head of loss/damage, but has either not kept the receipt or proof of payment. Practitioners should inform the claimant at the first interview when the claim is discussed to start looking for receipts and to keep the same if any further costs are incurred. They should also be told that if receipts are not kept then it may well not be recoverable against the defendant who will almost certainly insist on proof of payment/purchase. Practitioners can assist clients with their record keeping by providing them with a document such as that set out below on the back of an A4 envelope so that costs incurred can be noted and the receipts kept inside the envelope. Even if the claimant has not kept receipts for past expenditure that has been incurred if he is able to produce bank or credit card statements to prove payment for the items then these may well assist in recovering the sum so long as the table below is filled in and the statements are placed inside the said envelope.

Date	Receipted item	Comments on item of expenditure	Cost

12.3.2 Details of the claimant's employment

If the claimant was employed at the time of the accident then he may well have kept copies of his payslips. Alternatively the practitioner can obtain earnings details from the claimant's employer (who in some cases is the defendant). A practitioner should usually ask for the claimant's gross and net figures for the 13 weeks prior to the accident. If the practitioner believes that this period may not necessarily be representative of the claimant's earning potential or lost salary, then he should ask for the figures a longer period. Such circumstances may arise where for example a bonus is paid annually and the last 13 weeks do not record this payment. Alternatively, if the claimant's income is seasonal, it is worth analysing the claimant's salary over the same period in the preceding years before the accident. The following information may also be of use to the practitioner and should be requested from the claimant's employer:

- any changes in rates of pay or hours of work since the accident;

- the claimant's P60 and/or P45;

- any additional overtime payments (if these are not detailed in the salary information);

- any additional bonus payments (if these are not detailed in the salary information);

- any additional holiday pay (if these are not detailed in the salary information);

- promotional opportunities – including how many had arisen prior to and post-accident which the claimant may reasonably have applied for and had a chance of being successful;

- pension details – to include the analysis of the lump sum and periodical payments 'but for' the accident and the position as a result of the accident;

- the claimant's personnel file;

- the claimant's medical/occupational health file;

- a copy of the claimant's contract of employment; and

- confirmation regarding whether the claimant is obliged to repay any sick pay payments as a result of a third party's negligence.

12.3.3   Self-employed claimant

If the claimant was self-employed at the date of the accident, he should be asked to produce copies of their business records, business accounts and tax returns for the relevant period of incapacity, together with material that will enable a comparison with previous performance. This will usually involve an examination of any annual accounts, copies of tax returns and in most cases may need the claimant to ask his accountant or tax adviser to compile up-to-date figures so that the relevant information can be analysed and entered into the schedule of loss.

12.3.4   The unemployed claimant

If the claimant was unemployed at the time of the accident but was either studying or training with a view to starting a new job or was just about to start a new job at the time of the accident, the claim for loss of earnings is more commonly claimed as a 'loss of chance' or, if the disability is longer term, for a disability on the labour market. This latter claim will, in such cases, closely resemble a claim for continuing loss of earnings as opposed to the more limited *Smith v Manchester* claim. In these cases the practitioner should obtain and collate as much information and evidence as possible in order to support the claimant's assertion that he would have succeeded in their chosen career. The claimant's training, qualifications, knowledge and experience should be ascertained in relation to the job. Details should be obtained regarding salary, promotional opportunities and pension entitlement. Where there is a concrete job offer available to the claimant, documentary evidence, such as the contract of employment, should be obtained, if possible, in order to see whether or not the claimant would have been subject to a probationary period or whether any unusual terms would have applied. Evidence should also be sought from the claimant's previous employers regarding the claimant's skill, abilities and general employability, and from the prospective employers regarding their opinion of the claimant's suitability for the position.

12.3.5   Employment evidence

One of the most useful sources of evidence in order to prove a loss of earnings claim (particularly concerning rare or unusual jobs, where statistical information is in short supply) is to obtain evidence from a comparator. Where the claimant loses a job that someone else is now doing or there are comparable positions in other companies, the court will be greatly assisted by evidence from a comparator stating the level of salary he receives, including all benefits and perks, as well as any increases or bonuses that have been received prior to the trial or which are likely to be received. Alternatively, such evidence may be obtained from a human resources employee or an employment consultant. A note of caution should be made here – the comparator must be in materially the same position as the claimant.

If there is any doubt about the claimant's employment history, the practitioner should request a copy of the claimant's employment history from HM Revenue and Customs. Since 1 October 2003, HM Revenue and Customs will supply employment history free of charge for a criminal injury compensation or personal injury claim.

12.3.6 Details of the claimant's care

When a practitioner is considering a claim for care it is important to bear in mind that the court will require cogent and clear evidence that the regime implemented for the benefit of the claimant is and was 'reasonable'. The general principles regarding mitigation of loss will be relevant. The test for judging the claimant's actions is not particularly high and is usually judged objectively, taking into account only matters known at the time. It is important to remember that a 'reasonable' course of action that is taken by the claimant does not necessarily have to be the cheapest.

When considering the reasonableness of a claim for care, consideration must be given to the following matters (amongst other things):

- the nature and severity of the claimant's injuries (including any special needs or challenging behaviour);

- the suitability of the care regime to the claimant's needs;

- whether the claimant has been shown to benefit from the care regime in question;

- whether there were any cheaper alternatives which would have adequately met the claimant's needs;

- whether there has been any overlap in the care provided to the claimant;

- whether the care regime was instituted on the advice of treating health professionals;

- the claimant's background, culture and religion.

The majority of people who are injured do not have sufficient funds to pay for professional nursing care, and are therefore reliant upon friends and relatives in order to meet their care needs. The law recognises that a claimant is able to recover damages for the value of nursing services provided gratuitously by a friend or relative. As such the loss belongs to the carer and not the claimant. However, as the carer cannot bring a direct claim against the defendant wrongdoer, such a loss is claimed by the claimant on the carer's behalf.[4] The object of the award is to enable the voluntary carer to receive proper recompense for his services. However as there is no conventional way of quantifying this loss, it is often left for the judge to decide on the appropriate level of award having regard to all the circumstances of the case, in particular the severity of the injury, the period of disability/functional difficulty and the duration of the care and assistance reasonably required. An approach often used is to make an award based on what a professional provider of such care would have charged, subject to a reduction to reflect the tax and NIC aspect foregone (the reduction is usually in between 20–25 per cent but there is no hard-and-fast rule).

In more serious cases, it may be necessary to appoint a care manager whose duties may well include the following:

- implementing and managing the claimant's care regime;

- hiring, firing and disciplining of carers;

- arranging contracts for carers and organising payroll;

- carrying out CRB and background checks on potential carers;

- carrying out risk assessments;

- helping to draw up job descriptions, staff rotas and information packs;

- helping to select an appropriate care agency and then liaising between the claimant and the claimant's care manager at the agency (if care is sourced through an agency);

- liaising between the claimant and different healthcare professionals (such as medical experts, physiotherapists, speech and language therapists, carers, occupational therapists and the like);

- ensuring that the claimant's care needs are being met and recommending any changes to the existing system;

---

[4]   *Hunt v Severs* [1994] 2 AC 350.

- managing the claimant's financial affairs and ensuring entitlement to state benefits;

- helping to plan appropriate holidays;

- dealing with accommodation issues, including helping to find suitable alternative accommodation and assisting with locating suitable architects and builders with a view to carrying out necessary adaptations;

- ensuring that the claimant is adequately insured;

- attending multi-disciplinary team meetings.

The more structured the claimant's environment – such as residential accommodation – the less likely it is that a care manager will be justified. Furthermore, the practitioner should keep a close and careful eye on the costs of any care manager, to ensure that the same is 'reasonable' and accords with any previous estimate given.

12.3.7 Details of aids, equipment and appliances

So long as an expense can be shown to have arisen out of a genuine medical or therapeutic need and is reasonably necessary for the claimant, the cost of such item(s) is likely to be recoverable. However, the following questions should be considered when advancing such a claim in order to ensure that appropriate evidence has been obtained to support the expense/loss:

- Is the claim for an aid, appliance or item of equipment supported by the medical evidence?

- Does the claimant have the necessary capacity to use and benefit from the aid, appliance or item of equipment claimed?

- Does the claimant and/or the litigation friend understand the need for and actually want the aid, appliance or item of equipment claimed?

- Might the aid, appliance or item of equipment claimed have been purchased by the claimant in any event?

- Is the expense of the aid, appliance or item of equipment unreasonably disproportionate to the anticipated benefit that it will bring to the claimant and his quality of life?

- Are there less expensive alternatives, and could the claimant make do with something he already has?

Answers to the above questions may well be obtained from a care report that is compiled by a qualified nurse or occupational therapist. It should also be noted that as long as it is reasonable to purchase the aid, appliance or item of equipment, it is not necessarily relevant that the same is or may be available on the NHS.[5]

12.3.8   Details of accommodation and housing expenses

Typical alterations to a claimant's home that are usually claimed for include the installation of ramps, lifts for wheelchairs, alterations to the internal layout of the premises, installation of a hoist, tarmacking the drive and creating extra storage space to accommodate wheelchairs, aids and equipment. On the other hand the claimant's existing accommodation may well not be suitable for the necessary alterations to be carried out and as such the claimant will need to purchase new accommodation. Where new accommodation is purchased the following expenses are recoverable:

- the cost of acquisition (or extension) of the new house and the sale of the old one;

- the cost of any necessary alterations;

- the cost of providing accommodation for the claimant's carer(s);

- the cost of providing any necessary additional furnishings and fittings such as carpets, curtains and fitting out a room for a full-time carer.

12.4.   EXPERT EVIDENCE

12.4.1   The need for expert evidence

A comprehensive discussion in relation the need and role of expert evidence in personal injury/clinical negligence cases is set out in a separate part of this book and the practitioner is referred to in Chapter 6.

The purpose of this section is to set out the types of expert that a practitioner may come across and have to instruct in an appropriate case:

- *Medical expert.* Expert medical opinion will often be required regarding the extent to which the injury can be attributed to the

---

[5] See s 2(4) of the Law Reform (Personal Injuries) Act 1948, which provides that '... there shall be disregarded, in determining the reasonableness of any expenses the possibility of avoiding those expenses or part of them by taking advantage of facilities available under the National Health Service'. See also *Eagle v Chambers (No 2)* [2004] EWCA Civ 1033 and *Pinnington v Crossleigh Construction* [2003] EWCA Civ 1684.

index event, the condition and prognosis of the claimant, the need for any further treatment and/or surgery, the need for care, life expectancy, the level of disability generally, the ability to continue with current employment/occupation, any disadvantage on the open labour market (*Smith v Manchester* award) and the risk of developing future problems such as arthritis or epilepsy.

- *Quasi-medical expert*. These include physiotherapists, chiropractors, osteopaths, acupuncture therapists and speech/language therapists. They are usually instructed to report upon specific treatment needs and the cost of such treatment. They may also be used to report upon the effectiveness of current treatment and to review the need for further treatment.

- *Care expert*. These experts are widely used to calculate a claimant's gratuitous and professional care needs, both past and present. They are usually either qualified nurses or occupational therapists. These experts may also assist with evaluating the cost of DIY, decorating and gardening expenses.

- *Aids and equipment expert*. These are usually occupational therapists by qualification. Where a claimant is significantly disabled, evidence might be required regarding items necessary in order for the claimant to lead a more 'normal' life. The aids and equipment needed vary from case to case and are usually injury specific. For example, in a back injury case an orthopaedic pillow, mattress, a back roll support or perching stool may be recommended. In a more serious case, details of wheelchairs, hoists, special bathing and showering equipment and other home and mobility aids will be needed.

- *Care managers*. In catastrophic injury cases, a case manager is often needed to organise and co-ordinate the efforts of the claimant's carers. The case manager is responsible for advising on the care needs of the claimant, ensuring that an appropriate care plan is adopted, and keeping the situation under review. A clinical care manager owes his or her duties to the claimant alone (on unilateral instructions) and is a witness of fact and so is not constrained by an expert's duties. The care manager can attend conferences without privilege being waived in the discussions. However, in certain (more serious) cases, there might be justification for claiming the costs of two care managers, one acting care manager, and the other reviewing care manager who reports to the court. Adopting this approach permits an independent and objective assessment to be made of the ongoing care regime.

- *Employment expert*. These experts help to quantify the claim for future loss of earnings or disadvantage on the labour market in difficult cases. Care must be taken, however, not to be seduced into using such an expert where the case is relatively simple – e g someone on a fixed salary scale or in a local authority service – where the courts will expect the practitioner to be able to provide calculations themselves.

- *Accountants and financial expert.* These experts are often used to calculate loss of earnings in complex cases or to assess future pension loss.

- *Mobility expert.* Such an expert is used to assist with assessing the particular transport needs of the claimant. These experts are usually occupational therapists or nursing care advisors by profession and may be able to match mobility needs with suitable aids and equipment.

- *Housing/accommodation expert.* These experts are usually surveyors or architects by profession and are able to advise on the claimant's housing/accommodation needs where his current residence is no longer appropriate following injury. These experts will be able to assess the particular housing/accommodation needs of the claimant and, in particular, whether their present accommodation can be modified in order to suit the claimant's needs or alternatively whether new accommodation must be found and, if so, at what cost.

- *Education expert.* In cases where the claimant will require special schooling or training, these experts are able to identify the claimant's special needs and to calculate the value of the claim in accordance with the facilities available in the local area.

- *Statistician/life expectancy expert.* Where the claimant has suffered an injury that may affect his life expectancy, it may be that an expert can examine a statistical database and prepare a report on the claimant's predicted lifespan, though in some cases this has been said to be a clinical rather than a statistical issue.

12.4.2   Problems with particular experts

In this day and age of judicial case management, judges often have to be persuaded by cogent arguments to permit the use of certain expert reports, particularly where the case has been allocated to the fast track. Where an expert has been instructed prior to the start of proceedings it is often easier to convince a judge about the usefulness of that evidence. Where, however, the expert in question has not been instructed, the court will often look much more closely and critically at the need for and the costs associated with obtaining such expert evidence. Gaining permission to rely on the following experts has created much difficulty and, as such, the following guidance is offered regarding their instruction.

12.4.3 Care experts

It is often suggested by judges that the claimant's representative should be able to estimate the amount of care required by the claimant and apply applicable professional rates (subject to a probable discount if the care was provided gratuitously). Such an approach is certainly both justified and proportionate in a straightforward case involving a limited care claim. However, the instruction of a care expert would tend to be indicated in the following situations:

- where there has been a significant amount of past care provided over an extended period involving numerous different applicable hourly rates;

- where there is an ongoing need for care which requires assessing and costing for the future;

- where the claimant has suffered an unusual type of injury and his care needs are not readily identifiable.

In a small claim, it may well be appropriate for a care expert to provide a brief report in summary form first, before deciding whether or not to seek a full report. In a small to medium size claim, it might be appropriate for the care expert, assuming that the expert is suitably qualified, to provide a joint opinion in relation to care needs as well as the need for aids and equipment. Some care experts will even address the claimant's needs regarding domestic assistance, DIY, decorating and gardening within one comprehensive report. This approach keeps the costs down, while making the judge's job easier by having everything in one document. For catastrophic injury claims, the same approach is not generally recommended. In such cases, there is more likely to be a dispute regarding the individual heads of loss due to the sums of money involved and small differences of emphasis between experts may result in very large differences in cash terms. It is therefore prudent to have separate experts providing detailed reports concerning their own specialised area.

12.4.4 Employment consultants

The instruction and use of these experts has faced regular and sustained challenge by defendants. Their evidence is often criticised as speculative and unnecessary. There are no hard and fast rules regarding when an employment consultant should be instructed in particular cases. Such evidence is usually most helpful in the following scenarios:

- where the claimant is unable to continue in his chosen occupation by reason of the injuries, but has an undefined residual earning capacity which might involve retraining or requalifying;

- the claimant is a minor and it is necessary to predict what the claimant's earning capacity would have been but for his injuries;

- the claimant had an unusual or unique job for which there are no average earnings statistics;

- the claimant had a professional job with a set hierarchy and pay structure, eg an army officer, a civil servant or a teacher, but there were clear opportunities for moving up the ladder, yet there is limited information to show what level the claimant would have eventually attained and how long it would have taken to get there. In such a case it might also be beneficial to find a comparator who started at the same level as the claimant;

- the claimant had a job that provided remuneration far in excess of the national average for that type of work. For example, a chef working in a prestigious London restaurant might have earnings way above the average earnings for cooks/chefs suggested by the Annual Survey of Hours and Earnings. Another example is that of a successful fashion photographer, who is likely to earn far more than the average wedding photographer;

- there is a real risk that the claimant will lose his job in the foreseeable future by reason of his injuries and it is unclear what alternative work he would be able to do in the local area and how long it would take him to find such work;

- where there is reason to think that the available national statistics are too compressed in the categories they offer to allow for an accurate comparison. An example might be architects and many manual building trades that are classed generally under broad headings that fail to reflect a great variability of earnings.

When considering whether to instruct an employment consultant, the following checklist may provide a useful guide. The more questions to which the answer is 'yes' the less likely it is that the instruction of an employment expert is justified:

- Are you able to predict the loss of earnings up to the time of trial and future career earnings including promotions, advancement and redundancy?

- Are you able to comment on the possible effects of the local labour market and the vicissitudes of the relevant industrial sector?

- Does the claimant's disability now exclude him from the labour market?

- Are you able to assess the claimant's job search period, training options and future earnings?

- Are you sure the other factors such as planned changes in sheltered employment provision etc are not going to affect the claimant's future employability?

In smaller or more straightforward cases, employment consultants can be asked just to provide or endorse some statistical data in order to help calculate the loss of earnings claim. In these cases, the relevant material might be in the public domain but it would take the layman a disproportionate amount of time to find the source. The employment consultant thus takes on the role of adviser and does not provide a full report or give evidence to the court. In an advisory capacity, the employment consultant may also offer assistance with a number of other matters, including identification of the central issues in a case, consideration of any Part 36 offers, and seeking to persuade the court why a full employment assessment might be necessary.

12.4.5   Forensic accountants

Forensic accountants have often been involved in the past to help calculate loss of earnings in difficult cases and to assist with quantifying pension loss. In relation to loss of earnings the assistance of a forensic accountant is generally helpful in the following situations:

- where a self-employed claimant does not have a steady pattern of earnings, and projection of future loss is not straightforward;

- where the claimant was a partner in a multi-party business and it is necessary to evaluate his lost share of the profits;

- where the claimant was a director or owner of a company whose profitability is significantly affected by reason of the claimant's injuries.

With regard to pension loss, this is no longer considered the preserve of accountants unless the terms of the pension are particularly complicated. As such the court usually expects the practitioner to assess this loss themselves.

12.5   THE SCHEDULE OF LOSS

The two principle heads of damage are pecuniary and non-pecuniary loss. The former has to be itemised in a detailed schedule of loss. Pecuniary loss is divided into two parts:

(1)   pre-trial expenses/losses (past expenses/losses); and

(2)   post trial expenses/losses (future expenses/losses).

By virtue of para 3.14 of the Personal Injury Pre-action Protocol ('PI Protocol'), a claimant is obliged to send to the defendant as soon as practicable a schedule of special damages with supporting documents, particularly where the defendant has admitted liability. The primary purpose of this provision is to allow the defendant to know the case it has to meet in so far as specific losses are concerned as well as to allow the parties to narrow the issues between them at an early stage of litigation in order to further the overriding objective.

The PI Protocol at para 3.19 also requires a claimant involved in a clinical dispute to provide sufficient information in his letter of claim to enable the defendant to commence investigations and to put an initial valuation on the claim. In addition, under para 3.22 any offers to settle that are made at an early stage should generally be accompanied by a medical report and a schedule of loss, together with supporting documentation.

In addition to the pre-action protocols, CPR Part 16 and the Practice Direction thereto also provide guidance to a practitioner involved in a personal injury case. For example paragraph 4.2 of the Practice Direction states: 'The claimant must attach to his particulars of claim a schedule of details of any past and future expenses and losses which he claims.' This rule is also said to apply to clinical negligence claims, though in those cases there is often insufficient evidence/information at the time of issue to allow a practitioner to provide a fully pleaded and evidenced schedule of loss due to the absence of a definitive prognosis.

12.5.1   The purpose of the schedule of loss

The schedule of loss is an important document for a number of reasons:

- It will often determine the jurisdiction and track of the case ie whether the claim should be issued in the High Court or county court and be allocated to the small claims track, fast track or multi track.

- It will provide the defendant with an insight into the losses being claimed, how such losses are calculated, the evidence in support of the same and the reasonableness of the heads of loss being advanced. A schedule that has 'to be confirmed' ('tbc') against most items of loss claimed is unlikely to assist or impress a defendant or court, whereas a carefully drafted, calculated and thought-out schedule is likely to reflect a claimant who is serious about proving and recovering all the heads of loss claimed.

- A properly pleaded schedule of loss that includes calculated figures supported by evidence is a helpful template for a judge when coming to assess the value of the claim and his approach to the same.

Three simple tips that the author can offer to a practitioner is:

- Identify the heads of loss the claimant wishes to or is entitled to claim.

- Quantify each head of loss as best and as reasonably as is practicable given the information/evidence before the practitioner.

- Explain each head of loss so that the defendant and the judge are aware of the legal/factual basis upon which each head of loss is being advanced and any evidence in support of the same.

As the judge will be looking to make an award that is 'fair and just' to both sides, a head of loss which is not properly pleaded, supported or explained may be disallowed even though the practitioner with a little more care and application would have been able to adduce sufficient evidence to plead and prove the head of loss.

12.5.2 The contents of the schedule of loss

The CPR do not require or provide any guidance as to the basic contents of the schedule of loss and so a practitioner is left with looking at what practice has developed over the years in relation to the basic contents that should be included in a schedule of loss. The following is intended to provide some assistance but a practitioner should bear in mind that if their claim involves additional items/heads of loss or information which they feel should be included then the simple answer is 'include it':

- the claimant's date of birth;

- the claimant's pre-accident occupation (if any);

- the date of the accident;

- the claimant's life expectancy (if relevant);

- the date of the schedule;

- the (assumed) trial date or window;

- the heads of past loss;

- the heads of future loss;

- an indication as to whether or not future loss is claimed as a lump sum or by way of periodical payments (or both);

- any relevant multipliers;

- details of interest claimed on general damages;

- detailed of interest claimed on past expenses and losses.

The schedule and any subsequent amendment to the same must be verified by a statement of truth, as strictly speaking it is a statement of case and is capable of standing as evidence itself without needing to be proved by a witness statement. However, it is always sensible to cover the items claimed in the witness evidence.

12.5.3   The layout and form of the schedule of loss

When drafting a schedule of loss a practitioner should bear the following in mind:

- The layout of the schedule should provide a focus for the claim being advanced.

- It should be user-friendly, easily understood and followed.

- It should have a logical progression.

- It should supply a short summary of the case including facts, injuries sustained and impact on the claimant's life that justifies the heads of losses being claimed, both past and future.

- It should be drafted in a tabular format so that the defendant and the judge are able to insert their figures on the same document.

- It should be flexible enough to incorporate amendments, additions, deletions and accommodate new information for changed circumstances.

The structure of the schedule will depend very much on the complexity of the claim. In a more complicated or less obvious claim, the schedule should contain a narrative for the court, explaining the reason for the expenditure/loss and why (with reference to the trial bundle, where this is to hand at the time of drafting) it is alleged that the items claimed are recoverable. Where a deduction needs to be made, for example where there is an element of contributory negligence that is alleged or agreed between the parties, this should also be set out in the narrative. Past losses should be separated from future losses so that interest can be claimed on the former as opposed to the later. Past loss, by its very definition, has not been incurred and as such does not attract interest.

Any schedule that is pleaded is only as good as the information/evidence that has been gathered by the practitioner in order to advance and prove the same. This is why the steps discussed above in relation to the gathering of quantum evidence are so important if losses are to be recovered. Once the information/evidence has been collected and arranged under each head of loss being claimed, it is usually down to the expertise and skill of the practitioner as to how best to present the available evidence so as to advance what will be perceived to be a 'reasonable' claim as opposed to a speculative or fanciful one. One of the major dangers with not collecting the necessary or in some cases sufficient information/evidence is that some heads of loss may not be claimed (in error) or claimed but not sufficiently substantiated so as to be recoverable. In each case the claimant stands to lose out on his damages under that head and, as such, the practitioner should be alive to the need to ensure that every reasonable head of loss is considered, pleaded and evidenced. However, practitioners should also be realistic and at times advise the claimant to do the same when it comes to items of loss that he wishes to claim. This may involve not including items in the schedule which are either not supported by evidence or unlikely to be viewed as being 'reasonable' by a judge or the defendant in the circumstances of the case. Exaggerated or unsubstantiated claims are likely to have an impact on the credibility of the claimant as well as the recoverability of other heads of loss. These are likely to be viewed with some suspicion by a defendant and/or the judge where other claims are felt/held to be exaggerated or unsubstantiated. Quite apart from those issues, practitioners have professional obligations not to overstate or plead heads of loss where there is no supporting evidence.

Finally a schedule that is 'easy on the eye' is more likely to find favour with the court. Drafters of schedules should experiment with different styles of layout in order to achieve the most attractive and efficient way of setting out the relevant information. The schedule of loss must be user friendly. It is helpful, therefore, in the larger claims where the schedule is likely to run well into double figures in page length, for the schedule to be split into various sections including an index, a summary of the claim, a list of important information, and possibly a chronology of important dates.

CHAPTER 13

EVIDENCE ON APPEAL

Christopher Goddard

13.1   THE EXISTING EVIDENCE

There are two aspects to consider in respect of the evidence that it is desired to put before the court on an appeal. They are different sides of the Civil Procedure Rules ('CPR') coin. The first consideration should be what evidence that was used at the first hearing or trial is required for determination of the issues that arise on appeal. It will frequently be the case that whole sections of the original evidence are not required on the appeal. The court has power to limit the issues to be heard and to impose conditions (CPR 52.3(7)). The courts have been keen to emphasise that they do not wish to be burdened with unnecessary documentation. Practice Direction 52 para 5.6A(2) makes it clear: 'all documents which are extraneous to the issues to be considered on the application or appeal must be excluded'.

The key is for the parties to apply their minds as to what is really necessary and come to an agreement in good time about the contents of the appeal bundle.

13.2   FRESH EVIDENCE

The second aspect of evidence on appeal is the more difficult question of the introduction of fresh evidence. Before the introduction of the CPR, following a trial on the merits, further evidence could only be admitted if there were special grounds. The introduction of the CPR gave an opportunity to change or develop the previous judicial approach, but the opportunity was not taken. The provisions of CPR Part 52 are simple and bold. There is no practice direction which accompanies the provisions.

CPR 52.11:

(1)   Every appeal will be limited to a review of the decision of the lower court unless:

    (a)   a practice direction makes different provision for a particular category of appeal; or

(b)   the court considers that in the circumstances of an individual appeal it would be in the interests of justice to hold a re-hearing.

(2)   Unless it orders otherwise, the appeal court will not receive:

(a)   oral evidence; or
(b)   evidence that was not before the lower court.

(3)   The appeal court will allow an appeal where the decision of the lower court was:

(a)   wrong; or
(b)   unjust because of a serious procedural or other irregularity in the proceedings in the lower court.

(4)   The appeal court may draw any inference of fact which it considers justified on the evidence.

(5)   At the hearing of the appeal a party may not rely on a matter not contained in his appeal notice unless the appeal court gives permission.

Thus, in applying the provisions of this part the question arises to what extent the principles used in the pre-CPR cases are to be applied. Lord Phillips MR provided the answer at an early stage in *Hamilton v Al-Fayed*.[1]

> 'We consider that under the new, as under the old, procedure special grounds must be shown to justify the introduction of fresh evidence on appeal ... The question (of the introduction of fresh evidence) must be considered in the light of the overriding objective of the new CPR. The old cases will, nonetheless, remain powerful persuasive authority, for they illustrate the attempts of the court to strike a fair balance between the need for concluded litigation to be determinative of disputes and the desirability that the judicial process should achieve the right result. That task is one which accords with the overriding objective.'

The old cases derive from the principles set out in *Ladd v Marshall*.[2] The special grounds that were set out were:

•   The evidence could not have been obtained with reasonable diligence for use at the trial.

•   The evidence must be such that, if given, it would probably have an important influence, though it need not be decisive, on the result of the case.

---

[1]   [2001] EMLR 15.
[2]   [1954] 1 WLR 1489.

- The evidence must be such as is presumably to be believed; it must be apparently credible, though it need not be incontrovertible.

More recently, in *Re U (a child)*[3] the wording was recast, but without apparent effect on the overall meaning. There are essentially three requirements:

- The evidence could not have been obtained with reasonable diligence for use at the trial.

- The evidence would probably have had an important (though not necessarily decisive) influence on the result of the case.

- The evidence must be credible (though it need not be incontrovertible).

In *Evans v Tiger Investments Ltd and Moore*[4] the Court of Appeal refused to admit fresh evidence in circumstances where it was clear that the evidence could have been obtained for use at the trial if reasonable diligence had been exercised. The court took the view that the principles set out in *Ladd v Marshall*[5] still fell to be broadly applied, despite the rule change to the CPR, but that in an appropriate case, some relaxation of those principles might be justified in light of the overriding objective.

In a case concerned with trade marks for Smirnoff vodka, there were appeals from the rejection by a hearing officer of 14 applications for revocation or declarations of invalidity in respect of registered trade marks. It was sought to adduce further evidence on the appeal. The court considered the relevant material and applied the principles in *Ladd v Marshall*. Pumfrey J held that the evidence could and should have been filed earlier and indeed was available. The effect of the application would have been to reopen the evidence stage of the applications, for which there was no possible justification. The court was impressed with the argument that the effect of admitting the fresh evidence would be to start the proceedings from scratch. The application was dismissed (*Smirnoff v Diageo North America Inc*[6]).

In a clinical negligence case a claimant was permitted to adduce fresh evidence collated between trial and appeal (*Jones v South Tyneside Health Authority*[7]). The claimant had a difficult birth, was unable to breath and suffered brain damage that caused him permanent disabilities, both mental and physical. It was a case with a substantial value. The claimant

---

[3]   [2005] EWCA Civ 52.
[4]   [2002] EWCA Civ 161.
[5]   [1954] 1 WLR 1489, 1491.
[6]   [2002] EWHC 2911 (Ch). The full title of this case was *Zakritoe Aktsionernoe Obchtechestov Torgovy Dom Potomkov Postavechtchika Dvora Ego Imperatorskago Velitschestva PA Smirnova v Diageo North America Inc.*
[7]   [2001] EWCA Civ 1701.

was unsuccessful at the trial. Following the trial the claimant's mother used the internet to locate the doctor who had performed the birth delivery and who had not given evidence at the trial. The doctor was found living in retirement in Oregon, America. By the time of the appeal the doctor had suffered a stroke. It was sought to adduce the doctor's evidence in the form of taped telephone conversations, letters and a video deposition. The fresh evidence was admitted but the main appeal failed because the fresh evidence was held to be wholly inconclusive on the relevant issues.

In another clinical negligence case the principles were applied with the result that the new evidence should not be admitted (*Toth v Jarman*[8]). It was desired to mount an attack on the evidence of one of the expert witnesses in the case. It was held that the evidence as to an expert witness's experience and expertise could have been obtained with reasonable diligence before the trial began. It was further held that the new material would not have had important influence on the outcome of the trial.

The court is always mindful of the need to provide some finality in the judicial process. In *Riyad Bank v Ahli United Bank (UK) plc*,[9] a witness at the trial was later subjected to cross-examination by correspondence. The application to admit the responses as fresh evidence was refused.

In *Al-Koronky v Time Life Entertainment Corp*[10] there was an application for security for costs. On the application to admit fresh evidence the court determined that there had been ample time in which to produce the evidence for the original hearing. Accordingly, the application was unsuccessful.

The efforts to obtain the evidence may be subject to some scrutiny: *Transview Properties Ltd v City Site Properties Ltd*.[11] A potential witness, now resident in Scotland, had refused ultimately to co-operate with the preparation of a witness statement for use at the trial. However, her attendance could have been compelled, nor had there been any attempts to adduce her draft statements as hearsay evidence. The court held that it was not fresh evidence. Furthermore the court was not satisfied that the evidence would have been decisive.

There is some difference in approach where there is a rehearing rather than a review of the decision. The difference may need to be considered at the outset. The basic principles apply to both; the difference is one of emphasis. The provisions of the CPR mean that an appeal from a master is not by way of rehearing but is a review of the decision, and that in

---

[8] [2006] EWCA Civ 1028.
[9] [2005] EWCA Civ 1419.
[10] [2006] EWCA Civ 1123.
[11] [2009] EWCA Civ 1255.

those circumstances it is necessary to consider the principles before admitting fresh evidence (*Aylwen v Taylor Joynson Garrett*[12]).

13.3 INTERLOCUTORY APPEALS

In *Electra Private Equity Partners v KPMG Peat Marwick*,[13] it was said that in interlocutory appeals some relaxation of the strictness of those conditions might be appropriate, according to the nature of the interlocutory hearing and the individual circumstances of the case. That would particularly be so where the battleground or its timing were not of the appellant's choice.

> 'The proper question was whether, regardless of the form of the proceeding, there had been a judgment after a hearing in which the issues for determination in the cause of action had been considered and determined on their merits in the decision challenged. That was not to say that there should be no restriction on the introduction of further evidence on appeal from interlocutory orders where the hearings on which they were based were not hearings on the merits. It should be a matter for the court's discretion, according to the nature of the interlocutory hearing and the individual circumstances of the case. Even where the Ladd v Marshall conditions had been applied to interlocutory hearings, there were signs that the courts had recognised the need for some relaxation of the reasonable diligence condition where, at an early stage of the litigation it was unjust to expect a party to have all his case ready, as would be the case here.'

The following pre-CPR cases were referred to with approval: *Langdale v Danby*,[14] *The 'Gudermes'*,[15] *Canada Trust Co v Stolzenberg (No 2)*.[16]

13.4 FRAUD

Where a judgment at trial has been obtained by fraud the question of the admissibility of fresh evidence often arises. In the context of this book, namely personal injury, the fraud is usually an allegation that the claimant has been faking the extent of his disability. The question arises as to how to deal with the new evidence that, for example, the claimant can move and work normally.

There are a significant number of cases outside the field of personal injury where the issue is the parallel one of fraud by means of forged documents. The application of the principles is the same. It has been observed that where there is some evidence of forgery or fraud, the requirement to do justice points strongly towards admitting the fresh

---

[12] [2001] PNLR 38.
[13] [1999] EWCA Civ 1247; [2001] 1 BCLC 589.
[14] [1982] 1 WLR 1123, HL, per Lord Bridge at 1133D–F.
[15] [1984] 1 Lloyds LR 5, CA, per Ackner LJ at 10.
[16] [1998] 1 WLR 547 per Waller LJ at 1173.

evidence. It would be a reproach to the administration of justice if a party had set out to deceive the court and the other side were able to say, once his deception had been found out, that, if the other side had been more astute, the deception could have been discovered earlier. The object of an attempt to deceive is that the deception should not be discovered.

In *Daly & Daly v Sheik*[17] the issue at trial had been the date of the signing of a contract. Following the judgment and the discovery of the original contract, the opinion of a document examiner was sought, and the expert concluded that there was no evidence to suggest that the document had been signed on the date contended. The evidence had not been tested and on the appeal there was an application to adduce that new evidence. The court was of the view that there was a need to examine the authenticity of the original documentary evidence put forward at the trial. There was a need to do justice in the case and the overriding objective required the document examiner's evidence be admitted under CPR 52.11 and considered at a fresh trial.

In *Arundel Corporation v Hokher*[18] the Court of Appeal permitted fresh evidence to be adduced on appeal that was credible as prima facie evidence that, contrary to the evidence given by the claimant at trial, a valid counter-notice had been served in reply to his landlord's rent review notice. Although the case comes from a different branch of the law, landlord and tenant, it is of value in showing the working of the principles that are applied. The issue was whether following the service of a rent notice under the rent review provisions of the head lease, there had been the service of a valid counter notice. Evidence had been called at the trial to the effect that a valid counter-notice had been served. The fresh evidence that was intended to be put before the court was in the form of a number of documents and evidence as to how mail was collected and dealt with at the London office of Arundel. This evidence demonstrated the there was on the face of it credible evidence that no valid counter-notice had been served. This raised substantial questions that required investigation about the authenticity of the counter-notice produced in evidence at the trial and about the truthfulness of oral evidence given about service of the counter-notice.

13.5   FRAUD AT THE APPEAL

The situation normally encountered in personal injury litigation is that the fraud arises in the evidence at the trial. However, there may be circumstances where the fraud arises at the hearing of the appeal. If the court hearing the appeal has made its determination based on that fraud, the question arises as to what is the means to a remedy for the losing party. CPR 52.17 provides that in the Court of Appeal or the High Court

---

[17]   24 October 2002 per Chadwick LJ and Longmore LJ.
[18]   [2003] EWCA Civ 491.

the court will not reopen a final determination of any appeal unless: (1) it is necessary to do so in order to avoid real injustice; (2) the circumstances are exceptional and make it appropriate to reopen the appeal; and (3) there is no alternative effective remedy.

For the purposes of CPR Part 52, 'appeal' includes an application for permission to appeal. Permission is needed to make an application to reopen a final determination of an appeal even in cases where under CPR 52.3(1) permission was not needed for the original appeal. There is no right to an oral hearing of an application for permission unless, exceptionally, the judge so directs. The judge will not grant permission without directing the application to be served on the other party to the original appeal and giving him an opportunity to make representations. There is no right of appeal or review from the decision of the judge on the application for permission, which is final. The procedure for making an application for permission is set out in CPR Practice Direction 52.

The court in *Taylor v Lawrence*[19] considered the point: 'Fraud has always been treated as an exceptional case. If, however, it is arguable that the Court of Appeal is able to reopen a decision where it has been obtained by fraud, this opens the door to the argument that there is jurisdiction to reopen an appeal in other exceptional cases.' The view expressed there was that the appropriate course is to bring a fresh action to set aside the judgment based on fraud, rather than reopening, and thus rehearing the appeal. That had been the practice with judicial support from as long ago as 1877. However, now that we are well into the twenty-first century and mindful of the CPR and the overriding objective, the Court of Appeal remitted the fraud issue to the original trial judge (*Owens v Noble*[20]).

13.6   THE APPLICATION

It is vital to bear in mind the criteria by which the application to admit fresh evidence will be judged and to deal with each element with some care and with sufficient detail. The witness statement in support of the application must give a case summary so that the court can see the context in which it is sought to adduce the fresh evidence, and can see the importance of the fresh evidence to the issues raised in the case.

The witness statement will then need to deal with each of the three *Ladd v Marshall* special grounds. Bold assertions unsupported by detail are unlikely to win the day. There needs to be a detailed explanation of why the evidence could not have been obtained with reasonable diligence for use at the trial. That may be helped by an explanation of how the evidence did eventually come to light. Much will depend on the particular circumstances of the case. It may be that the party was not aware of the

---

[19]   [2002] EWCA Civ 90.
[20]   [2010] EWCA Civ 224.

existence of the evidence and only came to hear of it later. It may be that the evidence had been sought but it had not been possible to obtain it. In this latter circumstance, the efforts to find the evidence need to be set out in some detail.

In dealing with the second requirement, it is better to help the court with a straightforward explanation of why the evidence would have an important influence on the result of the case. Do not leave it to the court to work out the importance. Lead them to the point so that they have a clear and early view of the significance.

In many respects the third requirement may be the most difficult to deal with. There needs to be an explanation or demonstration as to why the fresh evidence is apparently credible. It may be that connections with other parts of the documentary or witness evidence will assist. Any connection should be explained and the relevant part of the evidence exhibited to the witness statement.

INDEX

References are to paragraph numbers.